THE WAGNER GROUP

Yevgeny Prigozhin's Mercenaries and
Their Ties to Vladimir Putin

OWEN WILSON

AUTHOR OF
THE KILLER PRINCE

GIBSON SQUARE

This edition first published by Gibson Square

rights@gibsonsquare.com

www.gibsonsquare.com

CONTENTS

PRIGOZHIN'S SLEDGEHAMMER

In early November 2019, *Novaya Gazeta*, the last surviving independent Russian newspaper secretly supported and protected by Mikhail Gorbachev, broke news about a gruesome 2-minute social-media footage from Syria that had first been released online on 30 June 2017. The video had been shot by soldiers, but leaked videos such as this one were rare as mercenaries were banned from posting about their missions on social media.

The clip showed a victim who had been identified as 32-year-old Mohammad Taha al-Ismail Abdallah by Arab news outlet *Jessr Press*. He was from Deir ez-Zor, Syria, and had fled to neighbouring Lebanon where he had found a job as a construction worker. Returning to Syria in April 2017, however, he was arrested and conscripted into the Syrian army of President Assad. In a phone call, he told his brother he would rather defect than fight. That was the last time anyone in his family had heard from him.

The video showed what happened to Mohammad. It seemed he had tried to desert while stationed at the al-Sha'ir oil field but was caught.

Accused of desertion, he is questioned before being pushed to the ground. Fellow soldiers laugh as they rain down blows with a sledgehammer on his legs, arms and torso. After being beaten and kicked unconscious, his head is cut off with a knife and his arms severed with a shovel.

'Cut him harder. Come on! Break his spine!' one of his tormentors shouts in Russian.

'Keep the legs. We'll hang him by the legs,' says another speaking the same language.

They wonder where to leave his mutilated body. 'Where the commander says,' one of them responds.

'So, shall we play football today?' asks another as he kicks the decapitated head. A second severed head was also in the video shot.

They hang Mohammad's body upside down by his feet and pose for a picture with the corpse before dousing it with petrol and setting fire to it.

While the killers had covered faces with masks at the start of the video, they remove them for the group photo with what is left of Mohammed.

'Don't worry, no one would watch this video,' one of them quips.

The head was left dangling from a fence. The body has the words 'For the VDV [Russian airborne forces]' scrawled across the torso.

In its news article, using face-recognition technology, *Novaya Gazeta* identified one of the tormentors as Stanislav Dychko, a former police officer from the Stavropol region of southern Russia. According to documents—including his ID—the newspaper had obtained, he had in 2016 become a reconnaissance gunner to 'defend the interests of the Russian Federation'.

It was a defining moment.

An employment questionnaire and a punitive non-disclosure agreement showed that Dychko had joined an entity called the Wagner Group PMC and their link to the video associated the private military company with casual brutality of the most inhumane, callously criminal nature.

The mass media around the world began to take a close interest in the Russians involved in this nebulous company and protected by Russia's impenetrable officialdom.

INTRODUCTION

To 21st-century Russians, 9 May is the most important date in the state calendar. It is Victory Day which celebrates the defeat of Nazi Germany in 1945. It occurs one day later than Victory-in-Europe Day as two separate surrender documents were signed by Germany with the Western Allies in Reims and with the then Soviet Union in Berlin. During the Soviet era, Victory Day was traditionally marked by a massive cold-war display of military forces parading through Red Square, intercontinental ballistic missiles and all. After the collapse of the Soviet Union in 1991, the parades were suspended, only to be revived in 1995, the year the golden jubilee of the victory was celebrated.

Although the parade on the 75th anniversary in 2020 was cancelled due to Covid-19, clearly 9 May was an important day for Russia's President Vladimir Putin. As Supreme Commander-in-Chief of the armed forces of the Russian Federation, it was his opportunity to follow Russia's leaders from Joseph Stalin onwards to take his place on the grandstand in front of Lenin's tomb to review the troops and deliver a rousing Victory Day speech about Russia's greatness.

While the parade was scaled back in 2023 (it featured just one tank), the Kremlin's rhetoric was not. Nor was Russian aggression abroad: some 200,000 Russian troops had been sent across Russia's borders to invade and capture Ukraine, more than the USSR had deployed in its attempts to conquer Afghanistan from 1979 (a failed conquest lasting until 1989). Likewise, fighting Ukraine's standing army of 400,000 had turned into a bloodbath.

'Today civilization is once again at a decisive turning point,' Putin proclaimed in his angry speech as if Russia was under a military attack within its borders rather than an aggressor beyond its country. 'A real war has been unleashed against our Motherland.'

Putin drew exotic parallels, describing Russia's small neighbour as if the country was an existential threat on the doorstep of the gigantic, hulking bulk of the Russian Federation. As he had done in crescendo since 2014, he labelled Ukraine's government 'neo-Nazis' and a 'criminal regime'—neglecting the fact that in Ukraine presidents stood after two terms and that he himself, following in the footsteps of Hitler, had absorbed all power since his first-ever election. Nor did he mention that during World War II Ukraine had paid a heavy price for helping defend Russia's landmass against Nazi Germany: half of the 27 million Soviet casualties according to some estimates were Ukrainians, then almost a third of the country's population. In 1961, the message on the same day was very different. Kyiv (then still called Kiev) was awarded the Order of Lenin for its resistance against the Nazi threat to the USSR and proclaimed a Hero City.

Putin welcomed the Russian soldiers present at the parade who had fought to invade Ukraine. 'We are proud of the participants of the special military operation. The future of our people depends on you,' he pontificated from the Red Square podium.

It was advisable for Putin's audience to choose their words carefully. Anyone suggesting that the 'special military operation' was actually a war waged by Russia against a dwarf state was liable to be arrested for subversion. Putin also blamed the West for 'destroying traditional values' and, in an even more outlandish slur, for propagandizing a 'system of robbery and violence'.

'The goal of our enemies, and there is nothing new here, is to achieve the disintegration and destruction of our country,' he fulminated as if resisting Russia's land grab by its smaller neighbours could break Russian culture and Russia's people. Concluding his fallacious speech, he exhorted: 'To Russia! To our brave armed forces! To Victory!' Audiences around Russia, having heard similar speeches for almost two decades, lapped it up.

While opposition leaders languished in jail or lay buried in their graves, and could not naysay him, dissent suddenly came from an unexpected quarter.

On the same day, 62-year-old Yevgeny Prigozhin, a shadowy figure once known as 'Putin's chef' and now head of The Wagner Group, a brutal private mercenary company fighting for hire in half-a-dozen countries—including on Russia's pay in the Ukraine—piped up and publicly labelled the Russian president a 'complete a******e'.

For weeks, gun-for-hire Prigozhin had ever-more vocally complained about Putin's invasion and even expressly exposed Putin's Nazi parallels as nonsense. He had darkly hinted that the invasion of the resource-rich Ukraine was motivated purely by private financial gain. On 9 May, he seized the opportunity to release a video tearing a strip off Putin himself, complaining that his men fighting in the eastern Ukrainian city of Bakhmut were being starved of ammunition and artillery shells.

His reference to Russia's leader avoided mentioning 'president' or the name 'Vladimir Putin' but was nonetheless a thinly veiled reference that did not leave room open for much misinterpretation.

'They're collecting them in warehouses—why, no one knows,' he said. 'Instead of spending a shell to kill the enemy and save the lives of our soldiers, they let our soldiers die—and the "happy grandfather" thinks this is good for him.' 'Grandpa in his bunker' was how Russian dissidents regularly derided the 70-year-old Putin.

'If he turns out to be right, then God bless everybody... but how will we win the war, if, by chance—and I'm just speculating—it turns out that this grandfather is a complete arsehole?'

It was a breathtaking public take-down of Russia's unchallenged ruler of 23 years. No Russian had even mildly contradicted Putin before and lived to tell the tale, and here was a seemingly fringe figure of the Moscow establishment who used the saltiest of language to criticize the president.

Prigozhin went on: 'The shells give freedom. And if they don't give freedom with the shells... if they keep holding onto them, then first we need to shove it up their a**e and then throw them in jail.'

The talk about ammunition was nothing new. For almost half a year Prigozhin had blamed Russia's defence minister Sergei Shoigu and General Valery Gerasimov, the chief of Russia's armed forces, for not providing his mercenaries in Ukraine with sufficient ammunition.

Days earlier, he had gripped the world press by threatening to pull out of the Russian frontline at Bakhmut in eastern Ukraine. He had also taken aim at the Kremlin 'breeding new PMCs'—*ad hoc* militias formed and paid for under Kremlin pressure by Russia's multinationals such as Gazprom and Rosneft. They were technically illegal in Russia—but were badly needed since the Russian military was defeated in its attempt to take Kyiv in 2022. The Kremlin was doing this instead of putting '200,000 soldiers, as I asked' under the command of the Wagner Group PMC, Prigozhin said.

Prigozhin had openly clashed before with Gerasimov—and other, lower-ranking army generals—over their leadership of the war. After planning the invasion of Ukraine, Gerasimov had briefly disappeared, but in January 2023 he was reinstated to Prigozhin's fury.

Prigozhin's approach to war was unorthodox. Recruiting from prisons, as Prigozhin did, was a Wagner Group speciality. But where usually recruiters seek out those who committed minor felonies, he chose to put weapons in the hands of the most dangerous criminals, including serial killers: men who felt no compunction to kill, loot and even torture.

With the official Russian army performing poorly in Ukraine, Prigozhin's dirty tactics delivered successes that made the army's failures that much clearer while making him an outspoken national hero for as long as the heavily controlled Russian media reported his words. By May 2023, he was thought to have become more popular than Putin though by now he was banned from Russia's state-controlled mass media. When he said explosively, 'We need to stop deceiving the population and telling them that everything is fine,' and, 'I must honestly say: Russia is on the brink of a disaster' only Russian war wonks on Telegram, Russia's twitter, could hear him say these anarchic words.

Since January 2023, officials in the Kremlin were taking down the Wagner

Group a peg without shutting the angry Prigozhin out entirely. Starving it of ammunition was one way to bump up its casualty rate and stymie the chances of success. Arrangements were also made for the Russian military to take over recruitment drives from prisons and for new 6-month contracts henceforth to be directly with the ministry of defence so that conscripts fell directly under defence minister Shoigu's chain of command. Meanwhile, the Wagner Group was also cannibalized as experienced fighters and instructors were being lured away.

Vlad Mykhnenko, an expert in the post-communist transformation of Eastern Europe and the former Soviet Union at Oxford University, did not hold out much hope for Prigozhin. He said: 'My money is on Prigozhin being found dead in a Russian state-staged "suicide," with a pistol in his hand and a ridiculous suicide note.' In an alternative scenario, Mykhnenko thought 'Moscow could also provide Ukraine with Prigozhin's precise geo-location within a 70km HIMARS rocket range to finish him off and provide a "heroic" propaganda recruiting boost to the "new" emasculated Wagner'.

But none of this happened. Prigozhin stood by his words but seemed to offer an olive branch to the Kremlin the next day as if he was the one in charge. Asked who 'the grandfather' was, he mockingly gave a cryptic multiple-choice answer that did little to dissimulate his challenge to the most powerful man in Russia.

'"Who might be the grandfather?" Option number one is Mizintsev who was fired for giving us shells and so from now on he is unable to give us more,' Prigozhin said in an audio post on Telegram.

Mikhail Mizintsev was a colonel general who served as the deputy defence minister for logistics until April 2023 and then joined Wagner as a deputy commander. Clearly, the man Prigozhin had hired as his new second in command was not the 'grandfather' or 'a*******e'.

'Option number two, chief of the General Staff, Valery Vasilyevich Gerasimov, who should give us shells,' Prigozhin said, repeating his refrain that 'we don't receive it in sufficient volumes but only get ten per cent [of what we need].

'And option three is Natalya Khim, who appeared on social networks offering us boxes of shells,' he said, referring to a reality TV star who was fighting in the Donbas region of eastern Ukraine and had claimed to have pushed for Wagner to be supplied with shells.

'Choose any of these options who I called the "grandfather",' Prigozhin said, as the answer to his riddle was clearly Gerasimov, but he repeated Putin's nickname one more time all the same.

In the face of Prigozhin's *lèse-majesté*, the Kremlin press secretary and long-time Prigozhin contact Dmitry Peskov remained remarkably coy later that day about his close associate's comments, playing down the Wagner leader's videos and claiming the Kremlin was 'too busy' to comment. 'You know what we were doing yesterday,' he told reporters. 'There were many guests, many events.'

Prigozhin had done something very unusual. He had poked the bear in the Kremlin without so much as a raised eyebrow in return. What was going on? He seemed to be able to behave with impunity towards the Russian president unlike any Russian before him for more than two decades. If he could defy Vladimir Putin, it begged the question—what was their relationship?

This book will set out that Putin was, in fact, Prigozhin's senior business partner and that Wagner Group PMC was just one of their private joint ventures (Prigozhin's online trolling factory IRA FAN was another). Through Wagner PMC, the two had deployed the power of the Russian state to carve out modern colonies for themselves in Syria, Africa, Crimea and Eastern Ukraine, guarded by Prigozhin mercenaries. Financed by one of the opposing sides in war-torn zones, and at the expense of the lives of Wagner troops and locals, it had been a brilliant scheme.

Once up and running, the expansion of the colonies financed itself through the grants of oil, gas, diamond and other mining concessions and nestling like a cuckoo in other areas in the world split by civil war. Apart from elevating war crimes to an industrial scale, it made Prigozhin a billionaire, turning the foul-mouthed minigarch into one of Russia's oligarchs. Putin's cut from their association would have been many billions in excess of Prigozhin's. Meanwhile, both could deny through the Kremlin the existence and criminal behaviour of Wagner PMC.

For years their tandem went from success to success, as they spread through the Middle East, Africa and Latin America, as Wagner Group PMC's operations remained cloaked in mystery. Nemesis came after the Kremlin's avaricious eye had fallen on Ukraine. Its neighbour was successfully weaning itself of Russian gas and oil imports and seemed to be slipping away together with its extraordinary Donbas-centred deposits of gas, iron ore, coal, manganese, titanium, bauxite, mercury, salt, as well as rich Crimea's offshore gas deposits in the Black Sea (estimated by NATO to be in the region of 4-13 trillion cm). When the 2022 invasion of Ukraine stalled after a few months, Prigozhin was called upon by Putin to deploy his privatised style of warfare and bring Russia badly needed victories. Prigozhin's carrot for success was receipt of mineral resources captured for his (and Putin's) Wagner Group PMC.

After 6 months, when Prigozhin failed, too, no one could untangle the Ukraine mess created through the involvement of his business partner but Putin himself. No one dared to lift a finger against the loud, small-time thug, lest their hand got caught in upper-Kremlin politics. To go against Prigozhin meant going against Putin and the private finances of the Russian president himself. Prigozhin's story is also the story of Putin Inc, and how the president of Russia likely enriched himself through Prigozhin's modern colonies, death and torture.

I

THE 'POLITE MEN'

Crimea was where the first sign of mercenaries connected to the Wagner Group appeared, just before Russia occupied Ukraine's peninsula between February and March 2014. 'The GRU led a lot of the way into Crimea,' said British military intelligence expert Philip Ingram, 'but the troops deployed beforehand were Wagner Group. They are current soldiers, who have been disavowed or temporarily retired of the GRU or *Spetsnaz* [Russia's equivalent of the Navy Seals and SAS], with former members that are brought together in a mercenary group, and put in as advance forces.'

In December 2013, Ukraine teetered on the brink of civil war. President Yanukovich's government buildings were occupied by protesters and his security forces had begun shooting with live ammunition as FSB 'advisors' invited by Yanukovich started arriving in Ukraine's capital Kyiv. The unprovoked shooting of close to a hundred Ukrainian protestors in cold blood on 20 February, led to complete disarray in Kyiv as Yanukovich fled to seek exile in Russia. Using the absence of a central government in Kyiv, Russia moved quickly into Crimea to occupy all strategic locations, install a puppet Crimean government and announce the results of a sham referendum at gun point that purported to proclaim Crimea's independence from Ukraine.

From December 2013, Wagner mercenaries were among the masked troops who appeared wearing army uniforms with no insignia in Crimea. They were armed with Russian weapons and drove trucks with no number plates. The Russian government denied all knowledge of them and speculated they were spontaneous Crimean 'self-defence forces' formed as a result of the chaos in Kyiv, while the heavily-supervised Russian media called them the 'polite men' as they disarmed official Ukrainian troops stationed in Crimea, took over government buildings and established roadblocks in a practically bloodless takeover.

With an impish sense of humour, because of their green outfits, they were also nicknamed 'little green men'. Other 'polite men' wore jeans, tracksuits and the orange and black ribbon of St George—a symbol of Russian military valour that these so-called 'pro-Russian self-defence groups' had taken as their battle badge. Although they all claimed not to have anything to do with the Russians, clearly their actions were co-ordinated. Meanwhile, local defence forces and the Ukraine's elite riot police based in Crimea remained in their barracks, after technically having been disbanded. In other parts of Ukraine, such as Donbas, similar plain-clothed Russian fighters turned up to foment conflict there.

The name 'Wagner Group' was anecdotal and no less spectral than any of the other 'green men' who started materialising in Ukraine's Crimea and other border regions with traditionally close ties to Russia. The name hailed from the call sign of its leader, Dmitry Utkin, a former lieutenant colonel in Russia's military intelligence, GRU. As a young man, Utkin had chosen to be called 'Wagner' after Hitler's favourite composer. The shaven-headed mercenary was reported to be a neo-Nazi and had Waffen-SS tattoos on his shoulder, SS lightning bolts on his neck and a Reichsadler Eagle—or German Imperial Eagle—tattoo on his chest in case anyone missed his infatuation with Hitler's sickening, criminal regime.

Utkin had previously led GRU units in battles during the first and second Chechen Wars (1994 and 1999 respectively) and as a result of his methods had gained a reputation for violent ruthlessness. Were these genuine 'wars' or merely provocations? According to Russian intelligence expert Yuri Felshtinsky, both were false-flag operations choreographed by the FSB/GRU to serve the Kremlin for cynical electoral expediency (*Blowing up Russia: The Return of KGB Terror*, written with former FSB colonel Alexander Litvinenko). Unleashing horrific violence such as Utkin's would have had exactly the desired effect in Chechnya.

The formation of the Wagner Group itself was entirely accidental. In 2013, Utkin retired from the GRU and enlisted as a mercenary in what was called the 'Slavonic Corps', a private military-security company (PMC) incorporated in 2013 in Hong Kong by Vadim Gusev and Pavel Sidorov. Ads had appeared on military websites recruiting ex-members of the special forces who had seen action in Tajikistan and Chechnya offering US$5,000 a month for a five-month contract starting in October. Gusev and Sidorov themselves worked for the Moran Security Group, a company with headquarters in St Petersburg, Moscow, Iraq, Sri Lanka and Guangzhou, China. Its website said it operated to the 'highest legal, ethical and professional standards'.

The CEO of Moran PMC, an ex-FSB colonel called Vyacheslav Kalashnikov, personally interviewed applicants (introducing himself as 'general') for the corps over the phone after which contracts were signed with the Hong Kong entity. Moran wasn't too picky according to RSB-group, a rival Russian PMC. It claimed that among the Slavonic recruits were criminals and ex-RSB troops who had been dismissed for poor behaviour. Utkin was team leader of the Corps and mustered in Beirut with others and then headed for Syria where they were to defend pipelines and oil installations.

The men were told that they would be working for the Syrian government and that the corps would grow to some 2000 troops. On Syrian soil, matters turned out to be a little different, however. The initial 267 mercenaries found themselves involved working for private warlords in the civil war raging against ISIL, the Islamic State terror group. The weapons they were given were ancient Soviet issue as all the good modern weapons had been taken by local Syrian troops. They had been promised T-72 tanks, instead they got obsolete T-62s as well as busses reinforced with metal plates and machine guns. And while they had been told that they were going to guard the oilfield at Deir ez-Zor, they found they were instead expected first to take the oilfield back from ISIL rebels.

The Corps' mission was a complete disaster. On the way to Deir ez-Zor, a Syrian air force helicopter happened to hit a transmission line and crashed into the column, injuring one of the contractors. They were then diverted to support the Syrian army, but soon found themselves under ISIL attack. They got into serious trouble in the city of As Sukhnah where they entered into an unequal battle with the jihadists. 'Participants told me that it was a magical battle, practically a counterattack for the city. Almost 2000 fighters against the 2 or 300 guards,' one Wagner employee said. The Syrian army had to come to the rescue of the Corps with support and the mercenaries were only saved from annihilation by a freak desert storm.

Following that, the contract between the customer and the Slavonic Corps was abrogated. They could not agree on payment for the fighting they were expected to do to reconquer the oil field. The 'Syrian bigwigs' refused to pay extra for more dangerous work and began to threaten the Russians, so the Slavonic Corps left Syria. Utkin's men had barely lasted a month and, following the disagreement between Gusev and Sidorov and the Syrian magnates, were returned to Russia without payment for their participation in the operation.

They headed back to Moscow in October where Gusev and Sidorov were arrested and charged with running an illegal private army, itself a highly unusual turn of events.

The two luckless men, in fact, made history as they became the first ever to be sentenced for the 'recruitment, instruction, financing, or other material support for a mercenary' organisation—a hitherto empty provision in Russia's criminal code dating to loftier times under Boris Yeltsin as President in 1994.

A whole Russian branch of industry consisting of PMSs had since ballooned under the code's gaping exemption for those 'assigned to perform official duties'—a provision that handed the FSB complete control over any Russian PMC activity on penalty of criminal prosecution.

Unfortunately for Moran PMC, ISIL had found documents clearly implicating Gusev and Sidorov in mercenary activities in Syria and had given these to media outlets. Given their incompetence in keeping their operations covert, it is possible that they were made an example of as a warning to Russia's PMCs to be more careful. The Kremlin had to decide whether to make public that the Slavonic Corps had been given an 'official duties' exemption from prosecution by the FSB, or to cut it loose. Evidently, the Kremlin thought better of admitting to government involvement in the debacle on foreign soil. Questions remained, however. The two men were given a sentence of only three years, even though Article 359 of the Russian Criminal Code states mercenary involvement in 'armed conflict or military operations, shall be punished by imprisonment for a term extending from four to eight years.' It also remained unclear whether they served their sentence.

As the 267 mercenaries themselves were never paid their first month's $5000 by the Syrian principal, they were not arrested on technical grounds. But the net result of the Kremlin's legal moves was both the corps' dissolution and that there was now a small army of mercenaries hungry for money after their Syrian misadventure.

From these November 2013 ashes of the Slavonic Corps rose the Wagner Group. As it happened, Utkin, though born in Soviet Russia, grew up in Soviet Ukraine and went to school in the Ukrainian town of Smoline in Kirovohrad Oblast, where his mother still lived. In November 2013, a crisis in Ukraine erupted when President Yanukovich—for no ostensible reason—dramatically vanished from a summit in Vilnius, Lithuania, and failed to sign an Association Agreement with the EU despite political promises dating back decades.

The unexpected turmoil indirectly created the need for bands of trained Russian mercenaries who could blend in among the Russian-speaking population of Ukraine in the east of the country and Crimea. Opportunistically, the looming civil war gave the Kremlin the chance to grab as many parts from Ukraine's control as it could. Given the friendly relations with Russia, in 2013, Ukraine had only a rudimentary, ineffective standing army and small militias could achieve outsize results.

As they were supposed to be Ukrainian militias claiming independence from Kyiv, the Wagner Group could not exist in any documentary shape or form. It should have no company registration, recruitment office or organizational charts, and filed no tax returns as this would show that they were Russian mercenaries stirring up trouble against Kyiv under orders from Russia. Any evidence that would prove their nationality and organisational structure—as ISIL had done when they handed documents of Moran PMC's Slavic Corps to the press—had to be avoided at any cost as it would defeat the covert role of the newly-minted group to be deployed in eastern Ukraine.

With Utkin as commander, the 'Slavonic Corps' was repurposed by the Kremlin as part of its secret Russian muscle inserted to peal away eastern Ukraine and Crimea and subsume these parts under Russian control. As Utkin was 'Wagner', his mercenaries became known as his musicians, or, as 'Wagnerians': in Russian, *Wagnerovci*. Whereas, Utkin had excelled in brutal savagery during the two Chechen invasions, on this occasion he had to operate with silk gloves and the least amount of fuss.

20 February 2014 was the starting signal for the Kremlin's covert operation. The killing of unarmed Ukraine protesters ignited the simmering civil war in which even parts of Ukraine's secret service, SBU, no longer supported the regime. The day became known as The Heavenly Hundred after the peaceful protesters who fell. In 2015, the head of the SBU, Valentyn Nalyvaichenko, stated that Russian snipers caused the bloodbath (though he was promptly contradicted by the government led by the new Ukrainian president Petro Poroshenko which denied that this was the case).

Russia moved in fast with its mercenaries acting under the guise of 'separatists' and seized, apart from Crimea. But they were not the only Ukraine locations by a long chalk. Attempts were also made to seize Ukrainian harbour cities Mariopul and Odesa, as well as Kharkiv, Zaporizhzhia and others with a substantial Russian-speaking citizenship.

The attempts to topple Ukrainian control over these towns failed (all would later receive punishing bombardments striking civilian targets after the 2022 invasion) for a mixture of reasons. Resistance by local officials was one of them, and another ironically the outdated equipment of the Ukrainian army. Orders to stand down issued for dubious reasons by generals based in Kyiv did not reach local units. Without waiting for central commands, Ukrainian troops began resisting Russian mercenaries masquerading as 'separatists' with extraordinary tenacity. But the results in Donetsk and Luhansk in Donbas, eastern Ukraine, were unequivocal.

After Crimea's annexation within a little over a month, the Wagner Group was moved on. The editor-in-chief of Ukraine's Information Resistance Group website, Yuriy Karin, was convinced that it was the servicemen of the PMCs who seized several airborne fighting vehicles from the advanced group of the 25th Airborne Brigade of the Armed Forces of Ukraine which entered Kramatorsk in the Donetsk Oblast in eastern Ukraine on 16 April 2014.

'PMCs recruit top-class subject-matter experts literally one person at a time. We remember the tricks performed by an airborne fighting vehicle on the square at the time. Are Donbas miners capable of performing such tricks, taking into account the state of our army at the time?' Karin asked.

These findings were confirmed in a later report on the use of Russia's private military companies on Ukrainian territory presented at the European Parliament in 2017. According to the SBU, Ukraine's intelligence agency, the Wagner's Group was most active in Ukraine between June 2014 and August 2015. Then, after suffering losses, it was deployed to Syria.

By late May 2014, the Wagner Group, with some three hundred men, appeared in Ukraine's Luhansk Oblast. Along with other Russian-led forces, it participated in the battles for Luhansk Airport and Debaltseve between May 2014 and January 2015.

According to the SBU, Wagner was responsible for the downing of the Il-76 military transport aircraft at 12.51am on the night of 14 June (13 June GMT) 2014 as it approached the runway at Luhansk Airport, resulting in the deaths of forty-nine Ukrainian servicemen. The SBU said it based this statement on Wagner's PMC's report to the Russian General Staff, which read: 'On 13 June 2014, group "B" destroyed the Il-76 military transport aircraft carrying enemy airborne troops, which prevented the Ukrainian troops from deploying a well-staffed group of troops to the territory of the LPR.'

The SBU said Dmitry Utkin personally gave the order to shoot down the transport aircraft. Anti-aircraft gunner Andrey Guralev, born in 1990, and senior anti-aircraft gunner Andrey Lebedev, born in 1974, carried out the order.

Ukrainian investigators issued a notification of suspicion on Dmitry Utkin for the downing of the Il-76 aircraft. It was sent to the Ukraine Prosecutor-General's Office. Earlier, the SBU had filed indictments against three people who ordered the downing of the plane, including the incumbent political leader of the outlawed LPR, Igor Plotnitsky.

The SBU said the Wagner Group distinguished itself during the fighting for Luhansk Airport in 2014, as well as in the Battle of Debaltseve in eastern Ukraine in February 2015. Some fifteen *Wagnerovcis* were killed when storming the airport. Another twenty-one were killed in the Battle of Debaltseve where new Russian BPM-97 Vystrel armoured trucks were seen, indicating that they had some sort of official Russian seal of approval.

The Wagner Group was also implicated in the assassination of insurgent leaders who had become inconvenient to the Kremlin's masterplan of making Ukraine subservient to the Russian Federation. Alexander Bednov, aka 'Batman', who had reportedly started to disobey the Kremlin's orders, was one of them. Bednov's motorcade was fired on near Lutuhyne, Luhansk region, on 1 January 2015. The fighters of the Batman battalion accused the head of the self-proclaimed Luhansk People's Republic, Igor Plotnitsky, of organizing the killing of their commander to get rid of an influential political rival. Alexey Mozgovoy, Pavel Dremov and other separatist commanders who found themselves with Plotnitsky were also thought to have been despatched by PMCs.

As Kyiv was still reeling, on 17 July, 2014, the Kremlin unleashed its next act of provocation and shot down a civilian airplane over Ukraine. It was Malaysian Airlines flight MH17 flying from Amsterdam to Kuala Lumpur as luck—for Ukraine—would have it, no Ukrainians were on board and the cold-blooded war crime had enormous international repercussions but failed to upset the febrile domestic balance Ukraine had regained in organising itself against Russia's presence.

Four years later, on 25 May 2018, the court investigating the downing of Malaysian Airlines M17 found that Russian citizen Oleg Vladimirovich Ivannikov—also known as Andrey Ivanovich, a high-ranking Russian military intelligence GRU officer—was the key person of interest. According to the open-source investigative search network Bellingcat, Ivannikov supervised the procurement and transport of weapons across the Russia-Ukraine border. He held these functions at the time MH17 was shot down. He also supervised the military activities of Russian militants and contingents of the Wagner Group. The Dutch-led Joint Investigation Team, JIT, said the missile that downed the plane resembled another Russian-made Buk missile that crossed into Ukraine from the Russian city of Kursk four weeks prior to the incident. Tried in absentia in 2022, Igor 'Strelkov' Girkin, along with fellow Russian Sergey Dubinskiy and Ukrainian Leonid Kharchenko, were found guilty of the Malaysian Airlines MH17 carnage and ordered to pay at least €16 million in compensation to families of the victims.

Colonel Utkin's Wagner Group was not the only PMC in Ukraine that was part of this lawless landgrab by the Kremlin. At least seven other Russian PMCs were seen in the Ukraine. But the hungry *Wagnerovcis* of Utkin's Wagner Group were to become the pre-eminent organisation in close cooperation with the Russian state. Wagner troops would be seen supporting fighters in the self-proclaimed People's Republics of Donetsk (DPR) and Luhansk (LPR) in eastern Ukraine. Unlike in Syria, in Ukraine the former Slavic Corps were in their element.

More importantly, they were an important part of the Kremlin's hugely successful mission to expand Russia's borders. When 2014 drew to a close, Western countries and their belligerent media seemed to have accepted that the Russian Federation was going to keep the fruits of its deft silent warfare under the guise of local 'self-determination'. All that the Kremlin had deployed to achieve its astonishing military success and international acceptance was a trained army of discreet thugs applying pressure in the right places. It was publicity money simply couldn't buy. It gave the Kremlin new ideas what to do next with Wagner PMC in the summer of 2015.

2

SYRIAN MASSACRE

In the autumn of 2015, the *Wagnerovcis* underwent three months of training at the test range in Molkino in the Krasnodar region at the base of a GRU 10th *Spetsnaz* Brigade (Russia's SAS). After training, some 1,350 *Wagnerovcis* returned to Syria in August 2015 a month before the Russians officially stepped in with airstrikes and ground operations. The Wagner mercenaries joined pro-government forces fighting in the provinces of Latakia, Homs and Hama in the west of the country.

There were several compelling reasons for this new deployment of the Wagnerians by the Kremlin. Militarily, Syria was vitally important to Russia as it leased its Mediterranean submarine base in Tartus from President Bashir al-Assad's government (and likewise Khmeimim Air Base in Latakia). Ever since the Arab Spring of 2010, Assad had been battling local insurrections by ISIL-led groups and others, in desperation not shying away from chemical warfare which in itself had attracted the attention of US President Obama and had led to US military engagement to support certain insurgents. But mainly, Assad's regime was buoyed by ample finances from the oilfields it controlled and could afford to pay for Utkin's ruthless army of fanatical 'discreet' thugs that wasn't afraid of incurring heavy losses against the right price.

In December one Wagner unit, originally 93 strong, was down to 30 when it was withdrawn. The survivors were tasked with training local servicemen, reconnaissance activities to a depth of up to fifty kilometres, the repair of military hardware and arms, communication with the local population, as well as the evacuation of the wounded from the battlefield. Unlike the conflict in Ukraine at that time, Russia was officially involved in warfare in Syria, though its presence was supposed to have been limited to a relatively small aviation group. There were no Russian ground military troops fighting in Syria, but through the FSB-GRU's Wagner PMC the Kremlin was actively engaged in ground operations.

For its Syria mission, the Wagner Group quickly recruited former Russian servicemen with a variety of specialist skills, as well as men with experience fighting against the Ukrainian army in Donbas. By early 2016, the group included at least four infantry companies augmented with tanks, artillery and rockets, and supported by an extensive logistics network from the Russian military.

'No private military company in whole the world has such a heavy fire-power,' an SBU agent close to the service's investigations into Wagner's activities in the Donbas told the *Kyiv Post* on condition of anonymity. 'We're absolutely sure that the Wagner Group is nothing but a Russian GRU military intelligence unit that, given its unofficial status, can be used as a highly effective combat force overseas, without the Kremlin or Russia's official security and military agencies having any responsibilities for them.'

In total, Wagner's manpower was around five thousand, mostly Russian citizens but its troops included approximately a hundred Ukrainian citizens, twenty Serbs and ten Belarusians. Despite having no formal allegiance to the Russian army, Wagner commanders and combatants were awarded official military decorations for valour, the SBU official added.

Wagner focused on Syria's oil-rich central and eastern provinces, particularly on the ancient city of Palmyra, then occupied by ISIL and also on the banks of the Euphrates River. The profitable gas and oil fields, earlier captured and exploited by the Islamists, had to be retaken and delivered to Assad.

In March 2016, the Russian news website *Fontanka* reported that the 'highest losses for the group were said to have been in January and February during the fighting for Palmyra'. Just how many had died was unclear. Some put the number at around six hundred, though others put it as low as twenty-seven. Ukraine's SBU said sixty-seven.

The Battle of Palmyra was the souring of the tense relationship between PMC Wagner and Sergey Shoigu, Putin's inner-circle confidante, Russian defence minister and head of the military since 2012.

'Before Palmyra, everything was fine, the supply was [from the Russian] army. When Palmyra was taken for the first time, the PMC had T-90 tanks, howitzers, Tigers and armoured personnel carriers,' said a former Wagner Group fighter. 'But when Shoigu reported to the commander-in-chief [Vladimir Putin] "We took Palmyra", the director of the PMC Wagner was indignant: "We took Palmyra, not you!"'

'Wagner's PMC took all the heights around it, then the units of the Ministry of Defence calmly walked through the desert, meeting almost no resistance. All the hard assault work was done by Wagner's PMC.'

The former fighter said that, after the row, all decent military equipment was withheld and the Wagner Group had to rely on old or looted equipment.

By August it was reported in Moscow that the number of soldiers working for the Wagner Group had swelled to 2,500 and that mercenaries were costing Russia $150 million a month which came from the state as well as private funds. Apart from the fact that each contractor received 300,000 rubles (US$5,000) a month, compared to a monthly salary of 80,000 rubles (US$1,200) for Russian soldiers, additional costs included 170,000 rubles (US$2,600) for the mercenaries' accommodation, 67,000 rubles (US$1,000) for equipment per contractor and 800 rubles (US$12) daily to feed each of them. Salaries were paid in cash and contracts were perfunctory.

Fontanka said that the Wagner PMC itself was incorporated in Argentina as Russian law forbade private military companies, though, of course, this made tracing the Russian ownership of the group almost impossible. The Wagner Group base was believed to be in the southern Russia Krasnodar region, close to the 243rd combined arms-training range near the village of Molkino and the base where the GRU's 10th Special Operations Brigade was stationed.

There was some international blowback meanwhile for the success in Ukraine. Utkin and the Wagner Group were blacklisted by the US Treasury in 2016 for having 'recruited and sent soldiers to fight alongside separatists in eastern Ukraine' and maintaining a military base near Ukraine's border.

The view in Russia was different. On 9 December 2016, Dmitry Utkin was invited to a reception at the Kremlin to honour Heroes of the Fatherland. Russian presidential spokesman Dmitry Peskov said: 'Heroes of Russia and cavaliers of the Order of Courage were invited.' He could not say why Utkin had been granted the Order of Courage, other than saying it was given for acts of bravery.

Asked whether Utkin's Wagner Group fighters were now in Syria, Peskov said: 'I don't know whether he has fighters and don't know whether they are in Syria and I don't know whether they have any such status whatsoever.'

3

WAR CRIMES FOR SALE

But things were changing fast. Where discretion was once the better part of valour and PMCs operated in the shadows, on 14 December, there were now bigger plans. The Duma—Russia's parliament—passed a bill legalising 'short-term military contracts to fight terrorism abroad'. The 1994 blanket law against such contracts (subject to exceptions) was lifted, legalising the existence of Russian PMCs operating abroad when fighting 'terrorism', a potentially flexible term. As the Russian government was no longer involved, the bill created deniability of involvement by the Kremlin to the Western press and governments in the operations of Russian PMCs.

Alongside, the existence of the Wagner Group became a matter of public record as members stepped out of the shadows, even if it continued to be draped in an aura of mystery. One of its members, identified only as 'Oleg', gave an exceptionally candid interview to a Russian-language TV channel in Estonia. Given the onerous *ukase* to Wagner PMC mercenaries to avoid the limelight, someone must have greenlighted Oleg's testimony with a purpose in mind.

Oleg said he had been paid 300,000 rubles (US$5,000) a month plus bonuses and had fought against ISIL in Palmyra. On top of their pay, members got 300,000 rubles for being wounded, to cover hospital treatment. If they were killed, the family got five million rubles (US$80,000). While the Wagner's contract was a perfunctory piece of paper, Oleg said that every cent was paid, though he was still wary that this did not afford him protection from prosecution by the Russian state under the 1994 law.

He cast light on the division of Russian labour in Syria. While the Russian troops were there simply to train some units, supply weapons and provide air support, they officially had no combatants on the ground. The 'dirty work', Oleg said, was done by the Wagner Group and they did not just fight against ISIL but also against the 'Greens'—the various groups which the West considers the moderate opposition to the regime of Bashar al-Assad.

Asked why he went to Syria, Oleg replied: 'I was an employee, but I do not care about this war at all. I like this job; if I did not like it, I would not work there.' He was a hired killer.

'That is right, I went there for money,' he said. 'Could it really be simpler?'

'If you met him in the street, you would not recognise a soldier of fortune in him—Hollywood clichés do not work,' said Estonian TV interviewer Artur Zakharov. 'A regular guy. A jolly fellow whose eyes well up with tears when he remembers fallen comrades.'

Oleg went on to explain that the Wagner Group was no ordinary private military company. It was a miniature professional army. 'We had a full range of equipment—mortars, howitzers, tanks, infantry fighting vehicles and armoured personnel carriers,' he said.

From their GRU training base in Molkino, mercenaries were flown to Syria—not by Aeroflot, Oleg pointed out, but on transport aircraft of the 76th VDV [Airborne Troops] Division, which was stationed in Pskovskaya Oblast.

'Pskov planes took us,' he said.

It was a circuitous route to Syria. They first travelled by bus from Molkino to Moscow where they were issued passports. From there they went to the Chkalovsky Air Base outside Moscow. They flew to Mozdok in the Caucasus where they stopped for two hours for refuelling and maintenance. There followed a five-hour flight over the Caspian Sea, Iran and Iraq to land at the Khmeimim Air Base in Syria. They took this long way round as Turkey would not let them through their airspace, so they could not fly directly. Once they got there, they were billeted in a sports complex. Vehicles, including artillery and tanks, were taken by sea by the so-called 'Syria Express'—Russian Navy ships plying from Novorossiysk to Tartus.

The Wagner Group was sent to Syria twice—once for a short time in the autumn of 2015, then for a longer operation in the winter and spring of the following year. Each tour was carried out under a separate contract.

By and large Wagner recruits were hardened combatants who had seen fighting in a few conflicts. Although they could hardly put recruitment ads in newspapers, the group did not have problems finding specialists.

Oleg said he did not join Wagner the first time he was contacted—he was distrustful. 'In practice, people get there through personal acquaintance, and only that,' he said. 'There is no full recruitment. A couple of tests are run on recruitment—on the use of alcohol and drugs. Next, there are physical tests. Effectively there are no examinations.'

Those who carried on fighting alongside the troops of 'independent' states in Donbas against Ukraine also had to undergo a polygraph test. They were asked whether they were members of the FSB. Despite their closeness to the intelligence services, its officers and agents were not welcome in Wagner. The group had its own security department which aimed to prevent leaks of information. Pictures of Russian mercenaries were rare online. Posting them an offence which rendered the guilty party liable to serious penalties.

When asked, Oleg thought that the war in Syria was stupid.

'I have not yet seen a smart war,' he said.

In the government-controlled areas a predominately secular way of life prevailed. A woman wearing a burqa was a rarity, although many wore the hijab. In Latakia, which had returned to the government's control, the local population was rather pro-Al-Assad, Oleg thought.

'In Latakia, portraits of al-Assad and Hafiz al-Assad, the president's father, are all over,' he said. 'And locals do not show their attitude. This is a civil war—you are either for or against. If you try to be neutral, then it will most likely be bad for you.'

The locals seemed glad to see the Russians, while the Syrian military almost idolized them.

'To them we are the Rusi. You see, they are very pleased that the Russians came,' Oleg said. 'They are thinking that finally they can sit down again and drink *mate* [a type of tea]; let the Russians do the fighting. When we arrived in a city, they danced in the squares and fired into the air with joy all night. But they were upset when we left!'

The once-prosperous town Murak was abandoned by the Syrians after the departure of the Wagner Group who, apart from the operations around Palmyra, worked as a fire brigade in small groups.

'We were always where the dregs were to be found, very hell itself,' said Oleg. 'All that I saw—it was the most terrible hell.'

Oleg did not hide his contempt for the Syrian insurgent militias and the official military. It is impossible to distinguish between them, Oleg said. 'God forbid we should have such allies. Because they always f**k up a job. Always.'

Years of war exhausted the human reserves of the Syrian Arab Army. Lacking in fighting spirit, few units are combat-ready. 'First, they lack training,' he said. 'They do not even know how to shoot. Second, they have a terrible attitude to their weapons. They do not even clean them.'

In Latakia, nonetheless, the Wagner Group suffered heavy losses thanks to their Syrian comrades in arms. With ill-concealed irritation, Oleg repeated stories about the battle heard from Wagner peers. On the day, the Russians were to cover the Syrians' attack on a hill and to suppress enemy firing points on neighbouring heights. But after the artillery barrage, the Syrian army refused to attack. The Wagner Group had to take on the job. They climbed the hill without incident, but at the top they found themselves under fire from three sides.

'The hill was all bare. If you were not in trenches, it was the end,' said Oleg. 'People were wounded, they needed to be evacuated. How many people would have to pull out? At least two stretcher-bearers, others to provide cover. The track along which the boys went up came under fire, so they could not go that way. They had to go down a mined slope.'

Twenty Wagner men were wounded that day, though none were killed.

Eventually, they tried to make the Syrians attack using intimidation. They jumped into their trenches and shot at their feet, but still they would not budge.

'And the Syrians did not improve. It turned out that they were shooting our boys in the ass. It was hell,' Oleg complained.

In the autumn campaign the Wagner Group suffered about fifteen fatalities—half of them on one day due to an ammunition explosion in a tented camp. Oleg did not know how this had happened—whether it was detonated by a mortal shell or an American bomb. More losses occurred in winter and spring, but Oleg could not provide exact figures.

Their inability to fire was not the only reason Oleg disliked the Syrian government forces.

'They steal everything that is not nailed down,' he said. 'They haul away everything—pipes, wiring, they even tore off tiles. I saw a toilet being dragged off.' Oleg said he had heard of no penalties for looting by the Syrians.

He had little time for the opposition groups—who he called 'pricks'. According to him, the Free Syrian Army included hundreds of separate groups, including Islamic extremists, who periodically fight with each other for territory or for something to eat.

'The Greens are different,' he said. 'The Turkomans are good guys. Good, I respect them. They fight desperately because they are fighting for their villages. If they abandon a village, everybody will leave. They are totally different people. It would be advantageous for the Syrians to entirely displace them from Latakia. In fact it would be ethnic cleansing.'

In 2016 the Wagner Group was unified and transferred to Palmyra to fight ISIL. While in the autumn some six hundred mercenaries were fighting in Syria, in the winter and spring their number doubled.

'It was easier at Palmyra because we were all rounded up together and we were carrying out a single task,' Oleg said. There was no fighting, as such, in the city. The jihadists had pulled out of the ruins to the surrounding heights.

'Over the ridge there is a highway,' said Oleg. 'Our guys brought out tanks and started to destroy everything moving on it. Burned a bunch of cars. Then drove for trophies.'

ISIL proved to be fanatical fighters. They had sown fear among Iraqis as well as Syrians. Oleg also pointed out that Islamists from Europe probably fought well. The Arabs—what he called the 'Blacks'—were different.

'They have local militia,' he said. 'A combatant has a machine gun and nothing else. Such a "Black" does not know how to fight, either. There was a case where scouts reported unknown people arriving in vehicles, forming a wedge and moving towards us. They were covered by artillery, no one fired a machine gun—we got them all.'

After completing their mission, the Wagner Group pulled out of Palmyra, leaving the laurels to the Syrian troops who marched into the empty city. However, the government forces did not hold the victory won by the Russians: On 11 December 2016, the Islamists recaptured Palmyra.

The Wagner Group did not just fight on the front and seemed to provide a full military service. They also repaired equipment.

'In Hamah there is a huge military factory producing armoured vehicles,' Oleg said. 'Before our guys arrived, the Syrians were repairing two tanks a month. When our guys arrived, they immediately began to put out thirty tanks a month. They worked from morning till evening. The poor guys were not even allowed out in the city. They toiled like slaves—they were tuckered out at night. Our guys all left, and the repairmen, there they remained.'

Before the Wagner Group pulled out of Syria in the late spring of 2016, they had to conduct a house-to-house search of the neighbourhoods near the airport not far from Palmyra.

'Among the palm trees and the labyrinth of stonewalls,' Oleg said.

After the liberation of Palmyra, the Russian Ministry of Defence held a concert in the ancient amphitheatre of the city where Prokofiev was played. As the civil war in Syria continued it was entirely possible that the *Wagnerovcis* could be called back to the city again—that is, the musicians with guns. Oleg was ready.

'Of course I will go,' he said. 'I will even go to Africa. Actually, it does not matter where; I really like this job.'

Some *Wagnerovcis* continued to fight in Syria. In March 2017, the Russian national daily newspaper *Kommersant* reported that 23-year-old Wagnerian Ivan Slyshkin was killed in action in Syria, though he was supposedly not on active duty.

4

THE CONOCO BATTLE

While gung-ho interviews with Wagnerians such as Oleg began to appear, the Russian government's response to news from Syria otherwise followed a strict script. In July 2017, the Russian business daily *Vedomosti*, quoting analysts from the Russian opposition Yabloko party, said that the total cost of Russia's military operation in Syria might exceed 140 billion rubles (US$2.35 billion). This estimation did not include strategic aviation flights, Russia's sophisticated air-defence systems stationed in Syria or the upkeep of the Wagner Group. Adding in all of these, the real cost could be fifty per cent more. Despite Russia's vested interests in Syria, the enormous sum was presumably not covered by the Russian Treasury alone but also by Syria.

On 20 July, however, the state-owned mass-market TV station Rossiya 1 carried an upbeat correspondent's report from Syria on the government army capturing more oil wells in Raqqa province.

Only the most determined fact finding by the media would scrape away what was actually happening in Syria. An ISIL video was released on Telegram on 3 October, 2017, showing two captives in grey prison uniforms, one with an injury to one of his eyes, the other with handcuffs. Speaking in Russian they gave their names as Roman Zabolotny from Aksai District in the Rostov region in southern Russia, and Grigory Tsurkan, from Domodedovo District on the outskirts of Moscow. According to the ISIL video, the two men had been captured during a counterattack near Deir ez-Zor (the oil field where the Slavonic Corps had first been deployed), and where Syrian and Russian forces continued to try and push out ISIL.

Zabolotny was recognized by Russian MP Viktor Vodolatsky, who said: 'I know him well. He is from Aksai.' He also said that Zabolotny was 'active in the Cossack movement'. Ivan Vasilenkov, a Cossack leader from Aksai District, said the man in the video was almost certainly Zabolotny. 'He is certainly similar, but we met each other two years ago,' he said.

The citizen journalist group, the Conflict Intelligence Team (CIT, based since 2022 in Tbilisi, Georgia) pointed out that an account in the name of Tsurkan on the social media site carried a photograph showing him dressed in a Cossack uniform receiving an award from a Cossack commander. Paramilitary Cossack groups have helped keep order at events such as the Sochi

Olympics and played a key role fighting for pro-Russian separatist forces in eastern Ukraine. The Great Don Cossack Host, an organization of the traditional military caste, next confirmed that Tsurkan was one of its Cossacks but claimed not to know how he ended up in Syria.

The CIT later posted evidence suggesting that Tsurkan had been part of a group that had harassed supporters of opposition leader Alexei Navalny in Rostov-on-Don, which is near the Aksai District. It also highlighted a Twitter account, called Necro Mancer, which posted evidence suggesting Zabolotny had previously been involved in delivering supplies to the separatist-controlled area of the Luhansk region of eastern Ukraine.

'I could not watch the video, but that is my brother in the still,' his brother Roman Tsurkan told radio station Business FM.

His interview established the link between the two men and Wagner PMC when he went on to say that his brother Grigory was a former paratrooper who had more recently been involved with the Wagner group. He volunteered that Tsurkan had been in Syria in 2013, before Russia's official intervention in the conflict there. Tsurkan thus may have been one of the original first Wagnerians.

Roman Tsurkan said his brother Grigory had signed an agreement not to reveal what he was doing in Syria and complained that the Russian authorities did not stick up for contractors if they got into trouble. He added that he had been ordered not to reveal any information about his brother.

'They use them like meat, those who have combat qualities, the real fighters,' he told Radio Free Europe/Radio Liberty's Russian service. 'Illegally sending them to slaughter without any mercy.'

Further evidence of Tsurkan's earlier involvement in the conflict in Syria was posted on Twitter by Necro Mancer in the form of a screenshot of a 2015 social media post by the Domodedovo District branch of the pro-Kremlin veterans' group *Boyevoye Bratstvo* (Combat Brotherhood), which describes him as having seen active service in both Syria and Yugoslavia.

A Combat Brotherhood photo showed Tsurkan in a group with another member of the Slavonic Corps who admitted to fighting in Syria in 2013. The Combat Brotherhood confirmed that Tsurkan was one of their members and put out a statement saying it would do everything in its power to help him.

The evidence linking Zabolotny to the Wagner Group was more circumstantial. But a list published by the investigative website *Fontanka.ru* of forty Russians, many of them reported to be fighting with Wagner, said to have been killed in Syria over the past few years included at least two Cossacks.

When asked, the Russian Defence Ministry denied that any of its men had gone missing in Syria, but then the ministry did not acknowledge the existence of the Wagner Group either.

Denial was the Kremlin's default response to unscripted questions about

Syria. In May 2017, ISIL published a video of what it said was the execution of an FSB officer named Yevgeny Petrenko. At the time the Russian Defence Ministry also said that no members of their forces were unaccounted for.

Asked about the video, too, Vladimir Putin's spokesman Dmitry Peskov said that the Kremlin was checking the men's identities, but that the Great Don Cossacks Host's statement was not official information and proved nothing. 'Of course Moscow is concerned about the fate of these citizens, if they are citizens of the Russian Federation,' he told journalists.

Evidence in Syria turned up of a Russian company, Yevro Polis, which had signed in 2017 a deal with the Syrian government to take over the Shaer gas field. The contract ran for five years between Yevro Polis and Syria's state-owned oil and gas company General Petroleum Corp (GPC). The one unusual fact was that GPC didn't actually have possession of the gas field. According to the contract, Yevro would get 'twenty-five percent of the proceeds from oil and gas production at fields if its contractors capture and secure from Islamic State militants'. Yevro Polis was a company owned by a certain Yevgeny Prigozhin.

In December 2017, Putin publicly claimed Russia's victory over ISIL in Syria. In fact, the war there was far from over. On 12 February 2018, relatives and friends of four members of the Wagner Group killed in Syria came forward. They said the four 'were fighting not against ISIL, but against the Kurds' for 'oil producing and oil refining infrastructure'.

Many of them happened during an incident known as the Battle of Khasham of 7 February, 2018. The battle unfolded in the Deir ez-Zor province when mercenaries attacked with a large force loyal to Bashar al-Assad, supported by tanks and artillery. They advanced across the Euphrates and fired at a base of the Syrian Democratic Forces manned by Kurdish troops and American military advisors. US forces responded with AC-130 ground attack aircraft, Apache helicopters, artillery and B-52 bombers on a scale not seen before in the Syrian conflict. It was the first confrontation been the superpowers since the Vietnam war and it effectively wiped out the 'battalion-size' attacking force. Three days later, a US drone destroyed an advancing Russian-made T-72 tank from the same hostile force, a US military spokesman said.

The *Novaya Gazeta* put the number at thirteen killed and fifteen wounded. It said Wagner troops had been operating with a special forces unit known as the 'ISIL Hunters', even though the base had no ISIL troops.

Russian survivors warned their fellow mercenaries on social media to stay away from Syria. 'Whatever you do, don't come here,' a Chechen member of the Wagner Group wrote, confirming the link to the Wagner Group made by *Novaya Gazeta*. 'We are getting f****** butchered, every day.'

As news of the contractors' deaths milled around in various media, it remained largely unknown in Russia itself under a state television blackout. The website of the main state news programme published a report, only to delete it the same day.

As the numbers kept on climbing, the news circulated only on minor media. Igor '*Strelkov*' (shooter) Girkin, a former FSB officer who played a key role in the annexation of Crimea and commanded Russia-backed separatists in eastern Ukraine as the Donetsk People's Republic's defence minister in 2014, said a hundred Wagner fighters had died in the US-backed strike on the Russian mercenaries. Bloomberg quoted Russian sources as saying that two hundred professional soldiers, most of them Russian, were killed, while an American official told the publication about a hundred had been killed. Western officials in the region put the number at between 60 and 160, and 200 badly injured, with many being treated at military hospitals in Moscow and St Petersburg.

As mercenaries on short contracts fighting 'terrorists' were no longer formally breaking Russian law, the Kremlin could simply shrug its shoulders when queried. As, indeed, it did. After two weeks of dismissing this as classic disinformation, Russia's foreign ministry finally admitted that 'several dozen' Russian citizens had been killed or wounded, stressing that the combatants were not Russian servicemen and that no Russian military equipment had been involved in the fighting. The fighters had travelled to Syria 'of their own accord and for a variety of reasons', the ministry said, although it did not identify any of the dead or wounded by name. 'It is not the place of the foreign ministry to assess the legality and legitimacy of their decisions,' it added.

The numbers easily eclipsed previous Russian losses in the Syria civil war, a war Putin presented in the mass media as a largely bloodless conflict for the Russians at least. Russia strenuously insisted it did not have troops on the ground even though it admitted that small numbers of soldiers and mercenaries had been killed.

There were other casualties. After initial denials, Russia's foreign ministry admitted that five citizens were likely to have been killed in the bombing while fighting alongside pro-Assad Syrian forces on 7 February. One of them was Igor Kosutorov, a forty-five-year-old owner of a grocery shop.

'Igor was a former army sniper. He went to Syria because he was a patriot. He believed that if we don't stop ISIL in Syria, then they will come to us, to Russia,' said his ex-wife Nadezhda Kosutorova from her home in Asbest in the Urals region. 'He told me that if he didn't go, then the authorities would just send young kids, with almost no military experience.' Asbest is home to the world's largest open-pit asbestos mine. The average wage there is a tenth of what Wagner mercenaries get paid.

Nadezhda had remained close to Kosutorov after their divorce, but she claimed he had not told her who had arranged his contract in Syria.

News of his death had reached her through the grapevine. 'I'm collecting information bit-by-bit from different sources trying to find out where the bodies of the dead might be,' she said. When asked why Russian authorities had not contacted her, she said: 'This is a political game that I don't understand.'

Aside from Kosutorov, at least nine other men were believed to have travelled to Syria from Asbest and the surrounding region to fight with Wagner in the preceding months.

'I want everyone to know about my husband and about all the guys who died there so stupidly,' said Yelena Matveyeva, the widow of Stanislav Matveyev, a 38-year-old mercenary from Asbest. 'They just threw them into battle like pigs to the slaughter.… Wherever they sent them, they had no protection.'

She said Russian authorities should acknowledge citizens who die fighting in Syria, and wherever possible, help to repatriate bodies. 'There should be something in their memory, so that the wives won't be ashamed of their husbands and their children can be proud.'

The Kremlin's reluctance to acknowledge, let alone honour the Russians who died in the confrontation with US-led forces, was in a strange and stark contrast to the hero's funeral given to Roman Filipov, a Russian air force pilot shot down over Syria.

'One gets medals and honours, while others are buried quietly and forgotten about,' Nadezhda, another woman who believed her husband died while fighting as a mercenary in Syria.

Two other Russian fighters were killed on 7 February—Vladimir Loginov, a Cossack from Russia's western Kaliningrad region, and thirty-three-year-old Kirill Ananyev, a radical nationalist with the Other Russia party from Moscow who had also fought in eastern Ukraine.

'He went to Syria because he liked fighting—Russians are very capable of that,' boasted Alexander Averin, a spokesman for Other Russia and friend of Ananyev. He said that five hundred Russians were in Deir ez-Zor at the time and many were dead and wounded.

'They are there illegally, the government has disowned them, even Putin says our soldiers are not there,' said eighty-year-old Valentina Berdysheva. Her oldest son left to fight in Syria as a military contractor with five other men in October 2017, she said. At least one of them was killed and the whereabouts of her son were unknown. The group of men told friends they had found 'a gig' before travelling to the southern Russian city of Rostov-on-Don and later on to Syria. Her son had previously fought in Russia's two wars in Chechnya but struggled to find work afterwards, Berdysheva said.

The plight of a mother searching for her son after being told he was killed while fighting for a private military company in Syria was later taken up in the Russian-language film *Mama, ya doma* (Mama, I'm Home, 2021), produced by

Russian filmmaker Alexander Rodnyansky, known for the Bafta-nominated movies *Leviathan* (2014) and *Loveless* (2017). Director Vladimir Bitokov said the script for the film was inspired by several reports of family members of mercenaries looking for their loved ones. 'We read all we could on this and used real-life stories as details,' he added.

On the US side, military authorities provided arresting news that the Russian government could have avoided disaster. For a week beforehand the Syrian Democratic Forces and US troops had been aware of a build-up of pro-regime forces near the base.

The Americans said they warned the official Russian military via a 'deconfliction line' used by the two countries to avoid entanglement on a battlefield. Half an hour before the attack, Kurdish officials at the base said they had called their Russian counterparts to tell the mercenaries to hold fire. The Americans said the line remained in use as the Russian attack went ahead.

'The Russian high command in Syria assured us it was not their people,' Defence Secretary Jim Mattis later told a senate committee. He said he directed General Joseph F. Dunford Jr, chairman of the Joint Chiefs of Staff, 'for the force, then, to be annihilated. And it was.'

The dramatic day began with little hint of the battle that was about to unfold in four hours flat. A team of about thirty Delta Force soldiers and Rangers from the Joint Special Operations Command were working alongside Kurdish and Arab forces at a small dusty outpost next to Conoco gas field, near Deir ez-Zor, the largest in Syria.

Roughly twenty miles away, at a base known as a mission support site, a team of Green Berets and a platoon of US Marines stared at their computer screens, watching drone feeds and passing information to Americans at the gas plant about the enemy fighters who were assembling. At 3pm the Assad force began edging towards the Conoco plant. By early evening, more than five hundred troops and twenty-seven vehicles—including tanks and armoured personnel carriers—had amassed.

In the US air operations centre at Al Udeid Air Base in Qatar and at the Pentagon, other military officers and intelligence analysts watched as the scene unfolded. Commanders briefed pilots and ground crews. Aircraft across the region were placed on alert, US military officials said.

Back at the mission support site, the Green Berets and Marines were preparing a small reaction force—comprising sixteen troops in four mine-resistant vehicles—in case they were needed at the plant. They inspected their weapons and ensured the trucks were loaded with anti-tank missiles, thermal optics, and food and water.

At 8.30pm, three Russian-made T-72 tanks—vehicles weighing nearly fifty tons and armed with 125-millimetre guns—moved within a mile of the Conoco plant. Bracing for an attack, the Green Berets prepared to launch the reaction force.

At the outpost, US soldiers watched a column of tanks and other armoured vehicles turned and drove towards them, emerging from a neighbourhood of houses where they had tried to gather undetected at around 10pm.

A half-hour later, the Russian mercenaries and Syrian forces struck. The Conoco outpost was hit with a mixture of tank fire, large artillery and mortar rounds. The air was filled with dust and shrapnel. The US commandos took cover, then ran behind dirt ridges or berms to fire anti-tank missiles and machine guns at the advancing column of armoured vehicles.

For the first fifteen minutes, US military officials continued calling their Russian counterparts, urging them to stop the attack. When that failed, US troops fired warning shots at a group of vehicles and a howitzer. But still the enemy advanced.

The US warplanes arrived in waves. There were hunter-killer Reaper drones, F-22 stealth fighter jets, F-15E Strike Fighters, B-52 bombers, AC-130 gunships and AH-64 Apache helicopters. For the next three hours, scores of strikes pummelled enemy troops, tanks and other vehicles. Meanwhile marine rocket artillery was fired from the ground.

The reaction team sped towards the fight. It was dark and the roads were littered with felled power lines and shell craters. The twenty-mile drive was made all the more difficult since the trucks did not turn on their headlights, relying solely on thermal-imaging cameras to navigate.

As the Green Berets and Marines neared the Conoco plant at about 11.30pm, they were forced to stop. The barrage of artillery was too intense to drive through until air strikes silenced the enemy's howitzers and tanks.

When the commandos eventually reached the plant, they were pinned down by enemy artillery and burning through ammunition. Flashes from tank muzzles, anti-aircraft weapons and machine guns lit up the sky.

At 1am, with the artillery fire dwindling, the team of Marines and Green Berets pulled up to the Conoco outpost and small-arms fire. By then, some of the US warplanes had returned to base, low on fuel or ammunition. The US troops on the ground, by then some forty of them, braced their defences as the mercenaries left their vehicles and headed toward the outpost on foot.

A handful of Marines ran supplies of ammunition to the machine guns and Javelin missile launchers scattered along the berms and wedged among the trucks. Some of the Green Berets and Marines took aim from exposed hatches. Others remained in their trucks, using thermal cameras, screens and joysticks to control the fire of the heavy machine guns mounted on their roofs.

A few of the commandos, including Air Force forward controllers, used the radios to direct the next fleet of bombers flying toward the battlefield. At least one Marine exposed himself to incoming fire as he used a missile guidance system to acquire targets' location data and pass it on to the controllers calling in the airstrikes.

An hour later, the attackers started to retreat and the US ground troops stopped firing. From their outpost, the commandos watched the mercenaries and Syrian fighters return to collect their dead. There were no US casualties, though one allied Syrian fighter was wounded.

The number of casualties from the 7 February fight remained disputed. Initially, Russian officials said only four Russian citizens—but perhaps dozens more—were killed. A Syrian officer said around a hundred Syrian soldiers had died. Documents suggested two- to three hundred of the Assad forces were killed.

The Russian mercenaries and their Assad allies had grossly underestimated their opponents when launching a simple, massed assault on a US military position. Since the 2003 invasion of Iraq, the US Central Command had refined the amount of equipment, logistics, coordination and tactics required to mix weapons fired from both the air and ground.

'Right now in Syria, we're in the most aggressive E[lectronic] W[arfare] environment on the planet from our adversaries,' head of US Special Operations Command General Tony Thomas said, referring to electronic warfare. 'They're testing us every day.'

It was not clear whether the failure to halt the attack was a simple oversight by the Russian military, a test of American defences and willingness to retaliate, or deliberate disregard for the fate of the mercenaries. It was not even clear whether the Russian high command had bothered to pass on the messages received on the deconfliction line to anyone else.

'Of course the Russians were aware that the Wagner people were in the Euphrates river valley,' said Kirill Mikhailov, a CIT analyst investigating Russian casualties in Syria. 'They know Wagner is there at the oilfields and gas fields and they don't really care what happens to them.'

'What Russia needed was a highly professional, highly mobile force with deniable casualties,' Mikhailov said. 'There were no actual Russian soldiers fighting there on the ground in Syria, unlike in Ukraine, but Wagner took up that role.'

'Wagner can and should be regarded as Russia's shadow army in Syria, as it has been providing the vital frontline component to Russia's operations in Latakia and Eastern Syria.' Mikhailov added that the group's 'capabilities exceed any Western private military company by far'.

The Kremlin and Putin were only interested in the bombing campaign in Syria to create a television war by providing footage of impressive Russian air strikes without any body bags to ruin the mood of Russian omnipotence.

'The big battles, the intense battles with casualties, that's all Russian mercenaries,' said Ruslan Leviev of CIT.

Wagner PMC played a key role in the battle to retake the city of Palmyra from ISIL and helped oust insurgents ('terrorists') from parts of Deir ez-Zor gas and oil fields on behalf of al-Assad. But Wagner PMC mercenaries mainly acted to advance lucrative Russian interests in Syria. How they did it, the Kremlin had neither any intention of sharing with the Russian people, nor acknowledging to anyone outside Russia. Following the success in Crimea, the *Wagnerovcis* had become the Kremlin's wraiths for hire whom it sacrificed with little compunction to do its dirty work.

5

EXPANSION

The most detailed information on Wagner PMC came from Ukraine. In Donbas, the country was under constant attack from the mini-states Russia had formed, occupied and populated with Wagner mercenaries. Sharing the same language and able to tap into informal networks, Ukraine officials and media were able to put together the most complete picture of Wagner PMC's evolution as the Kremlin's go-to problem solvers.

The surprise came on 26 February 2018, when the Ukrainian News Agency reported that forty Ukrainian citizens were fighting with the Wagner Group in Syria. Igor Guskov, the chief of staff of the head of SBU, told the *Kyiv Post* that at least three Ukrainian nationals were killed in Syria in the spring of 2016, while more were likely to have been killed in the 7 February 2018 airstrike by the US.

From being mainly Russian, *Wagnerovcis* were increasingly being recruited from other nationalities. He revealed that Wagner Group had a special unit called the Carpathians, which comprised about a hundred Ukrainian and Russian nationals. The unit was formed in 2015 in the breakaway Donbas Oblast.

'They were initially trained for subversive and terrorist activity in Ukraine,' he said. He added that after Russia sent mercenaries to Syria, the Ukrainians were dispersed among other Wagner units. The three Ukrainian nationals killed in Syria in spring 2016 were Donetsk Oblast natives Eduard Prykhodko from Horlivka, Oleksandr Konashenkov from Novohradivka, and Oleksandr Kyyashko from the city of Donetsk. The first two were killed near Palmyra and the third in Latakia. All three had previously fought alongside the Russians in the Donbas.

It was not just a matter of swelling numbers. These non-Russians were paid less and were assigned the most risky jobs. Russian mercenary Mikhail Polinkov, who also fought in Ukraine, said in an interview with Roy-TV, a Russian ultra-nationalist YouTube channel, that the Carpathians unit, also known as *Vesna* (Spring), was one of three main forces in Wagner group's attack on 7 February 2018, and that ninety-four of its number were killed in the bloodbath.

'They were the attacking core,' Polinkov said. 'They went first—the Carpathians-*Vesna*. I don't know why, but they were always being sent into the attack first as cannon fodder. And they were also paid less than the others.'

The Kremlin deliberately created a martyr cult around slain *Wagnerovcis*. Polinkov said in the interview that he had visited some of the Wagner mercenaries in hospital in Moscow. While slain Wagner mercenaries received no benefits from the Russian government, they had monuments raised in their honour in Russian-occupied parts of eastern Ukraine and in the parts of Syria controlled by the Assad regime.

In early 2018, Donetsk-born journalist and blogger Denis Kazansky posted on his Facebook page photos of two identical monuments to Wagner mercenaries—one in Luhansk, Ukraine, one in Syria. Both monuments having recently been unveiled. The figures on the monuments were wearing the special medals that Russia has awarded to Wagner mercenaries. They received the Russian military Medal for Courage in Death, normally given only to members of Russia's regular armed forces and not to individual citizens.

Ukrainian activists from the open-source intelligence groups *InformNapalm* and Ikhtamnet_m0209, as well as the Ukrainian Cyber Alliance hacker group, identified twenty-five Wagner mercenaries who fought in a Russian tank unit, and twenty members of a Wagner group howitzer battery. *Inform Napalm* published their photos, military credentials, and names.

The Ukrainian nationals identified included Oleksandr Bohadyr, born in Mariupol, who served as an artillery commander, and Andriy Chemerys from Crimea, who was a gunner with a Wagner tank company. The commander of the unit—Russian citizen Sergey Kim, a former marine officer—had planned the failed Wagner attack on the Conoco base in Syria on 7 February.

'We didn't manage to find out if [these fighters] actually took part in the battle near Deir ez-Zor. But many of them have Russian military awards for taking part in the war in the Donbas—in particular, for the battle for Luhansk Airport.' That was where the Wagner Group had downed the Il-76 in June 2014 on orders of its commander Utkin, 'Wagner' himself. The Ukrainian activists said the Wagner mercenaries had been instructed not to leave traces in social media, unlike the Russian army soldiers who posted regularly.

InformNapalm website explained: 'The Kremlin uses the Wagner Group as an element of Russia's hybrid war in Ukraine, Syria, and probably in the Balkans in the short term. International mercenaries are united under the guise of the Wagner Group, but the basic core of this [force] is made up of retired Russian military servicemen carefully following orders from Russian high command.

They revealed how intimately the Russian President himself was involved in Wagner PMC. 'They are trained on the bases of Russia's [GRU] 10th Special Forces Brigade, and are given awards signed personally by Vladimir Putin… [In the Ukraine] the range of their tasks included the elimination of field commanders of militants who demonstrated independence. They get heavy weapons and equipment directly from the storage bases of Russia's Defence Ministry.

'From the notion of "regular serviceman of the Russian Federation," they are distinguished only by the wording of the contract and the amount of pay, as well as with the fact that it is easier for Moscow to disown them.'

Already in 2012, then prime minister Vladimir Putin had outlined that PMCs were 'an instrument of the accomplishment of national interests without the direct involvement of the state' and that 'thought could be given' to how to bring such activity into Russia's legal channels. In 2018, the growing number of casualties among Russian military personnel in Syria was putting pressure on the Kremlin to provide additional support to the armed forces fighting abroad. The same was true of Russia's 'non-combatant' mercenaries in Wagner PMC. In January, 2018, Sergey Lavrov, Putin's Foreign Minister, spoke of the need to 'clearly fix the legislative structure so that these people also be in the legal field and protected'.

Considering Wagner PMC a ringing success, the Kremlin now sought to expand the pool from which mercenaries could be drawn. The Russia-led Collective Security Treaty Organization (CSTO), formed by Putin in 2002 from 6 former states belonging to the USSR, was pushing for the legalization of private military and security companies. If adopted by other CSTO member states it would allow citizens of Armenia, Belarus, Kazakhstan, Kyrgyzstan, Tajikistan and Uzbekistan to take part in Russia's military operations abroad, i.e. Wagner PMC.

According to Ukraine's intelligence service SBU, eleven Belarusians were already fighting with the Wagner Group in Syria. Later it identified two other Belarusians involved in Wagner's operations in Sudan and other African countries. And by April 2019, the SBU had identified 125 Ukrainian citizens said to be involved in the Wagner group's activity in Ukraine, Syria, the Central African Republic (Central African Republic) and Sudan.

Full details of the proposed CSTO law on PMCs had yet to be made clear. However, Victor Ananiev, the director of the Moscow-based Institute for Security and Sustainable Development (ISSD), which was charged with drafting the legislation, outlined some key features. The law would confer non-combatant status on such organizations. The ISSD draft also mandated that a PMC (i.e., Wagner Group) contractor receive compulsory insurance in case of death, injury or damage, kidnapping and ransom demands, and that serving in a foreign country would not invalidate the insurance.

In a country such as Russia which, as of 2008, had compulsory military service, PMCs would now offer a more attractive career opportunity. In 2018, there were over five million retired and former military personnel who faced social and economic hardship in Russia. Qualifications to join up would be minimal.

It would be open to anyone over eighteen from any CSTO country who had completed at least vocational training and successfully passed the necessary exams. For example, young and middle-aged men from Kyrgyzstan and Tajikistan etc could sign contracts to serve with regional PMCs on the promise of lucrative salaries. If the Battle of Khasham was indicative, presumably, CSTO *Wagnerovcis* would become the cannon fodder of their operations. Potential customers included state executive bodies, foreign government agencies on the basis of bilateral agreements, and international organizations.

According to CSTO vice chairman Valery Semerikov, the context of this draft proposal was that the organization was planning to establish its own peacekeeping forces that would be able to operate under a United Nations mandate.

CSTO member states, however, questioned Russia's motives. Their agreement would help speed up Russia's ongoing domestic debate on passing its own PMC law. However, there was a suspicion that Russia wanted to employ PMCs in Afghanistan. While Moscow expected that PMCs might be employed against external aggressors or in counter-terrorism operations that raised the question of whether their functions would overlap with the existing Collective Rapid Reaction Force within the Russia-led regional alliance.

It might also advance the Kremlin's repeated attempts to push other CSTO countries into sharing more security responsibilities in Russia's broader neighbourhood. Of particular note were Russia's unsuccessful efforts to involve CSTO countries in a UN peacekeeping force in Ukraine as well as Moscow's wish to send troops from Kazakhstan and Kyrgyzstan to Syria. Allies were wary because Putin's belligerence, as opposed to a peace-seeking nature, was well known.

While Russia had said very little publication about Wagner's confrontation with the US in Syria on 7 February, 2018, Putin's response three weeks later was an animation showing missiles striking South Florida, particularly Mar-a-Largo, home of the then US President Donald Trump. It was screened during a speech launching Putin's campaign to be elected for a fourth term as president. By 10 June 2018, the number of Wagner Group mercenaries had swelled to at least 4,840.

Lethal suppression of unwanted information was stepped up at the same time by Russian officials. On 12 April 2018, 32-year-old Maksim Borodin, a Russian journalist working for the news service *Noviy Den* (new day) fell from the balcony of his fifth-floor apartment in Yekaterinburg, a major city in the Urals, and died from his injuries. He had been writing about the deaths of employees of the Wagner Group in Syria.

Russian investigators said they were not treating his lethal fall as suspicious. 'There are no grounds for launching a case,' the local investigative committee told the TASS news agency. The committee also told Agence France-Press that they would not comment on the incident to foreign media. His death was being treated as a suspected suicide by local police. A spokesman said Maksim's flat was locked from the inside and there were no signs of forced entry. There was, however, no suicide note, nor was there any alcohol in his bloodstream.

Polina Rumyantseva the editor of *Noviy Den*, said she did not believe Maksim had taken his own life. She said that the week before Borodin's fall, unknown assailants had attacked him from behind and hit him in the head with an iron pipe as he left his apartment block. He had to be treated in a hospital. What's more, he was about to get married and had a new job in Moscow.

'I know for sure this person was not planning to end his life, but rather to develop and enjoy a bright future,' she said.

Igor Pushkarev, a journalist who worked with him on the Syrian story, said both had received threats on the internet.

'If someone was going to be killed for this story, it should have been me,' he said, as he had tracked down the relatives of those killed in Syria.

In a lengthy Facebook, Maksim's friend Vyacheslav Bashkov claimed that Maksim called him at 5am the night before his fall.

Maksim had 'a worried voice,' he said and told him that he was 'surrounded by security officials'. There was 'someone with a weapon on his balcony and people in camouflage and masks on the staircase landing'.

Bashkov went on: 'Maxim expressed the opinion that in the shortest possible time they would come in, and now, apparently, they are waiting for the court's permission. Therefore, he needed a lawyer, which is why he called me.'

'Max's voice was alarmed, but not hysterical, not drunk. I immediately took everything seriously, promised to call anyone I can, and let me know as soon as someone responds.'

He called a number of lawyers and journalists but, an hour later, Maksim called him back and said he was 'mistaken', apologized and said that there had been some sort of 'training exercise' for the World Cup which was taking place in June.

'I didn't call him after that,' Bashkov wrote, 'although I was waiting for him to write something on Facebook. But he didn't write anything and on the 13th the media reported that Maksim had been found under his balcony and he was in the emergency room.'

After he heard his friend was in the hospital, Bashkov told the police about the call, but said they didn't question him further. Police hadn't contacted the lawyers and journalists he had called, he added.

'I think it's suspicious that those who spoke with Borodin the day before

12 April haven't been questioned,' he said. 'And of course many think that Maksim's death could have been linked to his publications about Syria and the Wagner private military company, but we can't assert anything until after the results of the pre-investigation probe have been announced.'

Harlem Desir, the representative for freedom of the media at the Organization for Security and Co-operation in Europe (OSCE) said Borodin's death was 'of serious concern' and called on the authorities for a swift and thorough investigation. Fifty-eight journalists had been killed since 1992, according to the Committee to Protect Journalists.

The following March when *Proekt*, an independent Moscow-based online news outlet which specializes in investigations, began to publish a series of articles looking into the role of the Wagner Group the editor-in-chief Roman Badanin said his journalists began to receive emailed threats of physical retribution for their work.

Hackers tried to break into his staff's personal accounts on Facebook, the Telegram messenger service and Google mail, he said, and one of his journalists was followed in the street by an unknown man who filmed her with a video camera.

'This is all simply an attempt to make us nervous, to distract from our journalistic work, to make it clear that we're under surveillance and that they're watching us,' Badanin told Reuters. He said he could not prove who was behind the harassment campaign, but said it peaked when *Proekt* ran an investigation into Wagner's new activities.

6

LIBYA, 2018

From 2014, *Wagnerovci* mercenaries built up a unique reputation for unscrupulous savagery and scary disregard for their own mortality. *Wagnerovci*, true to their founder's Nazi fascination, committed the most gruesome war crimes as part of their daily work. A British mercenary who had seen them in action in the Horn of Africa said: 'Their morality is not ours.' He described an incident he'd seen a few years earlier.

'The Wagner guys had caught some pirates,' he said. 'They tied them up, put them back in their boat, poured petrol over them and lit them. If you'd said something they wouldn't have thought there was anything strange. "That's what we do to pirates".'

They had two successes under their belt, Ukraine (Donbas, Crimea) and Syria. Whereas Wagner's operations in Ukraine had been a near impeccable exercise in stealth, their dogged fighting in Syria showed to any interested buyer of their services that, apart from brutality, they could alongside command the power of the Russian military (at a price). Unlike any other PMC, they were supplied through Russia's logistical network, deployed its military-grade weapons and were even able to call on the Russian airforce to support its 'private' operations due to the secret hand-in-glove co-operation with the Kremlin. Those interested in buying these services could count on maximum deniability as, according to the Russian Federation, right up to its President Vladimir Putin, Wagner PMC simply did not exist. The denial ahead of the Battle of Khasham bloodbath showed how far Moscow was prepared to go. And, with Putin personally behind the group, as well as the Kremlin itself invested in its commercial successes, it was a PMC like no other in the world—more a commercial branch enriching government officials than a private enterprise.

Apart from Russia's astonishing coup in Ukraine's Crimea, the Kremlin-Wagner promotors could also claim another unique selling point against its Western competitors: a willingness of its mercenaries to die for money at an unbeatable low price. Evidently, with kickbacks greasing the palm of every official involved, including Putin, the stage was set for Wagner aggressively moving into global combat zones that were dominated by Western PMCs. The world leaders were companies from the United States, Britain and Israel.

Governments contracted with private security companies to perform a wide range of operations, such as protecting cargo ships from pirates at sea, or safeguarding businesses with a global value of up to US$400 billion. For the Kremlin, there were not only these lucrative mercenary contracts up for grabs, there was also an Aladdin's cave of other potentially even greater spoils—as in Syria—that could be gained with Wagner PMC prepared to conquer them for Russia: oil and gas concessions, diamond and precious metal mining.

From 2017, Wagner PLC mercenaries started to turn up around the world, particularly in Africa and the Arabian Peninsula. In late 2017, according to SBU intelligence sources, a number of Wagner militants were spotted fighting in Yemen, in that country's civil war on the side of the Houthi uprising that started in 2014 even though Russia had declined an official request from the Houthi's leader, Mahdi al-Mashat. In January 2018, the US-based private intelligence company Stratfor also said that a number of Russian mercenaries had been deployed to Sudan to support the country's president, Omar al-Bashir, in his war against the breakaway country of South Sudan.

Libya was an exemplary case of the Kremlin's *modus operandi*. After the death in 2011 of Libya's leader Muammar Gaddafi, the previously stable oil-rich country had been plunged into a civil war with foreign nations discreetly fighting over the spoils by offering aid. Wagner PMC created the opportunity for Russia to have its cake and eat it by snatching the largest possible slice of mineral wealth it could.

In the autumn of 2018, Wagner Group mercenaries were first seen in Libya. General Khalifa Haftar, the warlord who presided over the Libyan National Army (LNA) and controlled much of the east of the country, had invited Russian 'private' help. *Wagnerovcis* were said to be scouting locations for a base in the ports of Tobruk and Benghazi.

In November 2018, Yevgeny Prigozhin was filmed sitting at the table during talks between Russia's defence minister and General Haftar. The Russian state-owned news agency *RIA Novosti* said Prigozhin and Shoigu were 'organizing the official dinner and participated in the discussion of the cultural programme for the Libyan delegation's visit'.

Following the talks some three hundred Wagnerites were sent, along with artillery, tanks, drones, ammunition and logistical capabilities. A British government source was quoted as saying: 'They are trying to secure the deep-water ports of Tobruk and Derna for the Russian fleet and also could control the flow of oil to southern Europe if they take over Libya's energy industry.' LNA spokesman Brigadier-General Ahmed al-Mismari described the reports of Wagner's presence as 'fake news', telling Russia's state-owned news agency Tass: 'Such assertions are ludicrous and absurd.' The Kremlin said the same.

However, in October 2019 *Meduza.io*, quoting an FSB veteran and a person close to Wagner, said that up to thirty-five mercenaries had been killed in the ongoing civil war in Libya. Seven Wagner mercenaries were killed in a strike on a building of the operational headquarters of Haftar's supporters in the city of Qasr Ben Ghashir, south of Tripoli.

In a separate development, Mohamed Gnounou, the military spokesman for the UN-brokered Tripoli-based Government of National Accord (GNA)— which Haftar's Libyan National Army was trying to oust from Tripoli—said that on 27 September GNA warplanes 'carried out air strikes over the previous two days targeting foreign mercenaries, including eight from the Russian Wagner group, who were preparing to mobilize against the capital'.

While *Meduza* had the names of several of the Wagner mercenaries killed, neither the Russian government nor Wagner itself had formally notified the families of any combat deaths. According to the Kremlin, the Wagner Group didn't exist and this omission was to be expected. But it was contrary to Wagner's normal practice, which was to send death certificates and any military decorations to the relatives of combatants who were killed.

Maxim Khlopin, head of the Urals branch of the Union of Donbas Volunteers, however, confirmed the names of two of those killed as Artem 'Hulk' Nevyantsev and Ignat 'Benya' Borichev. They were both from Yekaterinburg and both reportedly previously fought on the Russian side in eastern Ukraine.

Social media posts suggested that some of the other mercenaries killed in the Tripoli airstrike also previously fought in eastern Ukraine against the Kyiv government. Videos posted by Libyan troops of the UN-backed government showed possessions said to belong to them. One of the items was a bank card belonging to Vadim Bekshenev, a Wagner platoon commander.

Furthermore, Wagner fighters seriously injured in the airstrike were evacuated to Russia. Among them was Alexander Kuznetsov, who had been honoured by President Putin during a Kremlin ceremony in 2016. Kuznetsov was treated in a clinic in St Petersburg which had ties to Vladimir Putin and his family.

Under Russian law, all medical facilities are obliged to report combat injuries to the police for investigation as it was in principle illegal for a Russian citizen to participate in armed conflicts. The clinic was owned by a large insurance company AO Sogaz. Its general director was Vladislav Baranov, who had a business relationship with Putin's eldest daughter Maria Vorontsova, née Putina, an endocrinologist. She was co-founder and a board member of AO Nomeko, another medical company that listed Baranov as its general director. Vorontsova's AO Nomeko listed the Sogaz unit that ran the clinic treating mercenaries as one of its 'partners' on its website.

A Reuters correspondent found *Wagnerovci* Kuznetsov smoking a cigarette in the clinic's backyard in late October 2019. He told her that he had been in Libya where Russians were 'fighting international terrorism to protect Moscow's interests'. He was swathed in bandages and sported a metal device used to fix complex bone injuries. Another Wagner fighter at the clinic identified him as the commander of the assault unit fighting in Libya.

Kuznetsov did not know who was paying for the treatment he was receiving either. Quizzed, the mother of another severely wounded Wagner fighter treated there said that the treatment was free of charge and neither she nor her son knew who covered the expenses. She also said she had seen documents that put one of the medical services her son had received at 600,000 rubles ($10,000).

In fact, the Sogaz clinic had been treating injured Wagner fighters since 2016. A former Wagner fighter who had been injured in Syria said he had been treated there along with five or six other wounded mercenaries.

AO Sogaz generally provided Russian army personnel and members of Russia's National Guard—a new military unit formed in 2016 that reported directly to Putin—with life and health insurance, according to an official government database of state contracts. The insurance company had other ties to Putin. Its deputy chief executive is Mikhail Shelomov, who was Putin's second cousin. Putin's publicly acknowledged friend Yuri Kovalchuk and his wife also had a stake in Sogaz. And the chairman of the board of directors was Gazprom chief executive Alexei Miller who worked at the St Petersburg mayor's office alongside Putin in the 1990s.

While the Wagner Group were fighting alongside the Libyan National Army (LNA) in the east of the country, Putin played the Kremlin's double game. He invited Fayez al-Sarraj, prime minister of the official GNA that held the Libyan west, to a meeting of African leaders at Sochi.

Meanwhile, Ukrainian and Belarusian pilots and technicians thought to be employed by the Wagner Group were being used to carry out airstrikes on Tripoli and other cities held by the GNA on behalf of the LNA which had killed dozens of civilians.

Haftar had gained air superiority recently thanks to two F-16 fighter planes provided by the United Arab Emirates. A GNA source said: 'Haftar has changed the way he uses the Wagner Group after it lost a number of fighters recently south of Tripoli, including a prominent commander.' He added that Wagner had provided Haftar with pilots and technicians, who are present at the Watiya Airbase, west of Tripoli, and the Al-Jafra Airbase to the south of the capital.

Richard Norland, the US ambassador to Libya estimated that there were two thousand Wagner personnel in Libya which were being used 'to undermine the recognized government'. The GNA complained that the Syrian airline

Cham Wings was flying them in. Jalel Harchaoui, a Libya specialist and research fellow at the Clingendael Institute, a Dutch think-tank, said Wagner Group had sent about two hundred Russian fighters to Libya in the first three months of 2020.

The ingenuity of the Russians to drive down the cost per mercenary knew no bounds. The Wagner Group had been training former Syrian rebel fighters at the al-Assad regime's '18th unit' camp, eastern Homs province, they had recruited to fight in Libya. Wagner recruiters targeted former rebels who were being harassed by the security forces. They were offered $1,200 a month to sign up.

In Quneitra, an area close to the border with Israel, Elizabeth Tsurkov, a Syria expert at the Foreign Policy Research Institute who spoke to community members, said the men signed up because their families 'were going hungry'.

'This is only happening because of immense need,' Tsurkov said. 'They have no alternatives'.

'They were told the mission would be securing oil fields and Russian facilities. If they agreed, the security forces would stop the abuse against them,' said Syrian activist Omran Musalmah. 'But when they reached the training camps in Homs they learned they were going to fight with Haftar against the government in Tripoli. Most went home.'

Libya Al-Ahrar TV's Twitter feed suggested that there was 'evidence of recruitment of Syrian children in the Libyan conflict'.

Egyptian-Canadian photojournalist Amru Salahuddien said he witnessed on Wednesday several GNA fighters falling to the ground, 'slightly shaking and unable to breathe normally'. While receiving treatment in hospital he saw GNA fighters with 'no visible injuries' shaking and vomiting with 'epilepsy-like symptoms'.

The GNA's interior minister Fathi Bashagha also accused the Wagner Group of using banned chemical weapons in Libya.

'In the Salah al-Din front, our fighters were exposed to nerve gas from Haftar's forces, and were paralyzed and then sniped. This deed can only be carried out by Wagner,' he said.

Further muddying the water in the country, Moscow was also promoting Saif al-Gaddafi, Colonel Gaddafi's son and one-time heir apparent who had been trying to establish his own power base after being released from jail in the town of Zintan.

According to leaked documents, the Wagner Group had presented him with a comprehensive strategy to return to power in the summer of 2019. It also restarted Jamahiriya TV, a channel that had been used to disseminate Gaddafi senior's view of the world, and had moved to Cairo from where it had been broadcasting intermittently. Wagner also set up a dozen Facebook groups promoting both Saif al-Gaddafi and Haftar, using sophisticated methods employed in US elections.

The Kremlin's gamble to capture Libya's oil riches proved in vain. By 25 May 2020, it was reported that the Wagner Group had been forced into a humiliating retreat in the face of Turkish troops that had arrived in Libya to support the GNA. Hundreds of men were filmed driving south from the capital, Tripoli, towards the town of Bani Walid, after their local allies announced a pullback from a number of front lines. After giving up some of their last strongholds in the south of Tripoli, Wagner Group troops were filmed retreating through the desert. Pro-GNA media claimed that 1,500 Wagner troops had fled to Bani Walid, taking artillery and other heavy weapons with them. They were then said to have flown on to a remote airbase at Juffrah in the centre of the country.

GNA army spokesman, Mohammed Gununu, said they had withdrawn from three military camps in southern Tripoli and the suburb of Salaheddin. Three planes had been seen taking off, thought to be carrying Wagner elements. The US accused Russia of sending fourteen jet fighters to provide the Wagner Group with close air support, but the planes arrived too late to prevent the withdrawal. They had stopped in Syria to be repainted to conceal their origin.

Following the reversal, Libyan peace talks finally resumed. As GNA troops cleared the suburbs of Tripoli that had been occupied by the mercenaries, they came across the evidence of Wagner PMC's barbarous handiwork.

There were hundreds of landmines, IEDs and booby traps left in civilian areas. A teddy bear taped to a mortar shell hidden under a table was found in one home. It had six trip wires attached to it so it would explode when someone approached it from any direction. Mohammed Ali Abdallah, a senior adviser to the GNA, said that the teddy bear booby trap was 'straight out of the Russian Wagner Group playbook'.

Explosives were attached explosives to toilet seats and doors, designed to detonate upon touch, Libyan deminers say. They discovered 107 improvised explosive devices on a single street. One toilet was designed with a sensor to ignite nine pounds of TNT when a person sat on it.

Most devious were in empty soft-drink cans. Many young Libyans like to playfully crush them and the pressure plate would trigger the device with the weight of half an AK-47 bullet. 'They studied us, even how our kids played,' says Rabie Aljawashi, the head of the Free Fields Foundation, a Libyan demining agency. 'They know how we think.'

The deminers also report finding a range of innovative mines, including a Russian 'scattering mine' that deploys itself and self-destructs in 100 hours, an anti-personnel mine with laser beams as trip wires, and sinister combinations of mines, such as an arrangement in which one mine is a decoy and another explodes. One Ukrainian adviser said the devices resembled those used in the conflict in Crimea, where Wagner troops have also fought.

An independent fact-finding mission on Libya, commissioned by the UN Human Rights Council, said that there were 'reasonable grounds to believe' that personnel from the Wagner Group 'may have committed the crime of murder' by firing gunshots directly at people not taking direct part in the hostilities.

By the middle of June Wagner PMC was back in action, riding into the giant Sharara oilfield accompanied by Sudanese Janjaweed fighters in a show of force designed to protect territory controlled by forces supporting Haftar. Libyan National Oil Corporation (NOC) chairman Mustafa Sanalla called for them to leave.

'This group is a grave danger to our oil facilities,' he said. 'It is a grave danger to our employees. Our employees live in fear with this armed, foreign group present in our oil facilities. This is a big problem. We need this group to leave without delay and without negotiations.'

The Wagner Group were also interfering in the oil industry in LNA-held Libya. According to *The Wall Street Journal*, Haftar initially let ports reopen but promptly changed his mind when Wagner Group moved to the Es-Sider terminal.

Nevertheless, by 28 July, the US State Department was threatening Haftar with sanctions due to his connections to Wagner after the Pentagon released satellite images of Wagner troops and equipment—including Russian SA-22 air defence systems, IL-76 military cargo aircraft and mine-resistant armoured vehicles—on the front line at Sirte, a port city key to Libya's oil production. The Ukrainians also believed Wagner was tasked with testing new Russian weapons systems in Libya.

Novaya Gazeta analysed the photographs and identified some of the vehicles as an armoured version of the Russian Ural truck. The model seen in Libya was manufactured by Prigozhin's company Yevro Polis.

It was also reported that Wagner PMC was consolidating their presence at al Jufra airbase to the south of Sirte, deploying at least 14 MiG-29 and Su-24 fighter jets from Syria, and took control of the country's largest oilfield, El Sharara, and the exporting port Es Sider.

In September 2020, the UN envoy for Libya, Stephanie Williams, condemned violations of the arms embargo imposed on the country. Reuters reported that Russia had stepped up its logistical support for the Wagner Group in Libya with some 338 military cargo flights between November 2019 and July 2020.

In March the following year, a 550-page report by UN experts said that an array of international backers on both sides of the conflict had violated the arms embargo—including the Russian Wagner group but also US private military contractor Erik Prince.

On 11 August 2021, websites run by Patriot Media, a group owned by Yevgeny published more than a dozen articles taking aim at a BBC investigation into the role of Russian mercenaries in Libya. Patriot's flagship news outlet RIA FAN promised to 'debunk the BBC's pseudo-investigation'.

'Western journalists have once again published an assortment of inventions, rumours, falsified materials and fakes which have been disproved many times,' it said.

One post was headlined: 'How the BBC created a fantasy film about Russians in Libya'. In it, the BBC's film was described as a 'Hollywood-style' work of fiction 'shot-through with dramatism comparable to the level of sentimentality in a soap opera'.

RIA FAN's article dismissed evidence presented in the film, including the Samsung tablet left by a fighter from the Wagner group. The tablet stored a ten-page document from January 2020, which included a list of the weapons and equipment required for various sub-units within Wagner in Libya and codenames of senior Wagner staff. These include a 'director general' who the UN investigators said was 'highly probably Yevgeny Prigozhin', the man the Kremlin (and he himself) maintained was merely their go-to caterer.

The tablet also contained maps of the locations of thirty-five unmarked anti-personnel mines concealed in a civilian suburb of south Tripoli that was then a frontline area under Haftar's control, supported by Wagner, along with a list of requested items including drones and tanks that would violate the arms embargo if delivered. The failure to visibly mark the anti-personnel and anti-tank mines and issue warnings of their locations to civilians in these areas was evidence of a violation of international humanitarian law by Wagner and is considered a war crime.

RIA FAN, however, claimed the information on it was full of inconsistencies and falsehoods, and that it was likely that it had been tampered with, 'It is not clear where the tablet came from, or where and under what circumstances it ended up in the hands of the investigators.'

According to experts, there was no possible source for such items except the Russian military's stock. The device has Russian-language maps of the battlefront, video from drones. In addition, there were codenames belonging to mercenaries part of the organization, confirming Wagner PMC's presence.

There was also a ten-page 'shopping list' as part of a file provided by a Libyan intelligence insider and found at a site after Wagner had retreated. It was dated 19 January 2020. It suggested where the money and support for the mercenaries' activities could be coming from, and details items required for 'competition of military objectives'. Among the items on the shopping list were four tanks and high-end radar technology.

One expert said certain items on the list could only be acquired from Russia's armed forces. A second suggested it implicated Dmitry Utkin. Other references to Yevro Polis implicated Yevgeny Prigozhin.

Two *Wagnerovcis* spoke about the type of person who was willing to join up. It was warfare on a budget and money went before morals. One admitted they took no prisoners and instead killed whomever they captured: 'No-one wants an extra mouth to feed.'

One Libyan villager who played dead as his relatives were killed was able to identify two suspected killers. RIA FAN claimed to have spoken to the two suspected Russian fighters.

One of them, Fyodor Metyolkin, was quoted by the agency as saying: 'I'm simply shocked by where they put me. I've never been to Africa, I could not have been. It's just a fairy tale, tell it to someone and they won't believe it. They've shown my photo to a Libyan?! It's some sort of show! They've involved me in a war at the other end of the world. I'm now with a lawyer I know, I think I'll go to court because this accusation is just crazy. I'm just a worker at a construction site. Turns out they've found a strategic tablet at the other end of the world, with me on it, too. Just unbelievable. I never thought this was possible.'

The other one, Vladimir Andanov, was quoted as saying: 'I laugh out loud any time something like this gets published online. Photos of us having fun playing airsoft [a Japanese survival game] are all over the world now. We're meant to be militants. Come on, I've got gigabytes of these pics, I can send them to anyone who wants them. That's bloody ridiculous. Of course, I've never been to war. Any sane person will see that it's all turned upside down there. That's just crazy, unbelievable.'

RIA FAN said that allegations of its owner's, Kremlin 'caterer' Yevgeny Prigozhin, involvement was another 'invention'. It recited an official Russian Defence Ministry communique that said Prigozhin was present at a meeting between Defence Minister Sergei Shoigu and the LNA's Khalifa Haftar only because he was providing catering services.

Maxim Shugalei, head of the Russian Foundation for the Protection of National Values, said on his Telegram channel.

'Media like the BBC disseminate preposterous fakes which stand up to no criticism,' he said. 'Utter disgusting rubbish. There may be a reason why this film has appeared now. Another meeting of the UN or some other useless and little effective organisation must be coming up, because this is why hastily put together fakes are planted on their eve.'

Shugalei had previously been jailed in Libya on charges of election meddling and was suspected of working for Wagner PMC in Madagascar.

Russian officialdom widely joined in to denunciate Russian involvement in

Wagner PMC's Libyan war crimes, stating that it was part of Britain's dirty tricks campaign against the Federation to take advantage of Libya's oil.

State Duma member Sergei Vostretsov said that there was an information war going on aiming to drive Russia out of the Middle East, leaving the oil and gas for the US.

'Biased media do not have a single truthful argument,' he said. 'Therefore, they use fakes and slander to denigrate Russia.'

Another member of the Duma, Alexander Sherin, said: 'Cases which will be considered by the BBC or any other foreign channels mean no good for Russia, and they can often be fabricated.... English representatives have already put forward preposterous claims which were never confirmed. We remember English spies who hid stuff under stones. That country shouldn't engage in investigations. Britain is the first country to meddle in other countries' affairs.'

Frants Klintsevich, a member of the Duma's upper house, said: 'It's an attempt to discredit Russians. Fakes and provocations have become the norm for the BBC. I get the impression that American secret services first of all have become the main sponsor for that radio station. It receives most of its income via grants and affiliated companies, and that is why where there is the BBC, there is no honest journalism, they've long walked down the path of provocation and fakery.'

Russian Foreign Ministry spokeswoman Maria Zakharova weighed in and said: 'Unfortunately, the British media did not think it necessary to take account of the facts'.

RIA FAN own commentator Vadim Manukyan: 'The BBC mostly does fake news, they have been caught spreading it on numerous occasions, and they invented this story, too. What for? To denigrate Russia once again and slap some of their sanctions onto Russians.'

The agency's head Yevgeny Zubarev wrote a letter to the BBC's Director-General, Tim Davie, saying he was 'amazed' by the 'unprofessionalism' of the BBC's investigation.

RIA FAN's director general went on: 'It is doubtful that the BBC is capable of teaching other news outlets the standards of the world's democratic press. It is highly unlikely that anyone would want to learn from 'journalists' who ask for comments from anonymous speakers (played by actors) or find evidence at bus stops. But this is easily fixable: we welcome BBC staff as interns at the Federal News Agency.'

The message to other countries was loud and clear: whitewashing Wagner PMC's business was Russian Federation business. Unlike the Syrian war, Russian mass media simply ignored the events in Libya and its domestic audience was none the wiser.

7

PUTIN'S KEY TO AFRICA

At the same time when Libya's general Haftar was brought on board as a new client, the Kremlin convinced Sudanese President al-Bashir to engage the *Wagnerovcis*. In Sudan, the mission started after a meeting between Vladimir Putin and Sudanese al-Bashir in late December 2017 when the Sudanese president asked his presidential peer for military assistance. Bashir, who was indicted in 2009 by The Hague International Criminal Court for war crimes, needed powerful allies as he became increasingly isolated both at home and abroad. A meeting with President al-Assad of Syria, for what critics called 'a genocide summit', was thought to have been a favour to Russia, which provided a military flight from Khartoum to Damascus.

Russia twice hosted Bashir, who also agreed to help Putin realise his ambitions for greater influence in Africa. The Sudanese president promised to make Sudan Putin's 'key to Africa'. During his first reciprocal Russian visit to Putin in November, 2017, Bashir duly signed an agreement granting concessions for gold exploration and diamond mining in Haute-Kotto Prefecture to a company M Invest. It was this company, among others, that would later reveal how Prigozhin was the spider in the Wagner PMC web.

M-Invest, which had a Sudanese subsidiary called Meroe Gold, started its operations in Sudan after Omar al-Bashir first met Vladimir Putin, offering him the mining concessions and also allowing him to build a naval base on the Red Sea. It was then that Wagner moved to train and equip the Rapid Support Forces, with large quantities of weapons and equipment to Sudan, including military trucks, amphibious vehicles and two transport helicopters. At the time of the Moscow visit of Sudanese president al-Bashar to Putin in November 2017, Igor 'Strelkov' Girkin said: 'The first Wagner detachment has already been dispatched to Sudan.' They were also active in promoting misinformation and disinformation from Sudan to its African neighbours.

Russian mercenaries worked to secure key gold mines for Russian mining companies in Sudan and an estimated thirty tons of Sudanese gold was exported to Russia every year, protected by mercenaries from the Wagner Group. 'One of the things that we've seen when Russia started to deploy its Wagner personnel to Sudan is that they were very focused on protecting the gold mining efforts,' said Sim Tack, cofounder of Force Analysis, a Belgium-based consultancy that specialized in conflict. Sudanese gold might have been the working capital that funded Wagner PMC's wage bill across the world, facilitating its rapid expansion and domination of the supply of mercenaries globally at the expense of traditional rivals.

In a few short years, the Putin-Bashir cooperation blossomed and the Kremlin even went on to authorize civil nuclear energy projects in the Uranium-rich country as opposition against Bashir gained momentum. After rioting broke out on 9 January, 2019, opposition sources reported that Wagner Group provided strategic and practical training to the Sudanese intelligence and security forces. Images emerged in the Western media of dozens of white men, dressed in camouflage, and being transported in trucks to observe anti-government protests in Khartoum. In late January 2019, the SBU published on its website a list of 149 Wagner group mercenaries operating in Sudan on behalf of al-Bashir's regime, a charge denied by Khartoum and ignored by the Kremlin. A former mercenary confirmed that in February 2019 white men in camouflage photographed at protests in Sudan that month were Wagner mercenaries involved in training local police on suppressing techniques. Russia's payoff was thought to include, in addition to the gold mining contracts, natural gas exploration agreements and the possible construction by Russia of an oil refinery in Sudan with the capacity to produce 200,000 barrels per day.

The way the Kremlin positioned and moved Wagner PMC forward was exceptionally sly. It turned out that M Invest had paid for a trip taken by Nikolai Dobronravin, a Russian professor and Africa specialist based at St Petersburg State University, to Bangui, the capital of Central African Republic. He travelled with three Prigozhin employees, including Dmitry Sytii, the founder of Lobaye Invest, another company formed to exploit African resources that would turn out to be controlled by Prigozhin. Sytii worked for the Internet Research Agency (IRA), the St Petersburg media outlet owned by Prigozhin's Patriot media group. Travel and billing records and email correspondence indicated that Dobronravin worked as a consultant for at least two Prigozhin-linked firms.

Engineered by the Kremlin, a conflict of interest unfolded. In a diplomatic pincer movement by the Kremlin, Dobronravin went on to become Russia's representative on a four-person UN expert panel on Sudan, the UN body responsible for monitoring the security sector as well as human rights and arms-embargo violations in Sudan. The experts were uniquely placed to influence the lifting of sanctions and the opening up of Darfur, Western Sudan, for uranium and other mining. Lifting sanctions would be important to the usefulness of the concession granted to M Invest, as well as to the Sudanese military, Moscow's main ally in Khartoum, and militia groups trafficking gold across the Libyan border.

Dobronravin admitted he did a 'short consultancy' in the Central African Republic, but said the invitation was 'personal' and he only found out about the M Invest connection to the panel's terms of reference subsequently. He strenuously denied that his work for M Invest affected his current UN role, and said the firm had not been under sanctions at the time. Dobronravin added that, in any case, he himself had never written anything for the UN that favoured companies that consulted him. 'Any bias would be immediately seen by the panel,' he said. 'I'm proud of my work for the UN. It was done with all possible accuracy.' The Kremlin did however know the details of M Invest and Lobaye Invest.

A few months after the sponsored 2017 trip to Bangui, Central African Republic, Russia's foreign ministry had tried to get Dobronravin also onto a UN expert panel responsible for the Central African Republic. This had proved unsuccessful. A high-ranking Russian diplomat then coached Dobronravin and helped him with an application for the Sudan UN job, according to documents obtained by Mikhail Khodorkovsky's Dossier centre which tracks the criminal activity of the Kremlin.

Khodorkovsky's files suggested Dobronravin kept in touch with Dmitri Sytii afterwards, as well as with other Prigozhin-linked individuals in St Petersburg. Dobronravin said, however, that his travelling companions on the 2017 Bangui trip 'did not introduce themselves in detail', or reveal their surnames and Khodorkovsky's files were wrong.

In 2017, at the same time as the deployment to Sudan, and in early 2018 other groups of Wagner mercenaries were despatched to the Central African Republic, confirmed both Sukhankin of the Jamestown Foundation, DC, and 'Strelkin'. They were engaged to support the local government amid long-running ethnic and sectarian violence in the country, and ensure privileged access for Russian businesses to the country's resources.

Wagner PMC took a lease on the palace of the former head of state, the self-styled Emperor of Central Africa, Jean-Bédel Bokassa, where the late dictator was accused of feeding enemies to lions and crocodiles or cannibalizing their flesh himself for potency. It was said the *Wagnerovcis* were there to guard the country's main diamond mine.

The Russian foreign ministry itself stated they weren't mercenaries but non-combatant 'civilian instructors'. 'Responding to a request of the president of the Central African Republic, the Russians made the decision to render [the government in] Bangui gratis military-technical assistance' was the tight-lipped explanation the ministry gave regarding 'publications on the nature and content of the bilateral relations of Russia and the Central African Republic'.

There was nothing to see. Everything was in accordance with international law, Russia claimed. 'With the consent of UN Security Council Committee

2127, a consignment of rifle arms and ammunition at the disposal of the Russian Defence Ministry was supplied at the end of January-start of February of this year for the needs of the Central African army,' the ministry said. 'Five military officers and 170 Russian civilian instructors for training Central African Republic service personnel have also been assigned there with the consent of this committee.'

The so-called instructors, however, had 'military bearing' and replaced Rwandan servicemen from the UN peacekeeping contingent guarding the president of the Central African Republic, Faustin-Archange Touadéra. They appeared at a gala celebrating the second anniversary of his assumption of power. Touadéra admitted the presence in the republic of a 'detachment of Russian military specialists to beef up the security of the head of state'.

'Russian instructors training our armed forces will greatly strengthen their effectiveness in combating plunderers,' Touadéra told Russian state-owned media.

Neil Hauer, an observer of Wagner's activities based in Tbilisi, Georgia, said that the republic was a natural next step in the Kremlin's new foreign policy of pushing Wagner PMC.

'Add in the promise of lucrative gold and diamond resources and it's easy to see why the country would be an attractive target for Moscow and a profitable one for Wagner,' he said. All payments had to be made in cash as all banks in the Central African Republic made transfers through correspondent accounts in France which blocked Russia from making bank transfers.'

Meanwhile, Wagner's costs were going down as it had found a new pool of recruits. 'Interviews with families of deceased Wagner fighters, many of them drawn from central Russia's dilapidated Ural region, have confirmed the group's monetary allure,' Hauer reported.

Meanwhile, in the face of the growing number of recruits the mercenaries' pay shrank substantially—increasing the profits of Wagner PMC. The average Wagner monthly pay cheque had fallen in 2017 by a third from 300,000 rubles (US$5,000), its initial high in 2013, to 240,000 rubles a month (US$3,550). The rate in 2018 fell to 160,000 rubles (US$2,570), but still far outstripped the typical wages in provincial Russia.

To fund this Russia and the Central African Republic began joint 'exploratory mining concessions', while Wagner mercenaries 'guarded' gold and diamond mines in rebel-held areas. The two countries also signed a military cooperation agreement. France, the United States and Britain then placed a block on further arms shipments from Russia to the Central African Republic, although Moscow was allowed to send another sixty 'instructors'. By the following year, the Central African Republic's defence minister told state media that Russian instructors had trained 1,300 of its troops at an 'army educational centre' in Berengo, adding that this could be expanded.

What the truth of the matter was, was brutally suppressed. Three journalists, Orkhan Dzhemal, a well-known Russian war correspondent, Alexander Rastorguyev, an award-winning filmmaker, and Kirill Radchenko, a cameraman, went to the Central African Republic to make a film on Wagner's activities for the online news organization Investigation Control Centre (TsUR) funded by Mikhail Khodorkovsky. They tried to visit Wagner troops' reported headquarters in Jean-Bédel Bokassa's former palace. On 30 July 2018, however, they were shot dead when their vehicle was ambushed.

According to Russia's Investigative Committee, the Russian nationals were killed by locals wearing turbans and speaking Arabic during an armed robbery near the village of Sibut, about 185 miles north of the capital Bangui. The driver of the car they were travelling in was the only person to survive the attack. The official investigation stated that, 'The journalists were stopped by an armed gang of unidentified persons, who then cowardly killed them and stole some of their belongings.'

Central African Republic government authorities said they suspected members of Seleka, a group of mostly Muslim rebels that controlled more than half of the country, were responsible after the journalists had ventured past a government checkpoint into rebel-controlled territory despite warnings from soldiers. A Russian Foreign Ministry spokesman, furthermore, denied that the journalists' deaths were linked to their mission to investigate the presence of *Wagnerovci*. Russian investigators concluded the three men were 'attacked by unknown people who intended to rob them and were killed when they tried to resist'.

But Khodorkovsky's Dossier Centre said the evidence did not support that conclusion. The attack on the journalists appeared to be professionally planned. Attempts to say the murder began as an armed robbery stemmed from a concerted cover-up on the part of individuals controlled by the Wagner PMC leadership the centre countered. Also, the journalists' money and film equipment were left on the road, and robbery was evidently not the motive for the ambush.

It appeared that Russia was running with the hare and hunting with hounds in the Central African Republic, on one hand supplying arms to President Touadera's forces, but also using private security contractors to trade with the Seleka rebels opposing them. Footage obtained by France 24 news channel showed Russian Wagner operatives delivering field hospital materials to rebel groups by truck in a convoy that also carried weapons. The head of the opposition Seleka was former Central African Republic president Michael Djotodia, who was educated in Russia and was married to a Russian woman.

The murder and subsequent investigation were picked apart methodically by Khodorkovsky's team, revealing numerous discrepancies between the officially declared explanations and the actual circumstances of the crime. The findings were published in a lengthy dossier almost a year to the day after the murders. It concluded that the official explanation for the journalists' deaths was 'indefensible' and presented evidence that 'military instructors' employed by Wagner PMC were involved in the incident'.

Mobile phone records and other documents showed that the car of the three journalists was being followed by an officer of the Central African Republic's special forces, Emmanuel Kotofio. Before and after their killing, Kotofio repeatedly called the driver of the TsUR journalists and a Russian instructor under the command of Valery Zakharov, security advisor to the president of the Central African Republic, who was a former Russian state security agent and also had links to Russian mining companies registered there. Zakharov previously worked as a security consultant for companies belonging to Yevgeny Prigozhin, according to a joint report by *Fontanka.ru* and Prigozhin's own Federal News Agency (FNA). Previously, FNA had played a key role in promoting Russia's military operations in Syria. The journalists' driver, too, could be linked to Prigozhin's companies.

The journalists' editor had asked a Federal News Agency (FNA) reporter for help organizing the trip. That reporter put them in touch with a mysterious fixer named 'Martin,' who said he couldn't meet them but sent a former police officer to drive them.

Although the three men had been planning to travel east from Sibut to Bambari, their driver instead took them north, where they were ambushed and shot. Radchenko was severely beaten before being killed. The driver was unharmed. He said that they had been ambushed by 'Arab-speaking local men'.

Soldiers at a checkpoint later told reporters from Khodorkovsky's London-based Dossier Centre that Kotofio and three armed white men had come through twenty minutes before the journalists. The soldiers had been told to let the reporters' jeep pass. Following the killings, Kotofio was reportedly promoted.

Khodorkovsky's Dossier Centre said the three journalists had been put under surveillance and the murder was premeditated. No action was taken by Central African Republic law enforcers to investigate the crime and they had ignored or concealed the evidence they had received. Witness statements obtained by the Central African Republic investigators contained facts that mysteriously failed to make it into the official investigation. From the day the murders took place, a disinformation campaign impeded the independent investigation. Media controlled by Prigozhin played an active role in trying to dispel any suspicions around people connected with Prigozhin, according to the Dossier Centre.

At his annual end-of-year press conference in December 2018, Russian president Vladimir Putin was asked about the deaths of Dzhemal, Rastorguyev and Radchenko, and the activities of the Wagner Group in Central African Republic.

'It was certainly a tragedy,' he said. 'These people died and left behind families and friends. In general, unfortunately, a lot of tragedies are connected with journalists. I think we should never forget them, including the journalists who died in south-eastern Ukraine under fire, or were killed in gun attacks, practically assassinated. Please do not forget about them, either.'

'As far as I know, your colleagues travelled to Africa as tourists, not even as journalists, without notifying local authorities. According to the data available to date, some local groups are behind this attack.'

'As far as I understand, an investigation is underway. Unfortunately, there is no reliable information yet, but we strongly hope that it will be eventually obtained. We are on top of this situation through our diplomatic channels. I hope that at least at some point we will find out what happened there. My heart goes out to you, to all members of the editorial board and the families of the people who died there.'

Putin's words were taken as a veiled threat to Russia's media. Another Russian journalist, Sergei Kanev, was also working on the Central African Republic assassination for *The Insider*, a Russian opposition website. Fearing arrest, he fled Russia. Khodorkovsky said that Russian security service officials were planning to accuse Kanev of 'organizing a terrorist act against the head of state'. He added: 'We were forced to get him out of the country.'

Kanev was the journalist who had named Colonel Anatoliy Chepiga as one of the two alleged Russian intelligence agents who travelled with Novichok to Britain in March 2018 to try to kill Sergei Skripal, a former double agent living in Salisbury, and his daughter. Kanev had also previously written about Putin's eldest daughter Maria Vorontsova, who lived a luxurious life in the Netherlands with her Dutch husband, while most Russians lived on the breadline.

As for the Wagner Group itself, Putin dissimulated and told journalists: 'Everything must remain within the law, everything. We can ban private security firms altogether, but once we do so, I think you will be flooded with petitions demanding to protect this section of the labour market. Almost a million people are employed there. If this Wagner group breaks any laws, the General Prosecutor's Office will go ahead and give it a legal assessment.

'Now, about their presence in foreign countries. To reiterate, if they comply with Russian laws, they have every right to work and promote their business interests anywhere in the world.'

8

PRIGOZHIN

In February 2018, when the FBI posted the details of its US$250,000 reward for information about Prigozhin, Khodorkovsky jumped on the announcement. 'It's a pity that this is not yet for participating in the murder of journalists, but it is a good start,' he said in Russian on his blog post. From 2017, Yevgeny Prigozhin's notoriety around the world had been spreading fast, at that time, for reasons unrelated to Wagner PMC.

The impenetrable smokescreen created by the Kremlin had been so effective that few realised Prigozhin was Moscow's trusted backstage oligarch and discreet personal fixer who went above and beyond. Hiding behind Kremlin walls, he was the visionary mastermind who in 2013 invented and controlled Wagner PMC, coordinating and cutting kickback deals with Putin, FSB, GRU, and Ministry of Defence, as well as directing ex-colonel Utkin's troops, and taking over the bedraggled group's managerial role that Moran PMC's two arrested, convicted and incarcerated employees after their brief misadventure in Syria. It was, however, not the death squad with a reputation for kamikaze brutality that he had created that would make him infamous. It was his gift for digital warfare that would put him on the radar of Western law-enforcement authorities.

Some ten years younger than Putin, Prigozhin, too, was born in Leningrad in the Soviet Union—now St Petersburg, Russia—on 1 June 1961 (Putin's birthday is 7 October, 1950). Known by the diminutive 'Zhenya', he was brought up by his mother, a doctor who worked in a local hospital and later became a teacher. Prigozhin said that his father died while he was young and the family struggled to get by, while also caring for his sick grandmother. Both his father and stepfather were of Jewish descent. In later life, his mother took to painting and was the nominal head of some of her son's companies.

Like Vladimir Putin, Prigozhin was heavily into sports in his youth. He attended sports boarding school No 62 (now the College of Olympic Reserve No 1) that trained future Olympians where he studied with swimmer Vladimir Salnikov and gymnast Alexander Dityatin, three-time champion of the Moscow Olympics. Despite this privileged education, Prigozhin was not interested in joining the Communist Party and never joined. His preferred discipline was cross-country skiing. He was trained by his stepfather Samuil Zharkoy, a prominent instructor.

'We skied some fifty kilometres in a day,' he said in an interview with St Petersburg publication *City 812*. 'Alone with myself, I can go very long distances.'

But Prigozhin's sports career was derailed by his career as a petty criminal. In 1979, the year he turned 18, he was convicted of theft by the People's Court in Leningrad and sentenced to 2 and a half years in prison. This was suspended, though he was sent to live in a hostel in Novgorod, a hundred miles from St Petersburg, where he was put to work in a chemicals factory.

Back in Leningrad the following year, the nineteen-year-old Prigozhin teamed up with twenty-on-year-old Alexei 'Lesha' Bushman. With a tenth-grade education, Lesha was unemployed and had a criminal record, too, along with a child and an ex-wife he had recently divorced. They were joined by a previously convicted native of the Bryansk region, Valentina Makeko, and two Chelyabinsk residents—Vladislav Kopayve and Alexander E. (a minor at the time of the crimes so his surname was never reported).

In February 1980, Bushman and Prigozhin broke into the apartment of a Soviet citizen named 'Osipov' and stole a vase, a candy bowl, a napkin holder and some glasses with a value of 177 rubles, little more than the average monthly salary.

On 1 March, the drunken Prigozhin set out on a theft mission of his own. That night, he broke into an apartment where the Telitsin family lived. However, he was foiled by a local resident, who saw the young man on the windowsill of the first floor and raised the alarm. Prigozhin fled. The next night, he tried again with Bushman in tow. This time they were successful in stealing an Orbita tape recorder, a radio with an Orbita player, crystal, a denim jacket and a women's handbag containing makeup—in total, goods worth 980 rubles.

Valentina Makeko joined the two men on 14 March, guarding the door while they burgled an apartment on Bryantsev Street where the Rostovtsev family lived. They stole crystal, bonds, vases, fountain pens and automobile accessories worth 1,610 rubles. Although Alla Rostovtsev suspected Prigozhin of the theft, as he was a friend of her daughter's and had visited the apartment, the police had no evidence against him.

Five days later, on 20 March, the gang swindled a man named Kovalenko in a deal involving smuggled jeans, making off with 250 rubles. They were celebrating that night with Kopayve in the Ocean restaurant, drinking champagne and brandy. As they were leaving at midnight, Prigozhin spotted a young woman with an expensive coat and suggested they rob her.

Outside on the street Makeko stopped her by asking her for a cigarette. When she opened her handbag, Prigozhin grabbed her by the neck from behind and started choking her. Makeko also threatened her with a knife. She screamed for help until Prigozhin squeezed so hard that she passed out. They dragged her off the street and stole her boots and gold earrings.

It would cost the gang dearly as police heard her cries. They pounced, grabbing Kopayve while the others fled. However, the police turned up at the flat where Prigozhin and Bushman lived and found the handbag from the Telitsins' flat and property belonging to the Rostovtsevs. Witnesses had seen them in neighbourhoods of the Telitsins and Rostovtsevs. The amateur thieving gang had even taken a taxi to transport stolen goods after the break-in at the Rostovtsevs'.

In court, the gang tried to shield the others. Makeko took responsibility for the thefts, but the court did not believe her. Nor did they believe Prigozhin when he took sole responsibility for the scam involving the jeans. Bushman was sentenced to eleven years in a high-security penal colony, while Prigozhin got thirteen. An appeal to amend their sentences was dismissed.

It was in Russia's GULAG system that Prigozhin graduated to professional criminal. He was inculcated with the code of the Soviet *vorovskoi mir*— 'thieves' world', an underworld equivalent of the Communist Party. Its basic precepts were that you look after your own, never forget a slight and never back down.

After nine years, Prigozhin emerged from the GULAG into a country falling apart. On 26 December 1991, the Soviet Union was officially dissolved and the former Soviet states, notably Russia, had turned into a kleptocracy where oligarchs enriched themselves on privatised state companies and organised crime thrived.

Prigozhin started small but, remarkably, with seemingly respectable enterprises. Very little suggested that he was to become infamous around the world as a notorious merchant of death, hired by regimes wanting to kill their opposition.

He and his stepfather started selling hotdogs in the Aprashaka flea market in Leningrad. With McDonald's opening its first branch in Moscow, everything American was in demand and soon, he claimed, 'the rubles were piling up faster than his mother could count them in the kitchen of their modest apartment'.

With the help of a former classmate, he moved into the grocery business, running a chain of supermarkets in St Petersburg called Contrast. They also moved into gambling and, with businessman Igor Gorbenko, opened the first casino in the city. Licences had to be obtained from the Supervisory Board for Casinos and Gambling, newly established by the city's first elected mayor, Anatoly Sobchak. It was a first point of contact with the future President of Russia. The board's chairman was former KGB officer Vladimir Putin, who was also Sobchak's liaison with the local KGB and his director of city communications.

Money from Prigozhin's casinos provided capital for the Bank Rossiya, which was used by oligarchs to funnel money out of the country. The US Government later identified the bank as Putin's personal cashbox when sanctions were imposed on the bank by the UK and US after the invasion of Ukraine in 2022.

Meanwhile, Prigozhin and his two associates diversified further into construction, marketing research and foreign trade. With Kirill Ziminov, his supermarket Contrast's commercial director, Prigozhin opened in 1995 what became St Petersburg's first upmarket restaurant, The Old Customs House.

The venue's first incarnation was a wine club. Prigozhin brought in an English sommelier named Tony Gere who suggested that in the premise's vacant customs office he set up a German bar or an English pub serving good sausages and beer. No one came. They switched menus and started bringing in oysters and foie gras from Finland. Again it failed to attract a clientele. Next, true to his seedy former career, Prigozhin tried employing strippers to liven up the catering.

Business gradually picked up but for an unexpected reason. The increasingly respectable patrons of The Old Customs House said they enjoyed the cuisine but found the girls a distraction and they were ditched. Prigozhin later told the magazine *Elite Society* that the plain reason for his success was that the people of St Petersburg 'wanted to see something new in their lives and were tired of just eating cutlets with vodka'. Vladimir Putin, then one of St Petersburg's most influential officials, became one of the restaurant's regular patrons.

Two years later, inspired by the waterfront restaurants on the Seine in Paris, Prigozhin and Ziminov expanded their successful formula and through their company Concord Catering bought a rusty old ship docked on the Vyatka river and brought it to St Petersburg. They spent $400,000 remodelling it and converting it into a restaurant, which they called New Island. It soon became one of the most elite eateries in the city, immediately attracting businessmen and officials from the city and federal government. From petty criminal and GULAG jailbird, the rough Prigozhin seemed to have found his *metier* with an unlikely gift for wooing upmarket customers.

Two months after he became president of Russia, Putin paid a visit to Japanese Prime Minister Yoshir Mori. Prigozhin always made a point of serving distinguished guests himself. In the summer of 2001, Putin brought French President Jacques Chirac as well. Naturally, Prigozhin was on hand to serve the two heads of state himself.

'Vladimir Putin saw how I built up my business from nothing,' Prigozhin told *City 812*. 'He saw how I wasn't above serving two crowned heads. They were my guests, after all.'

As a result, Prigozhin earned not only Putin's respect but also the slightly derogatory nickname 'Putin's chef' or 'Putin's cook', though he was neither a cook nor a chef himself. Rather he hovered near his celebrated clients to be at their beck and call, sometimes clearing away empty plates, like a skilled *maitre-d*.

Later, after he had publicly admitted to leading the Wagner Group, Prigozhin, joked he ought to have been called 'Putin's butcher'. He certainly ran his restaurants with the same ruthlessness that he would treat his mercenaries from 2013. Prigozhin assaulted a chef after a complaint from a customer at one of his eateries about the quality of the food. The forty-year-old ex-employee of Concord Catering told the magazine that when a guest returned a dish because the tomatoes were not fresh 'the chef was taken to the cellar and pummelled to the point of being hospitalized for two months'.

In another incident, an unnamed witness—who is now in exile outside Russia—said he saw temporary employees who were accused of stealing food 'taken to a forest and beaten'. He added, 'I saw them do it'.

Prigozhin was initially 'a pleasant person, with a great sense of humour' but once you were under his orders he became swiftly terrifying, he said. 'One of his recurring jokes is to walk into his employees' office with guns in hand and say: 'Come on, let's talk, I'm going to kill you'. The possibility of dying in a car accident or being stabbed in the back on the street is something one has in mind when working at home.'

In May 2002, Putin dined with US President George W. Bush and his wife Laura on Prigozhin's New Island floating restaurant. The following year, Putin celebrated his birthday there. By then, Prigozhin had parted ways with his business partners and established himself independently in the restaurant and catering business.

It briefly appeared as if the formal criminal was turning a new leaf. While climbing the greasy pole, the ex-criminal, gulag-hardened businessman took time out to write a children's book. Called *Indraguzik*, it tells the tale of a little boy and his sister who live with their family inside a huge theatre chandelier. The story begins when the boy falls from the ceiling into the world of normal-size human beings below and follows his attempts to get home.

Ostensibly, the authors are Prigozhin's son and daughter, Pavel and Polina. However, the preface reveals that the book was a collaboration between Prigozhin and his children. It says that Pavel and Polina suggested the names of the main characters and persuaded their father 'to invent a story about a tiny boy named Indraguzik and his sister Indraguza'. The book was published by little-known publisher Agat in 2004. Inside its front cover, there is a photo of a beaming Prigozhin with his children and their mother, Lyubov Prigozhina. Just two thousand copies were printed and largely given away to friends and associates.

The ninety-page book is lavishly illustrated with colourful drawings attributed to Prigozhin, although there are no other public examples of the Wagner leader's artistic skills. According to the *Moscow Times*, the book ends with a poem that describes the story of Indraguzik's many adventures as 'funny and strange'.

Despite being a children's book, it is tempting to read it for incidents that may be relevant or prescient. During Indraguzik's adventures, he meets another 'small person' named Gagarik, who is described as an 'older man with a bird and a trench coat made from rough cloth'. Gagarik cooks soup for the boy. Eventually, Indraguzik ends up in the 'Big City' where he befriends a full-size human boy—aptly called Big Indraguzik—who helps his namesake and finds a balloon on which he can fly back up to the chandelier.

Along the way, the children discover that the chandelier is magic and can make people grow in size. Indraguzik offers to help the king of their native land by putting him in the chandelier, but they accidentally make him too big and he turns into a giant who is unable to rule effectively.

'How can I rule my people if they are so small? I could destroy them by mistake. Please make me the same king I was,' he says. 'Only a small king can rule the Izdraguziks.'

This was Prigozhin's only foray into the world of art and literature. He stayed in the catering business—for the time being at least.

In May 2008 his company Concord Catering won the contract to feed the guests at Dmitry Medvedev's presidential inauguration. With Putin forced by the constitution to temporarily take the role of prime minister and move to the White House on the Krasnopresnenskaya Embankment, Putin's chef maintained his position as a Kremlin insider throughout the Medvedev years. He catered for gala dinners for the then Prince Charles, Queen Sophia of Spain when she visited St Petersburg, Queen Sirikit of Thailand, Prince Philip of Spain, Chinese President Jiang Zemin and Italian Prime Minister Silvio Berlusconi, as well as catering for other high-level events, such as the celebration of the tercentenary of the founding of St Petersburg in 2003, laid on at grossly inflated prices.

Prigozhin opened a string of other upmarket, if kitsch, restaurants catering to the new moneyed classes in Russia. Nor did Putin forget about him. He also won contracts worth billions catering for government employees and school children. In the autumn of 2010, Vladimir Putin attended the opening ceremony of Prigozhin's 'Concord Culinary Line' factory outside St Petersburg. The factory was built specifically to supply schools with food. Putin's fingerprints were here, too. It cost roughly $53 million to build—$43 million of which came from the state-owned Vnesheconombank, which only granted credit in such generous proportions to construction projects tied to Putin's pet project, the 2014 Winter Olympics in Sochi. The bank was run by Putin's associate, Sergey Gorfov. It was reportedly a critical financial vehicle for oligarchs and served as cover for Russian intelligence operations overseas.

Soon, however, the parents of St Petersburg began protesting against the quality of food their children were being fed. They were concerned that all the produce provided by Concord claimed to have such a long shelf life that could only mean that it was full of harmful preservatives. In September 2011, the TV news show *Vesti* (news) aired a segment about several schools in St Petersburg going without any food. After this, Prigozhin mothballed his new factory, just one year after Putin had attended its opening.

The poor results in St Petersburg made no difference at all to Prigozhin's meteoric rise from petty criminal to starring in Russia's most inaccessible industry—government procurement. The company he fronted went on to win school catering contracts in Moscow. The three-year deal with the mayor's office was worth more than 10 billion rubles (US$154 million). Concord's next commercial coup dwarfed even this deal. The young company won the contract to supply food to the military worth roughly 50 billion rubles (US$768 million) a year. By 2012, more than ninety percent of all food orders for soldiers were supplied by businesses affiliated with Prigozhin. From Putin's chef, he had become the army's chef. Over two years, it was worth 92 billion rubles (US$1.4 billion).

In fact, Concord acted as a financial smoke screen for other activities. Prigozhin's so-called super contracts—worth at least $3.1 billion altogether according to information released by the Anti-Corruption Foundation, founded by a dissident politician and shuttered in 2021—were vital to enterprises far more lawless than feeding school children substandard food. The difference between the cost of supplying the food and the value of the payments was a Kremlin subsidy funding international operations organised by Prigozhin.

What were some of these 'operations'? On 26 February 2012, Moscow witnessed the 'Big White Circle' demonstration following contested parliamentary elections in December 2011. Uniting under the slogan 'For honest elections!' participants formed a ten-mile human chain around Moscow's Garden Ring road. It was a peaceful rally, and police didn't detain a single protester. But, curiously, hot tea and cookies were provided by a company run by Dmitry Koshara, the director of development for Prigozhin's Concord Catering. As a result of this seemingly friendly gesture, Koshara then reached an arrangement with the organizers that, at the next opposition rally, on 5 March—the day after the presidential elections—'security guards' from Concord would marshal the crowd.

Given Prigozhin's reliance on billions of Kremlin funding it would have been commercial suicide for any of his companies to be seen to provide assistance or even comfort to its detractors and certainly to opponents of his patron, Putin, in the presidential elections. It must have been another ghosting job organised by the Kremlin. Koshara could gather information about future rallies and about the leaders of the protest movement and insert its guards. Through them the Kremlin could control any disturbances, should they occur, without the need for police to get involved suggesting that the government didn't tolerate opposition.

And so it turned out. According to the independent Russian newspaper *Novaya Gazeta*—banned after the death of its secret protector Mikhail Gorbachev—Koshara was also collecting materials that would later be used in Anatomy of Protest, a documentary of the protests that aired on NTV, a television network closely associated with the FSB and since sanctioned by the US treasury. The documentary improbably accused the opposition of plotting a coup. Koshara himself boasted that every fifth account registered on the 'White-Circle' protest website, 26feb.ru, was one of his bots.

There were acts of more covert infiltration on behalf of the Kremlin. In September 2013, US President Barack Obama arrived in St Petersburg to attend the G20 summit. Obama was greeted by a demonstration of gay activists who stood with signs reading, 'Obama is with us' and 'Obama is our president'. The police dispersed the rally, but the demonstration, according to *Novaya Gazeta*, was the work of people linked to Prigozhin who wanted to control the protests. Later, these same people spread disinformation about the rally on the internet.

After a decade of such shady but highly lucrative on behalf of the Putin government, Prigozhin rapidly grew very wealthy. In 2016 *Delovoy Peterburg*, a Russian daily business newspaper published in St Petersburg, estimated Prigozhin's fortune at 7.14 billion rubles (US$70 million). The following year it listed him as ranking 83rd among the city's 304 ruble billionaires, with 11 billion rubles, or almost US$110 million.

Since the newspaper included only property listed in the public records, his wealth was even higher. If all property linked to him had been counted he would rank far higher. He had a 115-foot six-bedroom yacht costing $6 million, three private jets paid for in cash and a vintage powder blue Lincoln Continental, said to be Prigozhin's favourite car. Prigozhin's sprawling $105-million family estate outside St Petersburg to photograph had father-daughter mansions and various luxurious amenities, including a full basketball court and a helicopter pad.

The family also had a wooded compound near the resort town of Gelendzhik, where Putin has his 100-billion-ruble (US$1 billion) summer palace. Publicly Putin denied that the palace belonged to him, with the Kremlin saying that it was a private venture owned by various businessmen whose names could not be disclosed by the state for privacy reasons.

However, Putin as president did officially have a winter palace: the official residence of the president in St Petersburg, the Konstantinovsky Palace, which was originally built by the Romanovs, Russia's royal family. Prigozhin's daughter Polina was lavishly married there. 'The most difficult thing was to get millions of natural flowers,' she said, explaining how they cascaded from the palace's ceilings.

The favour Putin extended to Prigozhin's daughter was also extended to a—then—far more controversial couple. In September 2021, the wedding party of Grand Duke Georgy Mikhailovich Romanov, a hereditary pretender to the Russian throne, to Victoria Romanovna Bettarini, the daughter of an Italian diplomat, was also held at the presidential winter palace. It was the first royal wedding in Russia in over a century and a little over a century since the last Romanov Czar and his family were executed in 1918 in cold blood by Bolshevik revolutionaries, ostensibly acting on orders of Putin's predecessors.

The palace was now in the gift of Putin, who enjoyed receiving Romanov royalty and their 700 royal guests in his presidential quarters that had once been theirs. Putin's chef Prigozhin—then still a close ally of the Kremlin, rather than a rebel—as always looked after the presidential catering.

But behind this catering front there was always more to Prigozhin. He curried favour with everyone from the president's drivers to his security guards. Thus, by 2013, Prigozhin had become close to Viktor Zolotov, a former bodyguard who was elevated to become the director of Russia's new National Guard, known in Russia as 'Men in Black' because they wore black sunglasses and dressed in all-black suits, carrying a variety of weapons including portable rocket launchers. (Since the invasion of Ukraine, Zolotov mysteriously disappeared.)

Another one of Putin's bodyguards Prigozhin was close to was Roman Tsepov. After Putin left St Petersburg for Moscow, Tsepov provided security to a handful of crime bosses, including the family of the infamous mobster Alexander Malyshev. Despite being arrested on charges of illegal storage of weapons and drugs, and fleeing into exile in the Czech Republic to escape charges of extortion of US$70,000, Tsepov was present at the inauguration of Vladimir Putin in May 2000.

Like Zolotov's disappearance, Tsepov's fate was an ominous sign that working for Putin was risky business, a sign that Prigozhin was not to heed. Tsepov seemed to have had some clandestine role in Putin's administration, but he must have spectacularly fallen out of favour. On 11 September 2004, Tsepov visited colleagues at a local FSB office where he drank a cup of tea. Later that day, he fell ill. A *post-mortem* found, as if it was an ordinary line of inquiry, that the cause was poisoning by an unspecified radioactive material. His symptoms were very similar to those of Alexander Litvinenko, Putin's ex-KGB colleague, who died of Polonium 210 after it was administered in a cup of tea in November 2006. Tsepov died on 24 September, 2004.

9

TROLL FACTORY

There was something calculated about Prigozhin's stellar rise under Putin's wings. In St Petersburg, he had worked hard to impress the former FSB-officer to show that he was not above getting his hands dirty serving plates. The tireless dedication to gain Putin's trust since his St Petersburg casino funded Putin's Bank Rosiye paid off in many secret ways.

In his estimation, Prigozhin seemed to be Putin's action man. While he had no official position in the administration, in letters he referred to himself as an advisor to the presidential administration and a knight of the 'For Merit to the Fatherland' order, though there's no official record of him ever being publicly given such an award. Boris Vishnevsky, in 2018 an opposition member of the city council in St Petersburg, said the Kremlin commissioned the former criminal to organize and supervise operations that it didn't want the government to be seen to have an involvement in. The large-scale government catering contracts were simply a convoluted front to pay him for the type of services the Kremlin did want from their Mr Fixit.

Prigozhin had a gift for delivering what Putin desired, since his black-ops assignments rapidly expanded in importance and scope in proportion to the value of his government contracts.

They showed an innovative approach, combining offline and online warfare. In 2013, the same year that Prigozhin founded Wagner PMC, he set up an internet troll factory a few months before in St Petersburg called the Internet Research Agency (IRA). Its web warriors were known on the internet as the 'Trolls from Olgino'—Olgino being the district of St Petersburg where the IRA was located. Officially, the founder and CEO of the IRA was the retired police colonel Mikhail Bystrov, but the agency was created with the help of several people close to Prigozhin, including Alexandra Krylova who previously worked at Prigozhin's Federal News Agency (FNA).

In August 2013, an ad appeared on social networks saying: 'We need Internet operators! Work in a chic office in Olgino!!! Salary 25960 rubles per month [US$780]. Task: posting comments on specialized websites, writing thematic posts, blogs, social media…. Payment every week, 1180 rubles per shift (from 8.00 to 16.00, from 10.30 to 18.30, from 14.00 to 22.00). PAYMENTS EVERY WEEK AND FREE MEALS.'

Initially, the IRA worked under the radar. The project was known as 'Operation Lakhta' after the lake adjoining the Olgino district. Payments to it were accounted as for 'software support and development' and funnelled to it through the bank accounts of fourteen different affiliates. The IRA also set up a number of front companies to conceal its activities. By September 2016, the monthly budget for Project Lakhta submitted to Prigozhin's Concord company exceeded 73 million Russian rubles (US$730,000), including approximately one million rubles in bonus payments. Soon, however, the IRA boasted between four hundred and a thousand employees, some in-house, some working remotely.

The IRA's covert brief was wide-ranging. The Kremlin only permitted right-wing voices to make themselves heard in Russian media but it used Prigozhin's troll factory to then mitigate any criticism from these right-wingers. Its job was to write posts and comments on social media, praising Russian authorities and criticizing the 'opposition' for its extremist faults.

One of the Kremlin's severest right-wing critics was Alexei Navalny, the leader of a Russian nationalist party. He was also the founder of The Anti Corruption Foundation (TACF), which became a thorn in the side of the Kremlin by exposing the side deals and private enrichment of Putin and those around him. In August 2020, just before Russia's September elections, Navalny was poisoned and the foundation disbanded. He was becoming too popular or too critical and in 2022 received a nine-year sentence upon his recovery for embezzlement, increased by 19 years in 2023 when he continued to agitate against the Kremlin from inside his prison cell.

But in the years before 2020, Navalny was the subject of nuclear bombs launched by IRA troll. One typical phrase conceived and disseminated by the troll factory in Olgino read: 'Alexei Navalny, who calls himself a "truth seeker" and a "freedom fighter", has earned himself a reputation as a liar, a fraud and a traitor to Russia. Meeting with representatives of foreign intelligence services, Navalny once again proves that he's on the West's payroll.'

The scope of Prigozhin's IRA activities extended far outside Russia. After the murder of Russian dissident Boris Nemtsov near the Kremlin in February 2015, for instance, the trolls were given the following assignment: 'The main idea is that we're cultivating the view that Ukrainian players might have been involved in the death of this Russian opposition leader.... That now Russia has once again become a country that faces the West's hostility. This is an obvious provocation and an effort to create a surge of discontent among the opposition's leaders who will begin calling for protests and demonstrations with the aim of overthrowing the government.'

This occurred after Russia continued to be criticized in the West for its bloodless annexation of Crimea and after the illegal secession of the Donbas—

that is, the Donetsk and Luhansk 'republics' of eastern Ukraine—from Ukraine but before they were invaded and annexed by Russia in 2022.

Ukraine's government became a regular target of the IRA, but Prigozhin's operations were far more sophisticated than that. As his *Wagnerovcis* fought in the trenches to support al-Assad's regime, his trolls fired trenchant support for the Syrian government into the media.

IRA also interfered with elections in the western democracies in the US and Europe, and the Brexit referendum in Britain in 2016. Some 419 fake Twitter accounts believed to be run from St Petersburg published posts about Brexit, for example. Trolls crowed when some of their fake news stories were picked up by the British newspapers. With its effective web campaigns, IRA complemented the role of the Kremlin's otherwise legitimate worldwide TV channel RT which broadcast in English. In the UK, RT paid Nigel Farage over £500,000 for TV interviews before the Brexit referendum and was in the US the sole mass-media platform for the Green Party in the 2016 presidential elections that saw Donald Trump elected.

Prigozhin and his trolls provided the Russian authorities with tailor-made native propaganda-solutions in countries where it intended to deploy with (Wagner) boots on the ground. In November 2013, three months before the overthrow of the pro-Russian president of Ukraine Viktor Yanukovich, a news agency called Kharkov—after Ukraine's most Russian of cities—was founded in Ukraine and opened a branch office in Crimea. The agency advocated a pro-Russian position and, in its news reports, used the term *Novorossiya*—'New Russia'. This is an historical term from the era of the Russian Empire denoting a region north of the Black Sea which had suddenly re-entered the political lexicon when Moscow-backed separatists took up arms against Kyiv in 2014. According to the newspaper *Novaya Gazeta*, Prigozhin was the one who financed Kharkov. Journalists later discovered that Prigozhin's mobile phone number—listed as 'Yevgeny Viktorovich' (Prigozhin's first names)—was found among the contacts of Konstantin Kobzar, one of President Viktor Yanukovich's assistants.

As early as 2014, three months after Donald Trump first hinted at a presidential bid, the IRA created a new division called the 'Translator Project' which focused on the US, using social media platforms such as YouTube, Facebook, Instagram, and Twitter. According to an internal document obtained by Robert Mueller, the former director of the FBI who was appointed Special Counsel in 2017 to investigate Russian interference in the 2016 US presidential election, the Translator Project's expressly stated aim was to 'spread distrust toward the candidates and the political system in general'.

Using fake accounts, it attacked the leading Democratic candidate Hillary Clinton who was a particular anathema to Vladimir Putin since her days as

Obama's Secretary of State. Eventually, the staff of the Translator Project swelled to more than eighty dedicated to promoting Donald Trump. They began by studying groups on US social media sites dedicated to US politics and social issues, tracking the size and engagement of various online conversations, including the frequency of posts and the average number of comments or responses.

Three members of the Translator Project applied for US visas, saying they were travelling to America for personal reasons and concealing their place of employment. Two were approved and the trolls set off on a three-week trip in June 2014 through Nevada, California, New Mexico, Colorado, Illinois, Michigan, Louisiana, Texas and New York. They bought cameras, SIM cards and untraceable 'burner' phones, and their travels took them through most of the most populous electoral states in the country.

That autumn a third agent spent four days in Atlanta, Georgia, for further research. On returning to St Petersburg, they had a meeting with the manager of IRA's IT department, whose job it was to procure servers and other technical infrastructure inside the US to help mask the origins of the IRA's activity. Meanwhile, posing as Americans, the IRA contacted political activists in Texas who told them to concentrate on 'purple states'—that is, swing states that were neither Republican red or Democrat blue—such as Colorado, Virginia and Florida.

Those working for the Translation Project were considered the elite among the IRA workforce. One former worker in the troll factory said: 'They were totally modern-looking young people, like hipsters, wearing fashionable clothes with stylish haircuts and modern devices. They were so modern that you wouldn't think they could do something like this.'

Like Wagner PMC, Prigozhin's operation was extremely professional, and focused like a laser beam, and no cost was spared. The IRA opened hundreds of social media accounts, creating fictitious Americans whom they sought to fashion into leaders of public opinion. 'Specialists' were instructed to post content that focused on 'politics in the USA' and to 'use any opportunity to criticize Hillary and the rest (except Sanders and Trump—we support them).' Their goal was to enflame political passions through supporting radical groups, users dissatisfied with the social and economic situation, and social movements opposed to the mainstream. Working around the clock to ensure 24/7 coverage in the US, they researched American politics, drafted social media content and 'operated' US personas online to post on Facebook, Twitter and Instagram.

These pages in purple swing states amassed hundreds of thousands of followers, enough to influence election results that were expected to be on a knife's edge. They focused on US foreign policy, economic and social issues, creating group pages on Facebook and Instagram that targeted immigration—

one group was called 'Secured Borders'—and Black Lives Matter with a 'Blacktivist' page. Religious groups were targeted with 'United Muslims of America' and 'Army of Jesus', while geographic differences were exploited with 'South United' and 'Heart of Texas'.

They also built numerous Twitter accounts designed to appear as if they belonged to Americans, such as @TEN_GOP, aka 'Tennessee GOP'—that is, Grand Old Party (the Republicans). It amassed 100,000 followers and its tweets were retweeted at times by senior Trump aides such as Kellyanne Conway, Donald Trump Jr. and General Michael Flynn. Meanwhile, they created an intricate account hierarchy. Certain accounts would post original content while others would repost, amplify and promote it.

Trolls were coached on how to appear to be authentic Americans and were taught about the appropriate lengths of messages. They had lists of American holidays and were shown how to incorporate graphics and video into their posts. And VPNs—virtual private networks—were set up inside the US to make it look like the 'specialists' work came from inside the country.

Like any other digital marketing campaign, the IRA studied the response to these accounts—including the comments, likes and reposts—to work out what had succeeded and helped boost their audience. The Facebook group was upbraided for its 'low number of posts dedicated to criticizing Hillary Clinton' and was told 'it is imperative to intensify criticizing Hillary Clinton' in future posts.

Once the presidential election heated up a year before the elections in 2015, the IRA began to buy political advertising in the US. To pay for these, they opened PayPal accounts using the Social Security numbers of individual Americans, employing the services of an American fraudster who specialized in setting up bank accounts under false names. Cover identities were established using fake driver's licences and false and stolen IDs. The IRA were spending over $1.25 million a month on this campaign while their CEO, Mikhail Bystrov, was meeting regularly with Prigozhin throughout 2015 and 2016. Prigozhin had no problem with the illegal means his subsidiary company deployed.

The next stage in IRA's campaign to steal the US presidential elections was even more brazen. Using accounts like 'Trumpsters United' and 'Clinton FRAUDation', they communicated with genuine members, volunteers, and supporters of the Trump Campaign involved in local community outreach, as well as grassroots groups that supported then-candidate Trump. IRA trolls communicated with Trump campaign staff involved in local community outreach. Ads on Facebook and Instagram also promoted the rallies and fake personas encouraged real people to participate. One person was paid to build a cage on a flatbed truck, while another person was paid to play Hillary Clinton in a prison uniform.

Facebook ads promoted a 'Support Hillary. Save American Muslims' rally and a poster for the demonstration carried a spurious quote attributed to Clinton: 'I think Sharia Law will be a powerful new direction of freedom'. A fake gmail account sent out press releases for a 'Down with Hillary' rally. A Facebook account under the name Matt Skiber contacted a real US citizen to recruit for a 'March for Trump' rally, offering to 'give you money to print posters and get a megaphone'. In late July, the IRA used the Facebook group 'Being Patriotic', the Twitter account @March_for_Trump, and various fake US personas to organize a series of coordinated rallies in Florida, collectively referred to as 'Florida Goes Trump', to be held on 20 August.

The trollers' idiomatic use of English was impressive. One message sought to emulate Trump's speech patterns. It read: 'Hi there! I'm a member of Being Patriotic online community. Listen, we've got an idea. Florida is still a purple state and we need to paint it red. If we lose Florida, we lose America. We can't let it happen, right? What about organizing a YUGE pro-Trump flash mob in every Florida town? We are currently reaching out to local activists and we've got the folks who are okay to be in charge of organizing their events almost everywhere in FL. However, we still need your support. What do you think about that? Are you in?'

Another message said: 'My name is [the stolen identity of a real person] and I represent a conservative patriot community named 'Being Patriotic.'… So we're gonna organize a flash mob across Florida to support Mr. Trump. We clearly understand that the elections winner will be predestined by purple states. And we must win Florida.… We got a lot of volunteers in ~25 locations and it's just the beginning. We're currently choosing venues for each location and recruiting more activists. This is why we ask you to spread this info and participate in the flash mob.'

The same methods were used by Prigozhin's team to organize similar rallies in Pennsylvania and New York and elsewhere, displaying a remarkably sophisticated understanding of local political agendas. Ads said: 'You know, a great number of black people support us saying that #HillaryClintonIsNotMyPresident'; 'JOIN our #HillaryClintonForPrison2016'; 'Donald wants to defeat terrorism… Hillary wants to sponsor it'; 'Hillary Clinton Doesn't Deserve the Black Vote' and 'Vote Republican, vote Trump, and support the Second Amendment!'—which guarantees the right to bear arms. A week later, after Hillary Clinton had secured the Democratic nomination, the Russians flooded their accounts with an ad saying: 'Trump is our only hope for a better future!' And they adopted the hashtags: '#NeverHillary'; '#HillaryForPrison'; '#Hillary4Prison'; '#HillaryForPrison2016'; '#Trump2016'; '#Trump'; '#TrumpTrain'; '#MAGA'; '#Trump4President' and '#IWontProtectHillary'. Then came:

'Ohio Wants Hillary 4 Prison'; 'Hillary Clinton has already committed voter fraud during the Democrat Iowa Caucus' and 'We cannot trust Hillary to take care of our veterans!' And in the immediate run up to the election, the IRA ran: 'Among all the candidates Donald Trump is the one and only who can defend the police from terrorists' and 'Hillary is a Satan, and her crimes and lies had proved just how evil she is.'

After Trump was elected the IRA organized more rallies in his support, as well as anti-Trump rallies to increase the divisions in society. One held in New York in mid-November was called 'Trump is NOT my President'. Another held in North Carolina a week later was called 'Charlotte Against Trump'. The Translator Project continued past Trump's election and inauguration, reverting to the IRA's original purpose of spreading division and distrust generally in the democratic process.

IRA ran the entire amoral, but hugely efficient foreign operation with bureaucratic professionalism and precision and easily outran US cyber controls. But there was one telling personal touch revealing Prigozhin's handiwork. On Memorial Day weekend 2016, thousands of bikers rode into Washington, DC, for the annual Rolling Thunder rally. Wearing his red MAGA baseball cap, Donald Trump glad-handed the crowd around the Lincoln Memorial. Meanwhile, one American had been hired to stand outside the White House holding a sign reading 'Happy 55th Birthday Dear Boss'. It was Prigozhin's 55th on 1 June.

10

KREMLIN BEAR HUG

When asked about the possibility of Russian hackers meddling in foreign elections at St Petersburg's international economic forum on 1 June 2017, given the Mueller investigation in the US, Vladimir Putin was dismissive in a characteristically prolix manner and was at pains to address a different question—whether the Kremlin was involved? With Prigozhin's employees personally taking the risk of prosecution by the FBI for breaking US law and shielding the Russian government, the Russian President could say anything he wanted.

'Hackers can be anywhere,' Putin lectured. 'They can lurk in any country in the world. Of course, the general context of inter-state relations should be taken into account in this case because hackers are free people like artists. If artists get up in the morning feeling good, all they do all day is paint. The same goes for hackers.'

He enjoyed being able to speculate why, given that the Kremlin was 'not' involved, the hacks might originate in Russia: 'I can imagine a scenario when somebody develops a chain of attacks in a manner that would show Russia as the source of these attacks. Modern technology allows that. It is very easy.' The hackers might even be Russian, he mused: 'They got up today and read that something is going on internationally. If they are feeling patriotic they will start contributing, as they believe, to the justified fight against those speaking ill of Russia. Is that possible? In theory, yes.'

Knowing that Prigozhin had covertly been paid billions masquerading as 'catering procurement' by the Kremlin to troll the US elections and tilt Trump's election, Putin nonetheless claimed: 'At the government level, we never engage in this. This is what is most important.' And, despite Prigozhin's using the Kremlin's largess to target voting in purple states only, he said, 'What is most important is I am deeply convinced that no hackers can have a real impact on an election campaign in another country. You see, nothing, no information can be imprinted in voters' minds, in the minds of a nation, and influence the outcome and the final result.'

Having started out comparing hackers favourably to free artists, he suddenly changed direction and said that the Russian government was not keen on the results of this freedom and actively sought to stop what he had lauded as 'patriotic' and 'justified' behaviour moments before. 'We do not engage in this activity at the government level and are not going to engage in it. On the contrary, we try to prevent this from happening in our country. At any rate, I believe that no hackers can affect the election campaign in any European country, nor Asia or in America.' The fact that his words contradicted themselves was perhaps the most important conclusion to draw.

Despite the bragging, the moment US law enforcement started taking an interest IRA's employees in the US knew the game was up. When it was reported that Facebook was working with the Office of the Special Counsel Robert Mueller who had taken over from the FBI's investigation into Russian interference in the American election, the IRA promptly began to cover its tracks. Irina Kaverzina, one of the specialists on the Translator Project detained in its US offices, emailed a family member saying: 'We had a slight crisis here at work: the FBI busted our activity (not a joke). So, I got preoccupied with covering tracks together with my colleagues.'

Kaverzina added: 'I created all these pictures and posts, and the Americans believed that it was written by their people.'

On 3 August 2017, Mueller empanelled a grand jury in Washington, DC, as part of his investigation. On 16 February the following year, it handed down an indictment on the thirteen individuals, including Yevgeny Prigozhin, and three companies—the Internet Research Agency, Concord Catering and Concord Management and Consulting, which had already been sanctioned by the US government in connection with the fighting in eastern Ukraine.

'The Treasury is targeting the private planes, yacht, and associated front companies of Yevgeny Prigozhin, the Russian financier behind the Internet Research Agency and its attempts to subvert American democratic processes,' said US Treasury Secretary Steven Mnuchin. He then appeared on the FBI's Most Wanted list with a reward of $250,000 on his head.

Even so, Putin mocked the West for falling so low as to suspect 'a restaurateur from Russia' of influencing the US election.

Prigozhin himself publicly joined in with his patron's jeering and loudly protested his innocence. 'I am not upset at all that I ended up on this list,' he said. 'Americans are impressionable people. They see what they want to see. If they want to see the devil, let them see him.'

Another Kremlin crony piped up. Ramzan Kadyrov, the pro-Kremlin leader of Russian Federation republic Chechnya bated the FBI, saying he wanted to claim the $250,000.

'It would be silly to miss out on such a generous reward, so I officially announce: Yevgeny Prigozhin is with me as my guest in Grozny,' he posted on social media. The bounty would, however, have to be delivered to him in cash as his foreign bank accounts—that were bulging 'with millions of dollars'—had been frozen by western sanctions.

'Better to pack the reward in $20 bills in suitcases and pass them on through someone in Grozny. Everybody knows me here,' he taunted.

In March 2021, Prigozhin even was to write to the FBI demanding he be removed from its Most Wanted list, calling his appearance on it a violation of his human rights. A statement on social media network *VKontakte*, quoted him saying that he was the victim of mistaken identity: 'Fraudsters are fraudulently trying to accuse me, a squeaky-clean person, of fraud.'

As to IRA itself, already in 2014, hackers from online group Anonymous International corroborated the financial link between Prigozhin's Concord and IRA—which Prigozhin persistently denied. But in 2023, after the IRA was sanctioned for interfering with American elections, he finally came clean and revealed how comprehensive the scope of his involvement was. 'I've never just been the financier of the Internet Research Agency [IRA],' he bragged. 'I invented it, I created it, I managed it for a long time. It was founded to protect the Russian information space from boorish aggressive propaganda of anti-Russian narrative from the West.'

According to Andrei Soldatov, co-author of the book *The Red Web*, the FSB has employed hackers since the early 2000s, when a group of students helped authorities shut down a website associated with Chechen separatists during the Second Chechen War started in aid of Putin's election. The practice had never been discontinued by the FSB.

'Today, the Kremlin-backed cyber campaigns have an unorthodox chain of command. It is one in which non-state actors call the shots,' Soldatov said. This created the fiction of a Chinese Wall between the Kremlin and the hackers. Though, in truth, the Kremlin could at any time direct its catering and other procurement contracts to a different company and starve the band of hackers of cash. Since their hacking efforts had no commercial value to anyone else, if the Kremlin's indirect funding dried up overnight lay-offs would have to follow promptly as only Russian state officials were interested in foreign election interference.

Clearly, through IRA Prigozhin had become an essential cog in the Russian secret service's cyber operations which was one reason why he described himself as a government advisor even though, officially, he had no role in the Kremlin.

With the Mueller investigation turning on the heat in the US, in 2017, IRA rebranded itself as the Federal News Agency—FAN, or the Russian Information Agency FAN: RIA FAN. The new RIA FAN was part of the Patriot media group whose supervisory board was chaired by Yevgeny Prigozhin.

Given the company's well-known role in drowning out right-wing voices inside Russia, at home in Russia the company was not universally liked either by the right-wing political groups whose voices the Kremlin tolerated. Despite the name change to FAN, the company was targeted before the Russian presidential elections in March 2018, when Putin's fourth term was announced with 78% of the votes. On 9 October 2018, at 3am, a petrol bomb was thrown through the window. There were only a handful of people in the building and luckily for the FAN employees there were no casualties.

'I believe this is tied to FAN's activities,' said Yevgeny Zubarev, FAN's editor. 'We're most often attacked online but attacks have taken place offline.' Where the Kremlin itself could not be challenged, RIA FAN was a different matter. Like Wagner PMC, IRA/RIA FAN's Kremlin work was a risky business. Beyond Russian borders, the company was at risk from foreign law enforcement, inside it risked being the lightning rod for Russia's right-wing extremists.

Meanwhile, although he himself was not in the firing line, the risk premium of his companies' black ops made Prigozhin and his Kremlin backers ever richer.

As the Kremlin carefully insulated Prigozhin from international criticism, it did not take any action either domestically and had no interest whatsoever in how much Prigozhin scrimped on his government procurement to underpin his digital and military empire abroad. In December 2018, following problems in St Peterburg, there had been an outbreak of dysentery at his seven day-care centres and kindergartens in Moscow which left scores of children sick.

Inna Chepeleva, whose daughter attended daycare at School No 1357 and came down with pneumonia attributed to the dysentery outbreak, said she was shocked at the refusal of officials there to explain what happened.

'Something was going on, but we knew nothing,' she said.

Lyubov Sobol, who works for the investigative team of opposition politician Alexei Navalny and documented Prigozhin's rise, took up the case on behalf of the parents of the stricken children. She also had a five-year-old daughter in day care in Moscow. She claimed she faced a smear campaign by Prigozhin-controlled media, including the Federal News Agency, as well as harassment from unidentified individuals.

Parents sued the school authorities and the Concord Ready-Meals Factory, but Prigozhin began doling out large sums of money in compensation if they would drop their cases. The victims had consumed meals provided by another company called Vito-1 which also had connections to Prigozhin. An inspection reportedly found that the business violated multiple sanitary regulations and criminal investigations were opened.

Another of Prigozhin's companies, SP Concord, that supplied school means went into liquidation. A Moscow court then ordered that Vito-1 and Concord pay compensation. While the story was broken on social media and Alexei Navalny's YouTube channel, an editor at the state-owned Tass news agency felt she had been forced to resign after her report casting doubt on the safety of food provided to Moscow's nurseries and schools by Prigozhin had been spiked. She told the *Guardian* that Tass management had 'clearly named the reason for the withdrawal of my material from publication—it featured references to Prigozhin's business interests'.

Sobol's investigative video got more than 300,000 views. The Russian Federal Consumer Oversight Agency confirmed 127 cases of dysentery. In a written reply to Sobol's complaint, the agency said numerous inspections at Concord Ready-Meals Factory as well as other firms affiliated with Prigozhin found violations of 'sanitary standards' and some of the food tests at its facilities and schools produced 'unsatisfactory results.' The Meshchansky district court awarded 10,000-15,000 rubles ($180-240) per child.

When Sobol suggested that Prigozhin had ordered an attack on her husband who had been stabbed in the thigh with a near-deadly dose of a psychotropic substance in 2016, rendering him convulsing and unconscious, Prigozhin sued.

'I think a more logical version is that Sobol pricked her husband's buttcheeks herself while roleplaying,' Prigozhin retorted.

Prigozhin also sued Navalny and his Anti-Corruption Foundation (FBK) through the food company Moskovsky Shkolnik for saying it had caused scores of cases of dysentery among pupils and teachers because of the poor quality of meals it supplied to Moscow schools—and won.

He also announced that he had bought a 87,658,461 ruble (£880,000) debt owed by Navalny at the FBK, saying he hoped to 'unrobe and unshoe' Navalny and forcing him to dissolve the foundation.

By then Navalny had been poisoned with a Novichok agent and had been flown to Berlin for treatment.

'Of course, if Comrade Navalny goes to meet his maker then I do not intend to persecute him in this world,' said Prigozhin, adding: 'If Navalny survives then he must answer under all severity of the Russian law.'

On his Russian blog on Telegram and an English version on Facebook, Mikhail Khodorkovsky was one of the people outside Russia who had tirelessly been exposing the operations Prigozhin ran on behalf of the Kremlin. He produced slick videos accusing Prigozhin of running internet troll armies in Russia and a whole host of other 'criminal achievements'.

After the killing of the journalists who worked for his news outlet in the Central African Republic, he wrote 'Putin's chef's criminal record is well known'. 'You can take a guy out of a St Petersburg back alley. But you can't take the back alley out of him.'

Based in London, Khodorkovsky was out of the Kremlin's direct reach—unlike Navalny—and Prigozhin's press service took a leaf out of the Kremlin playbook. It flatly denied that the businessman had 'interests in military or civilian projects in the Central African Republic, including goldfields'.

Nonetheless, it was Khodorkovsky's posting about Prigozhin as mastermind behind the assassination of the three journalists in the Central African Republic that made Prigozhin himself strike back at Khodorkovsky directly, perhaps instructed by the Kremlin or, indeed, Putin himself wanting to needle the Russian oligarch in exile. Evidently, being exposed by the FBI as a digital hacker didn't trouble Prigozhin that much, but his control over his brainchild Wagner PMC had to be denied both in words and in action. He decided to counterattack by putting the bounty on Khodorkovsky's head.

In a statement published via his Concord company, he offered $500,000 for his rival's capture, adding that he would only pay if a Russian citizen caught him, because he did not want to pay money to the foreigners who had hit him and his companies with sanctions.

Prigozhin could afford to go on the attack. The revelations in 2017 of Prigozhin's impressive meddling in the 2016 elections of the most powerful country in the world had an unintended benefit for 'Putin's butcher' as he styled himself jokingly in private. The minute Mueller investigation had trumpeted around the globe that his military operations through Wagner PMC offered a revolutionary service to Kremlin customers. As his cheap daredevil *Wagnerovcis* committed atrocities, Prigozhin's internet trolls reached well behind the front line to infect the hearts and minds of the local population and create civil unrest behind enemy lines at the same time.

As the former colonial power in the Central African Republic, France discovered the effective power of Wagner PMC's trolling. France's Foreign Minister Jean-Yves Le Drian complained that the Wagner Group had a 'strong, active presence' on local social media networks and were spreading false 'anti-French' claims.

'These people are not in the army, they are back-up troops acting under the authority of a man called Mr Prigozhin,' he told senators. 'If you can hear me [Mr Prigozhin], know that we know you very well!'

Britain discovered the same in July 2021 when images from Syria turned up. While parliament voted not to allow British ground forces to enter Syria, this did not apply to Special Forces who were not subject to parliamentary veto. A small contingent of SAS and SBS soldiers had remained in Syria as part of a joint special operations task force who maintained a regional surveillance capability and keep an eye on jihadi prisoners guarded by Kurdish forces. They also acted as forward air controllers, identifying targets for RAF attacking the remnants of ISIL.

One of the image showed a Russian military contractor wearing a British combat shirt emblazoned with the Union Flag patch sewn onto the left upper arm. Wearing another nation's emblem directly contravenes a raft of international conventions including the Hague and Geneva and was technically banned even by the Russian Federation.

The image of a Russian mercenary riding on the back of an open vehicle in Syria with the Union flag clearly visible on his left arm was posted on a Russian language website used by current and former members of the Wagner Group.

A former SAS soldier said: 'When it comes to Russian mercs there are no rules. They don't care about international law, the United Nations or the Red Cross—all they care about is success and they will do whatever it takes. If that means pushing the blame for their covert actions onto others, all the better. When it comes down to it, all witnesses need to remember is the flag on the arm.'

Rob Lee, a former US Marine turned academic who specialized in Russian defence matters commented: 'Russian mercenaries have previously used camouflage with UK flags on them and worn them during training. In this case, I think the mercenary just purchased a multicam top and this one had a UK flag on it.'

International outrage about Wagner PMC or not, the support the Kremlin gave to Prigozhin did not budge. With Russia's top ministers on its brown-envelope payroll, no one in the Russian Federation was going to touch the goose that lay the golden eggs.

Only brave Russian journalists begged to differ. In early November 2019 *Novaya Gazeta* identified the mercenaries in the 2017 YouTube video set in Syria in which thirty-two-year-old Mohammad Taha al-Ismail Abdallah was pushed to the ground, sledgehammered on his legs, arms and torso and beaten unconscious, whereupon his arms were severed with a shovel and his head was cut off with a knife. Kicking his head around to play football, another decapitated head lay nearby. Taking off their masks, two soldiers posed next to the dismembered torso that was hung upside down from a fence with the words 'For the VDV [Russian airborne forces]' scrawled across.

Using face-recognition technology, *Novaya Gazeta* identified one of the men as Stanislav Dychko, a former police officer from the Stavropol region of southern Russia. He had joined Wagner Group in 2016 as a reconnaissance gunner to 'defend the interests of the Russian Federation', according to a document the newspaper had obtained. Journalist Denis Korotkov said: 'They're out of control, I don't think it's an isolated case.'

In March 2021, three human rights groups filed a case against the Wagner Group in Moscow.

'This litigation is a first-ever attempt by the family of a Syrian victim to hold Russian suspects accountable for serious crimes committed in Syria,' said a press release issued by the Paris-based International Federation for Human Rights, the Syrian Centre for Media and Freedom of Expression, and the brave Moscow-based Memorial Human Rights Centre. 'The complaint demands the initiation of criminal proceedings on the basis of murder committed with extreme cruelty, with a view to establishing the alleged perpetrators' responsibility for this and other crimes, including war crimes.'

The filing was carefully choreographed for fear the applicants would be arrested. The documentation was handed in four days before any announcement was made in an attempt to protect the litigants. The name and location of Ismail's brother, the complainant, was withheld as he could be targeted by the Kremlin whose assassins would have no problem killing him in Syria if they had his home address.

The brave act was largely symbolic and meant to illustrate the flimsy rule of law in the Russian Federation. There was little chance the Russian judiciary would act as the Wagner Group did not officially exist and, under Russian law, nationals could not be tried at home for crimes committed abroad.

'The state investigative committee has not started to investigate the circumstances of the murder even though all necessary information was handed over to authorities more than a year ago,' Russian human rights attorney Ilya Novikov told *Novaya Gazeta*. Russian authorities ignored the paper's call for an independent investigation into the killing that was filed in 2020.

The same day the case was lodged, unknown attackers targeted *Novaya Gazeta*'s Moscow office. 'In the morning a chemical attack was carried out on the building where our editorial office is located,' said the independent media outlet's editor-in-chief, Dmitry Muratov, who was awarded the Nobel Peace Prize in 2021. Muratov suspended its publication on 28 March 2022 until the end of Russia's 'special operation' in Ukraine due to increased government censorship. Seven of its journalists had been murdered. Its website was blocked in retaliation, its media licence cancelled and, after relocating to Latvia, the outlet was declared an undesirable organization, effectively an enemy of the Russian state.

Even though *Novaya Gazeta* had a minute readership compared to the enormous size Russian population covered by the three Kremlin-controlled mass-media channels, the Kremlin was concerned enough about independent domestic investigations and evidence of its government's blatant hypocrisy. While Putin's regime was unconcerned whether Russians trusted or mistrusted what officials said, it violently and aggressively restricted the proof of the latter that was discoverable to its citizens.

11

CAREFUL WHAT YOU WISH FOR

Under Prigozhin's leadership and with Kremlin's top officials invested in spreading its formula for successful propagation of Russian interests, the Wagner Group were now advising on military and election campaigns in ten African countries—the Central African Republic, Sudan, Libya, Madagascar, Angola, Guinea (bauxite), Guinea-Bissau, Mozambique, Zimbabwe (platinum) and the Democratic Republic of Congo—as Russia extended its influence in sub-Saharan Africa. All these countries share tense political situations—civil wars, military coups and armed conflicts—and a wealth of natural resources. Its hold over some of these countries was such that, in addition to Sudan, the Kremlin had also authorized civil nuclear energy projects in the Republic of Congo, Nigeria and Sudan. It led automatically to a reduction in complaints. 'Do not expect strident condemnations from those countries where there is a large Russian presence, especially from PMCs,' Steven Gruzd, from the South African Institute of International Affairs think tank.

Sudan, where local dictator Omar al-Bashir had so keenly advanced Russia's interests, soon discovered the downside of inviting the presence of a foreign military to sort out domestic problems. Wagner PMC was so deeply embedded that its role was unaffected when he was ousted by a military coup in April 2019. Prigozhin, in fact, criticized his former client al-Bashir for failing to follow Russian advice on how to crack down on the country's pro-democracy uprising. He wrote to him complaining that he had ignored Russian advice to paint protesters as 'pro-Israel,' 'pro-LGBT', and 'anti-Islam' in a bid to discredit them. In 2020, the US revealed that M Invest was owned by Prigozhin and served as cover for the Wagner Group.

Despite the fall of al-Basir, Russia did not pull out of Sudan and *Wagnerovcis* simply continued working for the Sudanese Transitional Military Council (TMC) that had ousted al-Bashir, backing new strongman General Mohamed 'Hemedti' Hamdan Dagalo's Rapid Support Forces (RSF). When negotiations to restore a civil government broke down, Dagalo's attacks on the Sudanese army directed by his rival General Abdel al-Burhan, Sudan's titular leader, sparked a civil war in 2023. Wagner PMC supplied rocket-support to Dagalo from Libya and also staged an 'online anti-revolution campaign' against a second wave of protests that have destabilised Sudan, further fuelling the unrest in Sudan.

Deprived of the regular shipment of gold to Moscow, a series of bloody raids on artisanal mines in the lawless border zones between Sudan and Central African Republic was evidence of how the Wagner Group was forced to plunder the region's valuable gold trade when making up a shortfall in cashflow. Dozens of miners were killed in at least three attacks and witnesses described 'massacres' by fighters they identified as being from Wagner, who swept through encampments full of migrant miners and mine workings during a six-week period.

Witnesses described 'massacres' by fighters they identified as being from Wagner who swept through encampments full of migrant miners and mine workings between the north-eastern town of Am Daga and the frontier over a six-week period. The fighters shot indiscriminately with automatic weapons, smashed equipment, destroyed buildings and stole motorbikes, they said. One described a mass grave containing more than twenty victims. Others spoke of hundreds dead or injured. The accounts have been corroborated by local civil-society groups and international officials.

The three biggest incidents took place on 13 March, 15 April and 24 May, 2022. Most of the victims were migrant workers from Sudan and Chad working in the goldmines, though some local civilians are also thought to have died.

Forty-two-year-old Mohammed Zain Mohamed Wadi said he was attacked in an area called Jabal a-Nar, about fifty miles west of the frontier with Sudan, by Russians, some in armoured vehicles, and soldiers from Central African Republic in pickup trucks or on motorbikes. Wadi said he helped to bury twenty-one of the victims, all Sudanese. Another six people were also killed.

'I'll never go back... actually I don't think anybody remained... The gold-mines there have been taken over by the Russians,' he said.

Thirty-five-year-old Jamaa Mohamed al-Habou was among those who were attacked in the last week of May in the village of Sankillio, near Andaha. He said he and other miners were 'chased off by Wagner' and that many were killed during a daylong assault. He fled into nearby woodland, abandoning a metal detector. Others left behind motorbikes and other vehicles, which were seized by the attackers. Members of armed groups opposing the government were also targeted, Habou said.

A third witness said as many as seventy people, including his brother and six relatives, died when Russians and Africans attacked the mine where he was working in March. 'I had to run for seven days. I saw them coming... to kill and rob everybody their hands could reach,' said thirty-six-year-old Adam Zakaria from Neyala in South Darfur.

He described the Wagner group as white people wearing grey military uniforms, travelling in pickup trucks, armoured vehicles and helicopters. Human

Rights Watch said that Russia-linked forces in Central African Republic did not wear a designated uniform with official insignia or other distinguishing features. They had beaten, tortured and killed civilians there since 2019.

'When we fled their attacks initially, we thought we were safe, but suddenly on our way they trapped us and started beating us, and near to Am Daga they laid another trap where they killed twenty-one people. We had to bury them in one big grave,' Zakaria said.

Inserting themselves as hired hands who offered a one-stop shop for all kinds of political, military and mining services, Wagner PMC had nestled itself like a virulent devastating and irradicable cancer in Sudan, metastasizing into the local fabric and thriving on provoking local rifts as it extracted mineral wealth while charging the local warlord for propping up their territory. Not that other PMCs were saints, but they would leave when the money ran out. Wagner PMC, however, was merely a means to an end, the end objective being permanent exploitation by the Kremlin of the host's natural resources by setting up a permanent military presence with a view to grabbing part of the local economy.

In the Central African Republic, the Wagner Group seemed to have been playing a double game as well. Wagner mercenaries were suspected of having supplied and trained Central African Republic militants from the 3R (Return, Reclamation and Rehabilitation) group in the use of anti-personnel and anti-tank mines, which are banned by a UN arms embargo. It was thought that this was the first time anti-personnel mines had been deployed in the Central African Republic.

As Faustin-Archange Touadéra was sworn in for a second term on 30 March 2021, a US working group alleged that the Wagner Group had committed human rights abuses in the Central African Republic while fighting alongside government forces. It said it was 'deeply disturbed' by the connections between Russian mercenaries and a series of violent attacks that have taken place in the Central African Republic since elections in December. As the country teetered on the edge of civil war, Wagner had assisted a successful counter offensive by Touadéra's army—*Forces armées centralafricaines* (FACA)—against the rebels.

The working group were even more disturbed to discover the foreign mercenaries were in close contact with UN peacekeepers MINSUSCA—the 15,000-strong United Nations Multidimensional Integrated Stabilization Mission in the Central African Republic which had been in place since 2014. There were regular meetings between UN staff and 'Russian advisers', visits by the Russians to MINUSCA bases and medical evacuations of wounded 'Russian trainers' to MINUSCA facilities.

'This blurring of the lines between civil, military and peacekeeping operations during the hostilities creates confusion about the legitimate targets and increases the risks for widespread human rights and humanitarian law abuses,' said Jelena Aparac, the chair-rapporteur of the UN working group on mercenaries.

The experts said they had received reports of 'grave human rights abuses and violations of international humanitarian law' carried out by Russian private military personnel operating jointly with FACA. In some cases UN peacekeepers were involved.

The alleged violations include mass summary executions, arbitrary detention, torture during interrogation and the forced displacement of the civilian population, about 240,000 of whom had fled their homes because of fighting in recent weeks. There were increased attacks on humanitarian organizations, as well as forced disappearances, the UN expert group said.

'Unacceptably, there seems to be no investigations and no accountability for these abuses,' said Aparac.

A 184-page report by the United Nations says supposedly unarmed 'military instructors' were really highly paid mercenaries running amok in the Central African Republic. Sorcha MacLeod, a law professor and member of the UN's investigating team, said: 'What we saw was very clear evidence of Russians involved in mass extrajudicial killings, people detained and tortured and the indiscriminate targeting of civilians—they systematically loot every town or village they go through. Russia says they're unarmed. They're not unarmed. We have evidence they're participating directly in hostilities and potentially committing war crimes.'

Kremlin spokesman Dmitry Peskov simply denied the charges, saying: 'This is yet another lie'. And left it at that.

The UN Office of the High Commissioner for Human Rights (OHCHR) was investigating several incidents. In December Russian and FACA soldiers allegedly opened fire on a vehicle that failed to stop at a checkpoint in Ouaka prefecture, killing three and wounding over a dozen, including six women and a child. They were also implicated in an attack on the al-Taqwa mosque in Bambari, the prefecture's capital, where retreating rebels and civilians had taken shelter after a battle for control of the town.

'They weren't trying to figure out who was a rebel and who was a civilian. They wanted to kill people,' a witness said. The Russian mercenaries were alleged to have summarily executed three young men, while at least fifteen people were killed by stray bullets, including children and elderly people. One young woman, aged twenty, whom several Russian mercenaries had abducted and raped her.

'They tortured me like an animal,' she said.

UN experts received reports that Wagner Group officers had committed rape and used sexual violence against women, men and young girls in many parts of the country. It was not clear how many people have been victims of sexual violence because survivors were terrified to seek justice for fear of retaliation.

'Being denied access to justice and to remedies is a sign of the impunity prevailing in the country,' the UN experts said.

They also confirmed with local officials or eyewitnesses the shooting of an unarmed man on 21 February, the killings of two disabled civilians and the shooting of two more civilians on 8 March, 2021.

Russians also were accused of widespread looting of money and mobile phones not only 'during house-to-house searches and at checkpoints but also after civilians had been killed'. One shopkeeper claimed a Russian had hacked off his finger. Another government soldier complained of being beaten to a pulp by Russians in a dispute over a motorbike.

UN documents obtained by Radio France listed at least twenty-six extrajudicial executions carried out by the group. 'Many civilians have been killed or injured although they are very far from legitimate military targets,' the UN said.

The rebels from a series of factions, which called themselves the Coalition of Patriots for Change (CPC), had also carried out atrocities, it was alleged. On 8 March they ambushed a convoy of government and Wagner troops in the village of Manga, on the highway between Bozoum and Bocaranga. Two Russian mercenaries were reportedly killed and a vehicle destroyed.

The UN working group lists three Prigozhin entities active in Central African Republic—Wagner, Sewa Security Services, which guarded the president and other top Central African Republic officials, and Lobaye Invest, Prigozhin's Central African Republic-based mining firm specializing in gold and diamonds that has been sanctioned by the US.

Captain Firmin Amoulo Malo, spokesperson for the Central African Republic's defence ministry, called the UN report a 'slanderous publication based on fabricated and unverified evidence… that aims to undermine the morale of our troops'. However, a Central African Republic government report found 103 incidents carried out by Russian 'instructors', as they are officially known, as well as its own troops and the rebels. These included extrajudicial killings, arbitrary arrests and torture.

'On the proven incidents, some are attributable to the Russian instructors,' the report said, without listing specifics or evidence. Some of the foreigners accused of abuse had been sent home, and evidence to support legal action in Moscow would follow, the report added.

Even Russia's spiritual friend China had to pay. A Chinese mining company in Central African Republic's Lamy-Pont area told the Corbeau News website that it was forced to pay a ransom of about US$103,000 to the mercenaries belonging to Russia's paramilitary Wagner group after they kidnapped a dozen employees. The website said the workers, whose nationalities were not identified, were abducted during an attack at their mining site by the mercenaries. The report did not indicate when the attack or payment took place.

It added that a Mauritanian businessman, who also lived in Lamy-Pont, was severely assaulted by mercenaries who 'arrested him' on 26 November. In another report, the mercenaries were said to have sexually assaulted a sixty-five-year-old woman on 24 November in the village of Dongue Douane, Corbeau News said. The woman reportedly died shortly after she was taken to hospital.

However, Russian mercenaries in the Central African Republic claimed they had foiled a coup attempt in April 2021 against President Touadéra. They said that it was the eleventh attempt since they arrived in the Central African Republic in 2018, allegedly that the French government was behind each attempt. President Emmanuel Macron suspended aid to France's former colony, calling President Touadéra a 'hostage of the Russian Wagner Group'.

'I think [the government] made a deal with someone and now they don't know how to handle it,' one foreign official in Bangui said. 'They can't control them.'

It was unclear how Russian fighters were paid by Touadéra but with international donors, led by the EU and World Bank, providing about half of the country's $400m annual budget. 'We can't rule out that donor money is going towards paying them,' said one foreign official.

The European External Action Service [EEAS] issued a thirty-five-page report between 15 and 22 November 2021 which said that about '2,600 mercenaries of the Wagner group have taken charge of Central African Republic army units', in particular those 'trained by the European Union' and that most FACA units currently deployed 'operate under the direct command or supervision' of the Wagner Group.

'We would need the guarantee that the soldiers trained by EUTM [European Union Training Mission] are not employed by the Wagner mercenaries,' an EUTM spokesperson told Reuters. 'For the moment, we don't have a response.'

The EU then suspended its training mission, fearing that the force had been taken over by the mercenaries.

Wagner's propaganda machine attempted to cast the mercenaries in a good light. More than ten thousand people attended screenings of the film *Touriste* at a red-carpeted premiere with an audience of ten thousand in a packed football stadium in the country's capital, Bangui, while trailers for the movie were watched millions of times online. The YouTube version had 7.6 million views. According to Russian media, the film was funded by Prigozhin and film rights were owned by his company Aurum.

In the stadium, along with posters for *Touriste*, stickers read: 'With the

Support of Evgeny Prigozhin' in Sango (the official language of the Central African Republic) above a heart-shaped Russian flag. *Touriste* T-shirts were given away. The film later aired on Russia's state-controlled NTV network. Other pro-Russian political groups sometimes wore T-shirts emblazoned with the words '*Je suis Wagner*'—'I am Wagner'.

The film told the story of a group of Russian military advisers helping train soldiers in the war-torn land, where Christian and Muslim militias had been fighting since rebels ousted former president François Bozizé in 2013. The Russian hero has deep blue eyes and is codenamed 'tourist'. He helps save a conflict-ridden African nation. The storyline features loud explosions and action-packed scenes filmed in the Central African Republic jungle, as well as swipes at Western armies.

'Americans are fighting for democracy, right? As for us, we're fighting for justice,' says an instructor in the movie.

Neil Munshi who visited Bangui for the premiere said, 'I talk to some of Wagner's alleged victims in the city's Muslim quarter: men and women who've fled rape, torture and killings in every corner of the country'. 'The most common refrain I hear about the mercenaries is: 'They have no rules.' The accusations were well known, their presence was obvious but as one young activist put it, 'There's really a kind of grey fog around them.'

Munshi said he met a Koran teacher from Bambari who said Russian fighters had arrested him at morning prayers with forty others, held him for a month, tortured him and stole his life savings, and a woman who says she feared she might have HIV after being raped by three Russian fighters.

'Two months after I left Bangui, a friend sent me pictures of a new sculpture that had been erected near the stadium,' Munshi said. 'It showed Russian and Central African Republic soldiers defending a cowering woman and two small children. Similar monuments to Wagner have cropped up in Syria and Ukraine.'

The local newspaper *Corbeau News Centrafrique* called the Bangui screening a 'success', though some Muslims who had had relatives killed by the mercenaries walked out, appalled by the violence, and even loyalists who welcomed Russian assistance complained that the film portrayed the Central African Republic's national army as cowards.

Prigozhin's mining company in the Central African Republic, Lobaye Invest, also produced a propaganda film for school children based on the Lion King. Besieged by a pack of rebellious hyenas, this cartoon lion, representing the Central African Republic, roars out for help, prompting the bear to journey from Siberia's snowy wastes to save him. The company also trained army recruits, ran the radio station Lengo Songo and even sponsored the 'Miss Central African Republic' beauty contest.

The paper's website later reported that the Wagner group were accused of killing ten people and torching fifty houses in Haute-Kotto (where Lobaye Invest had generous concessions to explore for diamonds and gold, like Prigozhin's other companies, it was on the US Treasury sanctions list), the north-east region of the country. Meanwhile, the Central African Republic Armed Forces (FACA) were also accused of carrying out human rights abuses in the central Ippy area, using 'the Wagner method'. Some of the abuses listed by Corbeau News included arbitrary arrests and mass executions.

In September 2021, the *Corbeau News* website reported the massacre of eleven civilians by private military contractors pursuing rebels at the Bo-Jou mining site, located between Kaga-Bandoro and Mbres. A Muslim village chief was also reportedly tortured because it was said he knew about the whereabouts of the rebels.

Also on 26 August, at least forty civilians belonging to the Fulani ethnic group were killed by Russian military contractors carrying out an offensive against the 3R rebel group, reports said. One hundred civilians remained missing, according to the local media. Meanwhile Wagner's mining branch had begun mining operations in the eastern region of the country. The Russians 'installed heavy machines' in the locality of Yalinga, Haute-Kotto, on the Nzako axis.

In the face of allegations of human rights abuses, Wagner pulled out of the eastern town of Bria to the residents' surprise. The motive behind the withdrawal was unknown but there was speculation that the mercenaries were reorganizing for counter possible attacks by Coalition of Patriots for Change (CPC) rebels on the capital Bangui, the site said.

'A convoy of eleven vehicles transporting Wagner mercenaries left the town of Bria on Wednesday morning [15 December] for Bambari, the capital of the Ouaka prefecture,' a witness was quoted as saying.

A month later, the Corbeau website reported that fifty people 'took to the streets to decry what they called the laxity of the UN force in the face of repeated killings of civilians in the Ouaka region of the Central African Republic'.

'In reality, it was a real manipulation of the people. According to local security sources, it was the Russian mercenaries of the Wagner company who asked people in Bambari to come to a meeting to register their names for the distribution of food. On arrival at the site, they were instead forced to demonstrate against MINUSCA to demand its departure from the town,' the website added.

An unnamed authority figure in the area was quoted by the website condemning the act.

'Asking people to come and register for food aid and then pushing them to stage a protest, I think these Wagner men have crossed the line. We've never seen this before in our country,' he said.

The EU said Wagner had intensified its presence 'in almost all areas of government,' including the military, customs, mining and the media. The group has also been accused of running disinformation campaigns against France. Local media sources reported that Wagner was behind a mass protest on 20 January 2022 in the capital, Bangui, calling for the departure of French forces from Mali, where the group is also carrying counter-insurgency operations.

Wagner killed more than sixty civilians in the village of Yangoudroudja on 9 February, 2021, and an unspecified number of others in the nearby village of Mouka. Soon after, it was reported that at least eight Wagner mercenaries were in a road accident in Nana-Mambere, north-west region of the Central African Republic, when the driver lost control of the vehicle while overtaking a motorcycle.

As Wagner slowly took control over the country in an act of post-modern colonisation, Wagner's civilian employees were at risk, too. In December 2022, Prigozhin's associate Dmitry Sytii, head of the 'Russian House' cultural centre in Bangui, Central African Republic, was taken to hospital after a parcel posted to him exploded in his hands.

A founder of the Prigozhin-linked mining company Lobaye Invest, Sytii had been sanctioned by the US in September 2020 for its operations in Central African Republic and Sudan. In 2021, a UN working group said it was 'deeply disturbed' by the connections between the Russian mercenaries, Lobaye and alleged human rights violations in Central African Republic, including mass summary executions, arbitrary detention, torture during interrogation and the forced displacement of the civilian population.

'At the moment, the life of Dmitry Sytii hangs in balance. Russian doctors are doing everything possible in the Bangui hospital to save him,' Prigozhin said in a statement posted by his catering company, Concord. It also brazenly described Sytii as a 'Patriot of Russia and Central African Republic'.

Prigozhin also simply claimed that the assassination attack was coordinated from France. 'I have already contacted the Ministry of Foreign Affairs of the Russian Federation so that it initiates the procedure for declaring France a state sponsor of terrorism, as well as conducting a thorough investigation of the terrorist methods of France and its western allies—the United States and others,' he said. The French foreign ministry in a statement denied any involvement.

12

GLOBAL ATTRACTION

Governments that disliked the US—teetering regimes without a free press by and large and leaders that refused to vacate their position—lapped up the news and flocked to Prigozhin's Wagner PMC to enlist the new *wunderkind*'s help. On 25 January 2019, *Wagnerovcis* travelled to Venezuela to provide security to the embattled president Nicolás Maduro.

'The order came down on Monday [21 January] to form a group to go to Venezuela. They are there to protect those at the highest levels of the government,' Yevgeny Shabayev, a Cossack leader and campaigner for the rights of veterans, a group that overlaps heavily with those who join mercenary groups in Russia. He said he had been told about the trip by the relatives of the military contractors. A Russian government spokesman did not immediately respond for comment about the report, although he had earlier told Reuters that the Kremlin had 'no such information'.

The news broke after the US threw its support behind opposition leader Juan Guaidó, who declared himself president on 23 January after the Venezuelan National Assembly refused to recognize the re-election of Maduro.

Russia and China, both of which had invested heavily in the country, ignored the National Assembly and attacked the US for encroaching on Venezuela's sovereignty. Putin accused the US of 'destructive interference from abroad' and his prime minister, Dmitry Medvedev, called Guaidó's assumption of the presidency as a 'quasi-coup'. As usual, the Kremlin denied the Wagner Group's presence.

Another Russian source, who was close to the Wagner group and had fought in foreign conflicts where it was active, said that Wagner Group mercenaries had arrived in Venezuela even before the presidential elections in May 2018, while another group had arrived more recently. Shabayev put the number at four hundred; the others spoke of smaller groups. He said they flew to Venezuela not from Moscow but from the other countries where they were conducting missions.

Citing contacts in a Russian state security structure, Shabayev said the contingent flew to Venezuela that week, a day or two before opposition protests started. He said they set off in two chartered aircraft for Havana, before transferring to regular commercial flights to Venezuela. Their task was to protect

Maduro from any attempt by opposition sympathizers in his own security forces to arrest him, Shabayev told the news agency. 'Our people are there directly for his protection,' he said.

Flight-tracking data showed a number of Russian government aircraft landing in or near Venezuela in the previous weeks. A Russian Ilyushin-96 flew into Havana late on 23 January after starting its journey in Moscow and flying via Senegal and Paraguay. Though a civilian jet, it was owned by a division of the Russian presidential administration, according to a publicly available procurement contract relating to the plane.

As to his own movements Prigozhin used the same cloak and dagger method to avoid being photographed by the press as he had been in 2017 with Sudanese president al-Bashir and Russian foreign minister Shoigu. *Novaya Gazeta* had been following the movements of Prigozhin's $2-million Raytheon Hawker 800XP aircraft, registration number M-VITO to place him personally at the locations of *Wagnerovcis*. On 4 February 2019, it bravely published its findings on its website.

On forty-eight occasions in the space of two years, business jet M-VITO had landed and taken off from Beirut, the capital of Lebanon, bordering on Syria. In the majority of cases, judging by the flight details, Beirut was being used as a Prigozhin transfer point. From there it departed for Syria or Africa a few hours after landing.

M-VITO was seen over the territory of Syria at great altitude. Lack of coverage in that zone meant it could not be seen lower, but in some instances it could be seen descending. The airspace over Syria is not closed to civil aircraft, but the European Aviation Safety Agency of necessity warns airlines of the dangers of entering Syrian airspace. As a result, very few risk flying there. However, Prigozhin's business jet had at that time been flown over Syria twenty-one times since 2016.

Also M-VITO flew to Africa after a stop in Lebanon. Almost the entire continent of Africa is a zero-coverage zone for devices that receive signals from aircraft. Prigozhin's aircraft was first spotted in Africa over Egypt on 10 November 2017 at an altitude of 11,000 metres, its standard cruising altitude. Otherwise the aircraft either proved to be outside the coverage zone or had turned off its transponder. Soon after this first flight, in December 2017, Moscow received permission from the United Nations to send weapons and instructors to the Central African Republic despite an embargo introduced in 2013. Since then, according to the tracking data, the business jet 'disappeared' twenty-seven times over Egypt, near or over Libya.

On 17 December 2018, M-VITO arrived in Nairobi, the capital of Kenya, from Sudan. The tracking data showed that it had flown from Berlin, stopping over in Beirut. Then, on the same day, the aircraft flew from Beirut and disappeared over Egypt. It turned out that the business jet overflew Egypt and called first at Khartoum, the capital of Sudan, before heading to Kenya.

The landing of Prigozhin's aircraft in Nairobi was confirmed to Kenyan journalists by Civil Aviation Director Gilbert Kibe. Five people were on board, but the Kenyan Government refused to say whether they included Prigozhin himself. Having spent three days in Kenya, M-VITO headed for Ndjamena, the capital of Chad, this time with seven passengers. It could be seen from flight tracking that the business jet reappeared over Egypt on 23 December, stopped in Beirut, then returned to Moscow.

While Russia celebrated its New Year on 6 January 2019 M-VITO arrived in Beirut from Saint Petersburg. Two hours later it headed for Africa, once again disappearing at high altitude over Egypt. On 8 January, after a stopover in Beirut, the aircraft returned to Russia. Two days later M-VITO appeared over Africa again, this time near Libya. It was impossible to say for sure whether Prigozhin was on board his aircraft during all these flights.

In a small *Novaya Gazeta* triumph, on 24 April 2018, Prigozhin was personally registered on one flight from Moscow to Khartoum on board another aircraft with the registration number M-NJSS. According to flight registration data, he travelled with two Wagner Group mercenaries whose identities were confirmed by *Novaya Gazeta*.

In August 2018, Prigozhin flew to Khartoum by private aircraft for a meeting with the leaders of Central African armed groupings for talks. Three days after this meeting a report, 'On talks in Khartoum on a settlement in the Central African Republic', appeared on the Russian Foreign Ministry website. It spoke about the signing of the Khartoum Declaration and announced 'the creation of the Central African Opposition Association to achieve long-term and stable peace in the Central African Republic'. The declaration's signatories included the leaders of 'major armed groupings, including organizations that were formerly part of the alliance of Seleka and Anti-Balaka'—the Christian militia in the Central African Republic.

Novaya Gazeta sent questions for Yevgeny Prigozhin about these flights to the official email addresses of the Concord group of companies, also to the email address press-mail@inbox.ru that was listed as that of 'the Concord Company's Press Service'. Journalists for various publications had been receiving replies from this address purporting to come from Yevgeny Prigozhin himself. His replies were forwarded by a certain 'Valeria Concord', whose identity could not be established. Prigozhin's replies to *Novaya Gazeta* were flat denials that said he did not own or use an aircraft with the registration number M-VITO. Indeed, the jet formerly belonged to the Beratex Group Ltd, a Seychelles company, which would not disclose its current owners.

On the other hand, Yevgeny Prigozhin's daughter Polina posted photographs of aircraft M-VITO on her Instagram page. Other photographs showed that Prigozhin's wife and children were repeatedly on board a business jet whose interior is identical to the Raytheon Hawker 800XP model of M-VITO. It was as far as Novaya Gazeta's evidence went.

The replies that appeared to come from Prigozhin also said that he had not visited African countries, Lebanon or Syria on board this aircraft, and could not talk about his interests in these countries. M-VITO made one more flight. From 25 through 30 January, 2019, the aircraft was in Africa and then returned to Moscow.

By May there were reports that Prigozhin was also called in to sway the South African presidential elections. He had allegedly drawn up plans to discredit South African opposition parties, including the pro-western Democratic Alliance. It was clear, Prigozhin hoped to secure lucrative assets in South Africa's mining sector and to sign a deal to sell its ruling government arms.

Earlier Margaret Thatcher's favourite PR Firm Bell Pottinger imploded when it became known that it had broken industry best practices. In Russia, Wagner PMC and Prigozhin were inured from any existential criticism. The Russian embassy in Pretoria simply denied the reports.

Demand for Wagner PMC continued to pour in. Employees of Prigozhin's flew to the Comoros islands in 2018 to exploit a long-running territorial dispute. France still directly governs Mayotte, one of the four islands in the Indian Ocean archipelago.

On the investment side, there were Russian plans for a trans-African road and rail-building schemes. Future African leaders were to be identified and cultivated and there were plans to revive 'pan-African consciousness' closely modelled on the idea of *Russkiy Mir*, or Russian world—a concept that had become fashionable under Putin and signifies Russian power and culture projected beyond Federation borders.

In February 2019, M-VITO was impounded in Berlin. The US listed the plane as 'frozen property' to which neither spare parts nor landing rights could be granted. Prigozhin was by now also on the sanctions list of the EU. It made little difference, he simply acquired another Hawker 800XP through the company Clubgroup Ltd. The plane was registered in San Marino, a microstate in Italy that does not have its own airport.

Prigozhin's new €2-million jet also visited Berlin on 30 October 2020, carrying Artem Stepanov who headed several front companies belonging to Prigozhin's shared pride of place with his employer on the US Treasury Department's sanctions list since April 2021.

By June 2021, this plane was also grounded in Berlin. It was to be overhauled there and was still standing in front of a hangar belonging to the hired firm 'Beechcraft Berlin Aviation' at BER (Berlin Brandenburg Airport) in June

2021.

Another private jet used by Prigozhin, a Gulfstream 550, was also detained at Luton Airport on 3 April 2022. The same plane had landed at Lagos airport in June 2021 when it was reported that Prigozhin was meeting senior military figures. The plane was operated by Sonnig International Private Jets, which had a base in Benghazi, Libya. The company said it took pride in flying to 'difficult destinations, hot spots and conflict zones around the world'.

It was unclear how many of Prigozhin mercenary pitches had gone forward, but the Wagner PMC media projects that were up and running gave an indication. These included a website, *Africa Daily Voice*, with its headquarters in Morocco, and a French-language news service, Afrique Panorama, based in Madagascar's capital Antananarivo. Meanwhile Prigozhin sat in on bilateral talks between Putin and Madagascar's outgoing president Hery Rajaonarimampianina.

13

MERCENARY COLONIES

By 2021, the Kremlin had nestled itself firmly with its own mines, trolling and military presence to defend Russia's neo-colonial interests in Libya, Chad, Sudan, Central African Republic. It was ready to propagate itself to another part of Africa to do the same. In September 2021, it was reported that the Wagner Group were closing in on a deal to send a thousand-strong force to shore up the junta in Mali that would earn it around $10.8 million a month. Its mission would be to train troops and protect the regime's senior figures in a country that has suffered two coups in the last year and faces an ongoing Islamist insurgency in the vast Sahel region.

'Syria gave [the Russians] the suggestion that they could be more active in that part of the world,' former NATO Secretary-General Javier Solana told The Associated Press. 'They have very good relations with Algeria and they have… the Wagner type of people in the Sahel, which is delicate.'

News of a deal came after President Macron announced the winding down of Operation Barkhane, France's five-thousand-strong Mali-based military effort against the insurgents. Troop numbers would be reduced for a broader international mission, he said. Wagner had also signed military co-operation agreements with the continent's most populous nations, Ethiopia and Nigeria, in the last two months. 'Moscow can bring real support to Bamako and extend its influence on the African continent,' Maxim Shugalei, who has ties to Prigozhin.

What happened in Mali was the same as what happened in Kurdish Syria. When Donald Trump abandoned America's Kurdish allies and pulled US troops out of northern Syria in October 2019, the Wagner Group immediately took over their base in Manbij, though they had fought to defend the city just months before at the cost of four American dead and three wounded. An official from the Kurdish-led Syrian Democratic Forces said: 'The Russians are in the American base in Manbij now, they helped escort the Americans out of the area and got their base in return.'

Footage posted online showed Russian war correspondent Oleg Blokhin, known to be following the Wagner group, smirking as he looked around the abandoned US base. He boasted: 'Yesterday it was them and today it is us here.'

A senior Pentagon official told Newsweek: 'It is essentially a handover.

However, it's a quick out, not something that will include walk-throughs, etc. Everything is about making out with as much as possible of our things while destroying any sensitive equipment that cannot be moved.'

The official explained: 'Having been in the area for longer, [the US] has been assisting the Russian forces to navigate through previously unsafe areas quickly.' A TV crew from Russia Today (RT) filmed the base, showing what the US forces had left behind, including a television, sofas and bunks with bed linen.

A special adviser to Malian transitional President Assimi Goïta, Baba Cisse, denied reports that the government had signed an agreement with Wagner, saying that 'no decision has been taken on the nature of this co-operation'. Mali's Defence Ministry also denied that an agreement had been signed, but confirmed that talks had been held with Wagner. But it was more a case of keeping up appearances. Mali's prime minister Choguel Maiga said that if France won't guard Mali, shouldn't Mali have a plan B. Evidently, Mali's politicians felt exposed without foreign protection.

While France, Germany and Britain condemned the proposed deal, Russian foreign minister Sergey Lavrov said that, with France drawing down its presence in the conflict-torn country, it was legitimate for the Malian government to turn towards 'private Russian companies' to combat terrorism in Kidal, northern Mali, where France had failed. Other members of the UN peacekeeping force in Mali threatened to pull out.

Nevertheless, on 21 December, the privately-owned newspaper *Le Nouvel horizon* reported that a Russian military aircraft had landed at Bamako international airport two days earlier. Another newspaper, *L'Indicateur de renouveau*, said that talks between Malian authorities and the Wagner Group had 'come true'. 'Here is the proof: the presence of the Tupolev TU-154M is a further sign of the progress of discussions between the two parties,' the paper said in an article headed, 'First Wagner combatants already on Malian soil?'

As always, Wagner's infiltration was shrouded in speculation. On 23 December a French government source quoted by Radio France Internationale (RFI) mentioned the presence of 'hurriedly set up facilities' at Bamako airport that 'can accommodate a significant number of mercenaries'.

'We are seeing repeated air rotations with military transport planes belonging to the Russian army and installations at Bamako airport to allow the arrival of a significant number of mercenaries,' the source said. A great deal of food had been ordered. 'The whole operation involved air transfers using Russian armed forces resources and was supervised locally by Wagner Group operators.'

The suspicious air rotations observed could have begun 'several weeks ago'. The landing in Bamako on 19 December of a Russian army Tupolev passenger aircraft, which had transited through Syria and Libya, raised many questions. An II-76 military airlifter transported equipment via this route, used by Wagner to deploy in Libya.

A number of men observed wearing fatigues and carrying AK-47 type rifles, estimated at around 40, arrived at the base a few days before. All of them were said to be Russian speaking, though doubts persist about their status.

Along with the installations at the air base next to Bamako airport, there were also a dozen military tents and a few troops transport lorries, along with about sixty armoured vehicles, some Chinese-made, others Russian-made.

As always, the Russian military was giving a helping hand to the supposedly independent contractors. Like the Libya-Chad-Sudan-Central African Republic triangle, any hope of peace returning to the region was gone. Wagner PMC's modus operandi was perpetual provocation to preclude that they would ever be required to move out.

'They're deploying there, supported by the Russian military. Russian Air Force aeroplanes are delivering them,' General Stephen Townsend, the head of US Africa Command, said in an interview on Voice of America. 'The world can see this happening… It's a great concern to us.'

William Linder, president of risk consultancy 14 North Strategies and an ex-CIA officer with experience in the Sahel, said: 'Mali's junta, wittingly or unwittingly, is making itself a pawn in Russia's game.'

A week later General Townsend reiterated: 'Our information is clear: Mali has brought Wagner to its territory.'

In an online press conference, he said: 'Several hundred men are on the ground, and this is a figure that could increase further. I have seen them in Syria, Libya, Sudan, the Central African Republic and Mozambique. After their departure, the situation is never better than when they arrived. It is often even worse.'

Asked about the $10 million a month the Malian government were said to be paying them, he said: 'I don't know where they get that money. I think they're going to have to exchange their services for natural resources like gold, minerals and precious stones.'

He told RFI: 'Although the international partners support the Malian government unconditionally, this is not the case with Wagner. They are there for their personal interests.'

Fifteen countries—Belgium, Canada, the Czech Republic, Denmark, Estonia, France, Germany, Italy, Lithuania, Norway, the Netherlands, Portugal, Romania, Sweden and the UK—condemned the deployment of the Wagner group, saying it 'can only further deteriorate the security situation in West Africa'.

'We are aware of the involvement of the Russian Federation government in providing material support to the deployment of the Wagner group in Mali and call on Russia to revert to responsible and constructive behaviour in the region,' the statement said.

Maliactu.net posted a report from *Le Patriote* on the arrival of an aircraft from Russia on 23 December with 'gifts for Malian children'.

'The Russian government has on several occasions sent gifts to Malian people affected by terrorist activities in the region,' it said.

It added that the partnership between Mali and Russia was 'developing quickly in various sectors—political, military, economic and others'.

Russia Today (RT) reported on its Russian-language website, citing a Malian resource, that Russia had delivered what was described as gingerbread and sweet gifts from the Russian city of Tula for Malian children 'as part of a cultural exchange', though no coverage had appeared on Russian state TV.

Novaya Gazeta reported the news in an article headed: 'Russian mercenaries in Mali, now—officially', citing African media, while RIA FAN published a story about Malian children who were given gifts from Russia ahead of New Year, citing posts by a local resident on Facebook.

However, it quoted senior state TV journalist Anastasia Popova as ridiculing the Western criticism on Telegram and praising the Wagner private military company.

'In the meantime, PMC Wagner entered Mali. In this regard, a hysterical communiqué from fourteen European countries plus Canada was published. They categorically condemned, and deeply regretted, that the Malian authorities are spending money, you see, not on their army, but on some overseas mercenaries,' she wrote. 'The appearance of Russians there will worsen the security situation, [the situation] with human rights (!), threaten the world and prevent the international community from providing protection to the civilian population. Then they say that our military planes fly back and forth, geologists walk around the airport, accuse the Russian authorities of all mortal sins and urge them to act responsibly and constructively in the region. Yeah, just as responsibly as all the French were stirring up there? I think the Malians know that with our [guys] it will be just the opposite, clearly and to the point.'

Vintage Wagner PMC carnage soon started. Rights Watch reported that in March 2022 Wagner mercenaries were involved in a massacre of three hundred civilians in the town of Moura in central Mali. The killings took place over five days, Human Rights Watch said. Local security sources told HRW that more than a hundred Russian-speaking men were allegedly involved in the operation, which HRW described as the worst single atrocity reported in Mali's decade-long armed conflict. Witnesses spoke of white soldiers talking in an unfamiliar foreign language they believed to be Russian. They went from house to house, detaining men and taking them out to be shot in small groups. They were buried in three mass graves, which the detainees had been ordered to dig.

The men were then shot while they sat or lay down next to the graves and some of the bodies were burned. One resident said: 'The sound of gunfire rang out in our village from Monday to Thursday.'

Giving testimony, survivors told HRW that helicopters carrying soldiers had landed near Moura's animal market on the morning of 27 March. The troops opened fire on thirty armed jihadis before reinforcements arrived and blocked off escape routes from the settlement, they said. Several lay dead, including two of the assault force, before deploying through the town.

The remaining Islamists fled on motorbikes, while the soldiers opened fire on people running.

'All of us started running in every direction, some into the houses,' said Amadou Barry, who lived in the neighbouring village.

These soldiers were then said to have rounded up hundreds of unarmed men from the market and from their homes. They were taken out to a dry riverbed nearby for interrogation. The men were held there with little food or water for four days, while soldiers periodically led groups of captives away to be killed, Barry and other witnesses said.

The prisoners were taken out of town and were forced to lie in the sun, HRW reported. Hundreds of the captives were murdered over the next four days, according to survivors, with town elders corroborating this figure.

Although it is not known why certain captives in Moura were killed and others were spared, some witnesses said members of the Peuhl, or Fulani, ethnic group had been targeted. 'The soldiers appeared to target the Peul and let the others go,' one local said.

Some villagers were released after their fingers and shoulders were inspected for signs that they had fired guns, but all men from the Peuhl ethnic minority were detained, Barry said. The Islamists had sought to recruit among the pastoralist Peuhl by exploiting grievances with the government and other ethnic groups. According to survivors, those killed in Moura were all from the Peuhl community.

Another man who was held captive said he had heard nine men being executed on 28 March and a further thirteen the following day, while a trader said he had witnessed two of his brothers being shot. 'They took them several metres away and executed them, point blank. Over the next few days, I saw others—in groups of two or three—killed the same way... nineteen in total,' the trader said.

'I lived in terror, each minute, each second thinking it would be my turn to be taken away and executed. Even after being told to go, I feared it was a trap,' one witness said.

A twenty-nine-year-old Fulani cattle herder named Hamidou said he was arrested at his home in Douentza village in central Mali with two other people in November and accused of being an Islamic militant. He was locked in a tiny room where he was bound, beaten and interrogated by 'white soldiers'.

'We were severely beaten daily. We didn't think we'd survive,' said Hamidou, who asked to be identified only by his first name for fear of reprisal, adding that most of those detained were ethnic Fulani, like him. 'From the day Wagner came to Mali until today, arbitrary arrests and killings of Fulani civilians have been increasing tremendously,' he said.

Héni Nsaibia, senior researcher at the NGO Armed Conflict Location and Event Data Project (ACLED), said between sixty and a hundred of those killed may have been unarmed Islamist militants, but the rest were civilians. ACLED said as many as 456 civilians died in nine incidents involving Malian forces and Wagner between January and mid-April 2022.

'We know that Wagner are deployed in central Mali, they've been assisting operations in lifting and bringing more soldiers to their positions in the region. I think it's pretty clear that it was Wagner that was conducting this operation,' said Ousmane Diallo, a researcher for Amnesty International in Mali.

Nsaibia said his own exhaustive research among survivors led to a similar conclusion, while a west African diplomat in Mali said 'inquiries into the events in Moura had confirmed that Wagner forces were working with Malian forces in central Mali'. In response Yevgeny Prigozhin, when queried said, this was all a case of 'fakes, outright lies and… falsification' and of trying to 'spit in the face of me, the Russian patriots, and the Malian people'.

'There is a proverb,' he said, '"Don't try to piss against the wind, you will get drowned in the splash." These atrocities are committed in your inflamed brain, infected with the disease called "Nazism".'

'You are a dying-out western civilization that considers Russians, Malians, Central Africans, Cubans, Nicaraguans and many other peoples and countries to be third world scum,' he added. 'Remember, this is not true…. You are a pathetic endangered bunch of perverts, and there are many of us, billions of us. And victory will be ours!'

The situation in Mali, he said, was the fault of 'the collective west, namely the USA, Britain, France and other countries trying to pursue a policy of enslaving Africa, have been planting and organizing terrorist groups in Mali for years'. This was being done, he said, 'in order to keep the population of this country in fear, to plunder its natural wealth and to write off the money allocated for so-called peacekeeping operations'.

Allegations that the Wagner Group and the Malian army were involved in massacres and other human rights abuses were false, Prigozhin said. 'Any terrorist killed by the Malian army, the collective west tried to pass off as a civilian… As to the atrocities, neither I, nor the men I know, nor the Malian army have committed them.'

He also accused the French of killing civilians and burying their remains not far from military bases.

US deputy ambassador Richard Mills said the first three months of 2022 had been marked by 'alarming accounts of human rights abuses'. He also called for an investigation into the 'execution-style killing of over thirty-five people' in the Segou region in central Mali on 2 March.

'This increase in reports of human rights abuses is exactly why the United States continues to warn countries against partnering with the Kremlin-linked Wagner group,' he said. 'Wagner forces have been implicated in human rights abuses, including execution-style killings, in the Central African Republic and elsewhere.'

Britain's deputy UN ambassador James Kariuki concurred. 'The United Kingdom is horrified by a surge of human rights abuses since the deployment of the Wagner group to Mali,' he said. 'Just as the presence of Russian mercenaries drove an increase in human rights violations and abuses in the Central African Republic last year, we fear we are now seeing the same in Mali.'

The French accused the Russians of trying to smear them by posting videos of Caucasians burying bodies at the base at Gossi in Mali which the French had just handed over to the Malians. According to French sources, the white men were most likely Wagner mercenaries. Several tweets with pictures of the bodies have been posted on accounts that support Russia or fake accounts created by Wagner. The tweets blame the French for the killings and the burials. One tweet from an account called Dia Diarra, allegedly created by Wagner, said: 'This is what the French left behind when they left base at #Gossi. These are excerpts from a video that was taken after they left! We cannot keep silent about this!'

But Wagner was not having it all its own way in Mali. On 25 April 2022, Islamist militants claimed to have captured one of their men.

'These murderous forces participated with the Malian army in an airdrop operation on a market in the village of Moura, where they confronted several mujahideen before… killing hundreds of innocent civilians,' a statement from the insurgents said.

New allegations surfaced about two shootings in villages around the town of Hombori in the central Mopti region, following the death of one or possibly two Wagner mercenaries accompanying Malian troops on operations against Islamist militants.

Aid workers, experts and human rights campaigners said one attack came after a military patrol was ambushed on the outskirts of a village at about 9.30am on 19 April. According to an internal Malian military memo, a Russian was injured by an improvised mine and died after being airlifted to the town of

Sevare. A medical official in Sevare described the man as a Russian in his thirties.

Another internal memo described a clash on 23 April between militants and 'a joint patrol of FAMa and Russian instructors' between the villages of Mondoro and Boni. FAMa is the *Forces Armées Maliennes* or Malian army. 'Provisional losses' amounted to 'two dead—one FAMa and one Russian—and ten wounded—six FAMa and four Russians', said the memo, sent some hours after the incident. Twelve other people, who may have been Islamists, were also thought to have died.

In 2022, dozens of miners are thought to have died in at least three major attacks this year allegedly involving mercenaries working for the Wagner Group.

'The operations that Wagner mercenaries are undertaking in many African countries are not really costly. They just need to supply a few hundred mercenaries with basic military equipment. They are paid back with resources from the state,' said Enrica Picco, Central African director at the think tank Crisis Group. 'Keeping those operations running means keeping a high profile on the continent and maintaining the rhetoric that Wagner mercenaries are successful.'

End-of-the-year tally made by ACLED said that more than two thousand civilians had been killed since December 2021, compared with about five hundred in the previous twelve months. At least a third of those deaths recorded in 2022 were from attacks involving the Wagner Group.

'They are killing civilians, and by their very presence, giving Malian security forces a green light to act on their worst inclinations,' said Michael Shurkin, senior fellow at Atlantic Council and director of global programmes at the consultancy group 14 North Strategies.

In June 2023, President Touadéra announced on Facebook that he was holding a referendum on constitutional reform that could extend his tenure to a third term. Opposition parties and civil rights groups said this was part of a Russian plan to consolidate Wagner's control of the diamond-rich nation and expand its influence in neighbouring countries. Wagner had at least 1,900 personnel there.

Reviewing the situation in Mali in December 2021, Concord told the *FT*: 'In just a year, thanks to the Russian instructors there, the situation has totally changed—the bandits have been destroyed and are surrendering in droves, are asking for mercy and a return to normal life. The great Russian military is saving the world from violence and injustice.'

And there was news from a correspondent on the ground. Maxim Shugalei, who had previously accused European forces, primarily French troops, of covertly training terrorist groups there, posted on Telegram on 20 December: 'I had to urgently interrupt my trip to Libya and fly to the Republic of Mali. It was not easy to get to Mali: the board, which had all the permits and approvals, was repeatedly denied overflight right in the air. In the Sahel, international treaties and rules have ceased to operate, and complete legal chaos is taking place. Obviously, NATO feels like masters in this territory.'

He again attacked France: 'They do not yet understand that the stage of the most serious opposition to their colonial habits has already begun. It is significant that the Malian authorities did not allow President Macron to enter the country today. The visit was cancelled. As I heard, the Central African Republic was not happy with this politician either.'

Next day, he posted a video from what he said was Bamako, but several hours later he made another post, suggesting that he had already returned home.

While Russia pledged to continue its support of Mali, the Russian ambassador there, Igor Gromyko, said: 'I have no information on the presence of the Wagner group in Mali. As the ambassador of the Russian Federation in Mali, I have not seen a single representative of this group. The Wagner Group is a private company that acts independently of the Russian government. We have no connection with this company.'

There were, however, 'Russian military specialists' in-country.

By 3 January 2022, RFI said that mercenaries from the Wagner Group, clashed with jihadists from the al-Qaeda affiliate, Katiba Macina, in a village situated between the towns of Bandiagara and Bankass. The previous week a reporter had seen Malian army vehicles carrying white men in military fatigues from the capital, Bamako, heading towards the centre of the country. However, the government in Bamako retained its position that no contract had been signed with the Wagner Group.

A week later, RFI reported that sources close to the French military had told them that 450 Wagner Group mercenaries were already deployed in Mali, including two hundred in Segou, central Mali, some two-hundred kilometres north-east of Bamako, on the Niger River. Others were in Timbuktu, Mopti and Sevare.

By 13 January there were reports that Wagner had suffered its first casualty in Mali. Menastream, a risk consultancy group that monitors militant violence in the Sahel, tweeted: 'It can now be said Russian military advisers/Wagner have suffered their first death in central Mali.'

The Russian mercenary was allegedly killed by an IED (improvised explosive device) in central Mali's Mopti Region.

'Footage from Nomono in Bandiagara shows the remains of a clearly white Caucasian IED victim dug up after being buried on site,' Menastream added.

The EU had also imposed sanctions on Mali's government after the arrival of the Wagner Group. Mali had already been suspended from membership of the Economic Community of West African States and sanctions imposed. Mali then closed its borders.

French Foreign Minister Yves Le Drian told French magazine *Journal du dimanche* that the Wagner Group were exploiting Mali's resources in exchange for security cooperation.

'In Mali... they are already using the country's resources in exchange for protecting the junta. They are plundering Mali,' he said. 'In the Central African Republic, they went to engage in predatory activities by exchanging the security of the authorities for the right to exploit mining resources with impunity. In Mali, it's the same. They are already using the country's resources in exchange for protecting the junta. They are despoiling Mali. Wagner uses the weakness of certain states to implant itself ... to reinforce Russia's influence in Africa.'

He also called the Mali junta illegitimate. The French ambassador was given seventy-two hours to leave.

After hundreds of Malians took to the streets of the capital Bamako on 4 February to demand the withdrawal of France's forces, it was reported that the government had signed an agreement with Wagner under which the company would deploy up on a thousand fighters in the country. On 15 February 2022, Le Drian confirmed that there were now a thousand Wagner mercenaries in the country.

'We absolutely expect an increase in Wagner numbers, to go up in Mali as the French leave,' a senior US defence official told Reuters.

A British defence source added: 'We strongly warned Mali government against engaging with Wagner. Wagner deployments elsewhere in Africa have largely been unsuccessful and frankly exploit the limited wealth of the countries that have engaged them.'

It was not long before Human Rights Watch reported on civilians imprisoned and tortured by 'white men speaking a strange language'. One herder said he was detained at a base in the central district of Niono, where he was hung upside down and subjected to acts of torture, including mock executions.

The man said that a white foreigner who was dressed in the same uniform as the Malian army 'forced him to drink a lot of water' before he tied 'electric cable around his toes' and electrocuted him several times.

'I and many others were beaten terribly by Malian and a few white soldiers speaking a language I'd never heard,' said another man.

In another case, Russian soldiers were present when more than thirty civilians, some of them children, were bound, doused in petrol and set on fire.

Pilots supplied by Wagner were seen flying Malian army helicopters and the group also provided officers who led Malian forces on bigger operations. Local witnesses accused both Malian and Russian fighters of killing civilians. Many victims had been tied and blindfolded, then shot, according to Human Rights Watch.

Refugees in the camp at M'bera in south-east Mauritania said they fled because the security situation in Mali had deteriorated since Wagner's arrival.

'Before, the Malian army was afraid to go too far [into the countryside],' said one man from the Timbuktu region, who arrived in the camp a month ago. 'But since Wagner has started coming with them, they have the courage to go further—reaching our villages.' He fled the country after a series of raids and attacks on markets in nearby towns, which he said were carried out by the Malian military and Wagner mercenaries.

Other new arrivals spoke of increased violence and extrajudicial killings since Wagner arrived. Human rights researchers and conflict analysts say this tallies with the scale of brutality they have documented as being meted out by the military and mercenaries.

The woman from Timbuktu said she has found peace at the camp, but at the cost of leaving her homeland, perhaps forever.

'I don't have any intention of returning,' she said. In M'bera, she has found security, and for the first time in a long time has had a peaceful night's sleep. 'I don't have Mali in my head.'

Since the Wagner group was invited into Mali in December, there had been an explosion of reports of massacres and torture involving Russian soldiers. Some thirty-five burned corpses were found near Diabaly, a town in the centre of the country, in March. Local sources said they were shepherds who were tortured and executed in a nearby Malian government camp where the Russians were operating.

At the village of Hombori, survivors said that Russians shot indiscriminately into a livestock fair on 19 April. They killed almost twenty people before rounding up about sixty into three trucks. Many of these, it was thought, were tortured or executed later.

'There were no jihadists. No men were armed. People fled in all directions. They killed several dozen people,' said a local merchant in a foreign interview. 'My older brother was caught in front of his store. It was white people, Russians, who arrested my brother.'

Just hours after the last French troops left Mali on 15 August 2022 jihadists announced that they had killed four Russian mercenaries belonging to the Wagner Group in an ambush in the central Mopti region.

While Wagner fought back against the Islamist insurgents, civilians suffered one more. On 30 October Agence France-Presse reported that thirteen civilians were killed in the Mopti region by Malian troops supported by 'white soldiers'.

'On Sunday in Guelledjé [near] Tenenkou … the Malian military came in force with white soldiers. There was shooting and arrests. At least thirteen people were killed,' a local politician told AFP. Those killed included a woman, her daughter and her granddaughter. A resident of Guelledjé said the village was attacked because 'the army and the white soldiers of Wagner consider it to be an Islamist extremist stronghold'. Another source that 'more than 20 civilians were killed and arrested'. Again the Peuhl seemed to have picked out.

According to the Armed Conflict Location and Event Data Project, a non-profit that tracks violence across the world, Wagner's deployment in Mali has 'entailed mass atrocities, torture, summary executions, looting, the introduction of booby traps as a counter-insurgency tactic, and influence operations in the information environment'.

Victoria Nuland, US undersecretary of state for political affairs, said terrorism had become significantly worse since Wagner had deployed to Mali.

'Terrorism is going up, not down, and we are firmly of the view that Wagner works for itself, not for the people of the country that it comes to,' Nuland said.

Meanwhile, the US State Department was looking out for the Wagner Group using false papers to purchase weapons and route them through Mali as a third party.

Having secured military strongholds in Mali— adopting an oil spill approach— Wagner PMC trained its attention to new mineral concessions on to Mali's neighbours. Following a military take-over in Mali's neighbour Burkina Faso on 23 January 2022, the head of the Wagner Group in the Central African Republic, Alexander Ivanov—also on the EU's sanctions list—wrote to the junta to offer assistance. Russian media also reported that Yevgeny Prigozhin had praised recent coups in west Africa. Prigozhin's trolls had also established their usual targets alongside the *Wagnerovcis* as pro-junta protesters in Burkina Faso were seen waving Russian flags.

Burkina Faso's private Radio Omega website quoted Ivanov as saying that the Russian mercenaries would be more effective in fighting Islamist militants. He also ridiculed the presence of French troops in the Sahel and said they had failed to defeat jihadists.

'I believe that if Russian instructors are invited to train the army of Burkina Faso, they will be able to do so effectively,' Ivanov was quoted as saying.

In his letter, Ivanov said that France had had 'no success' in the counter-insurgency. He added that his instructors were 'ready to share the experience acquired in the Central African Republic on rapid organisation and high-quality operations in order to build an army ready to combat and master the security situation in little time'.

Within hours of a second coup in Burkina Faso, Yevgeny Prigozhin posted a message on Telegram praising the mutinous soldiers for doing what 'was necessary' and the Wagner Group quickly moved in, whipping up anti-French sentiment with a stream of bogus social-media posts. Mamadou Drabo, executive secretary for Save Burkina, a civil society group that supports the junta, said: 'If today we say that we don't want Wagner then how long are we going to stay in this war?' Drabo said. 'We don't want Burkina to be turned into Somalia.'

It had already happened. Authorities were ordered to hand nearly $30 million in gold from its mines over for 'public necessity'.

'I believe mine in southern Burkina has been allocated to them as a form of payment for their services,' Ghana's President Nana Akufo-Addo said in 2022.

'To have [Wagner] operating on our northern border is particularly distressing for us in Ghana,' added Akufo-Addo.

Wagner was infecting social media in Niger and the Ivory Coast—two relatively stable countries in which Wagner had no domestic involvement—with its social-media propaganda. It depicted the French as zombies, snakes and in one case a fat rat called Emmanuel. In the latter video, a Wagner man appears with a sledgehammer marked with a 'W' to smash the rodent named after President Macron over the head.

Other posts circulating on social media in Niger accused France of arming jihadists who killed seventeen Niger soldiers in Intagamey. Another spread rumours of a coup against Mohamed Bazoum, Niger's president, while he was visiting France. Weekly news magazine *Jeune Afrique* reported that much was linked to 'the Lakhta project', a well-known troll farm financed by Prigozhin.

Mozambique, opposite Madagascar, proved one of Moscow's few failures. Wagner mercenaries arrived in the country with three Mi-24 combat helicopters after seeing off competition for the government security contract from an operation owned by Erik Prince, founder of Blackwater, the US private security company. They were to provide training and combat support in the northern province of Cabo Delgado which was under attack from ISIL. President Filipe Nyusi, was another ruler in distress. He was facing elections and had visited Moscow to sign energy and security deals with President Putin. Vast reserves of natural gas had been discovered off the province's coastline in 2010. Mali, Niger, Chad, Burkina Faso and Mauritania were among other countries that had asked Moscow to help them to fight threats from Islamic State and al-Qaeda.

As part of the Wagner script, Prigozhin deployed his expertise in trolling to good effect. But this time, Facebook took action against a disinformation campaign targeting eight African states as part of Russia's efforts to ramp up influence on the continent. The social-media company removed several accounts traced to Prigozhin. Three separate influencing operations linked to dozens of Facebook pages, accounts and groups targeted African nations with content that was sympathetic to Russia during elections or periods of political instability.

'Each of these operations created networks of accounts to mislead others about who they were and what they were doing,' Nathaniel Gleicher, Facebook's cybersecurity chief, said.

Researchers from Stanford University, California, who worked with the social media company on the investigation, tracked some accounts to the Wagner Group. The campaign in Africa was the first well-documented case of Russia 'franchising' its disinformation efforts to local parties. The reliance on native speakers or locally based subcontractors made the propaganda harder to detect. Parallel campaigns were undertaken in Madagascar, the Central African Republic, Mozambique, Democratic Republic of Congo, Ivory Coast, Cameroon, Sudan and Libya.

The news followed an Africa summit held in the Olympic Park in Sochi, attended by more than forty African leaders. It was hailed as Russia's return to the continent as it had a strong influence with African liberation movements during the Soviet era. Dictatorial African leaders lapped up what Prigozhin had to offer.

It did not go well, however, in Mozambique. In its densely forested Cabo Delgardo province, seven Wagner mercenaries were killed by ISIL-backed militants in two separate actions. On 7 October 2019, while on patrol with the Mozambique Defence Armed Force (*Forças Armadas de Defesa de Moçambique* or FADM), two Wagner mercenaries were killed in an ambush.

Then on 27 October, Islamists set up a roadblock and began firing on the Wagner convoy. Four mercenaries were shot dead at the scene and beheaded, taking a leaf out of the *Wagnerovci* playbook. A fifth was shot and wounded, and died later in hospital. Twenty troops from FADM died in the same encounter.

The *Daily Maverick* reported on 29 November that eleven of the Wagner Group's soldiers were killed and a further twenty-five injured, in three separate battles with the militants.

Despite using advanced warfare tactics, drones and data analytics, Wagner were forced to back off. Security consultant Olivier Guitta told the BBC: 'After suffering a series of ambushes and nearly a dozen reported deaths in several battles in densely forested districts of Cabo Delgado, the Russian private military contractors have gone into a strategic retreat.'

They left behind headless corpses piled high in the streets. Thousands had fled and French energy giant Total's multi-billion dollar gas project closed.

The *Moscow Times* said that Wagner was struggling and some believe its mercenaries were in way over their heads in Mozambique.

'You have to realize this is one of the toughest environments in the world,' said Al Venter, a veteran South Africa journalist who has written extensively about mercenaries on the continent.

'The consensus is that Wagner has almost no experience of the kind of primitive bush warfare being waged in there. They are going to come very badly unstuck'.

Military experts said the Russians were 'ill-prepared' for the mission, and that 'attempting to apply a European or Russian style of strategic approach to an African conflict was a recipe for disaster.' The mercenaries' relationship with their host, FADM, broke down after several of the Russian fighters were killed in 'friendly fire'.

Nevertheless, new competitor PMCs sprang up, such as Vega, Shield and Patriot, the latter allegedly directly linked to the Russian defence ministry and its contractors reportedly potentially earning up to one million rubles a month—'an unthinkable sum for anyone living outside Moscow's Garden Ring,' according to Neil Hauer of *The Atlantic*.

'It remains to be seen exactly what role Patriot, Wagner, or any other imitators will play in Africa, Syria, and elsewhere going forward, but it appears as though the private military company as an instrument of Russian foreign and domestic policy is here to stay,' said Hauer.

One of the security firms that lost out to Wagner was OAM, headed by John Gartner who served in the special forces of what was formerly known as Rhodesia. He had proposed a deployment of fifty men at a cost to the client of $15,000 to $25,000 a month per man. The Wagner Group's tender was far lower, but the Russians underestimated the scale of the job, he said. Professor Mark Galeotti, Russian security expert at University College London, linked its rising body count to Wagner's brisk expansion to meet Russia's international ambitions: 'This means being less picky with recruits'.

Wagner retreated to the port city of Nacala, 360 miles south of the insurgency hot spot, which would give them space to 'regroup, resupply and restrategize', according to Gartner. The *Daily Maverick* online said: 'The soldiers left in Mozambique have retreated as far as their base in Nacala where they were retraining, acclimatizing and gathering intelligence.'

There had been some three-hundred attacks over the previous two years and at least 450 people were killed, mostly civilians. ISIL claimed involvement in about a dozen incidents. Ending the bloodshed had become urgent for the government as it negotiated investments worth at least £30 billion for the natural gas fields discovered off Cabo Delgado.

Wagner trolls meanwhile interfered in the elections in Mozambique on 15 October. A survey published at the end of the campaign by the International Anticrisis Centre putting the ruling party Frelimo in the lead 'created suspicions'. International Anticrisis Centre, however, was a think tank with ties to Yevgeny Prigozhin and its research was worthless. It was sanctioned by the US

Treasury.

Frelimo denied any connection, while Moscow denied reports that there were any Russian mercenaries in Mozambique.

'I would file such reports in the notorious "fake news" category. They are not true when it comes to Mozambique,' Andrei Kemarsky, head of the Russian Foreign Ministry's Africa department, told the *RIA Novosti* news agency.

Nevertheless ISIL released a video of a helicopter initially thought to have belonged to the Wagner Group being shot down during fighting on 10 April 2020. It might have been true. Wagner pulled out of Mozambique in March to be replaced by the Dyck Advisory Group. Reports in the South African press said that the helicopter belonged to DAG and that it encountered mechanical problems and was forced to land.

Mikhail Khodorkovsky's news website MBK Media said Wagner had failed in its mission in part because of 'poor co-ordination' with government forces. Some $60 million (£44 million) had reportedly been invested in Mozambique by Prigozhin as Moscow aimed to profit from the country's lucrative natural gas resources.

As Wagner pulled out of Palma, leaving the town to the insurgents, three SAS men were sent to search for Brit Philip Mawer who was understood to have been with around two hundred other expatriates at Palma's Amarula Lodge hotel in a convoy of around seventeen vehicles trying to escape when it ran into a militant ambush. At least seven were killed.

DAG mercenaries spotted a body believed to be Mawer's in the wreckage of a car. They tried to an angle grinder to cut his corpse free. The SAS team was poised to go in with them, but was ordered to stand down at the last minute.

It was a rare failure. 'Wagner frequently oversell their capacity,' said a western defence source. 'Repressive regimes make Faustian bargains with them, using their nations' natural wealth to buy security but finding themselves trapped with an expensive, unreliable and untrustworthy partner'.

14

MORAL HIGH GROUND

To other countries with leading PMC companies, the outline of Putin's modern colonialisation programme through Wagner PMC's *Wagnerovcis* and digital trolls was now very clear. At the Munich Security Conference in 2019, Britain's Minister of Defence Gavin Williamson said 'the infamous and unaccountable Wagner group allows the Kremlin to get away with murder while denying the blood on their hands'. Grzegorz Kuczynski, director of the Eurasia programme at the Warsaw Institute and an expert in Wagner's activities, said that unlike other mercenary companies: 'The Wagnerists are ready to carry out any order at the behest of the Kremlin.' The Russian authorities can use them for 'wet work' in various parts of the world, officially refusing to admit having ties with them.

The Kremlin's aims were clear. A trove of Wagner documents containing a map dating to December 2018 showed the level of cooperation between the 'Company'—aka the Wagner Group—and African governments, country by country. Symbols indicated military, political and economic ties, police training, media and humanitarian projects, and 'rivalry with France', until 2014 the dominant military force in this part of Africa.

Five was the highest level; one was the lowest. The closest relations were with Central African Republic, Sudan and Madagascar—all put at five. Libya, Zimbabwe and South Africa were listed as four, with South Sudan at three, and the DRC, Chad and Zambia at two.

Other documents contained the Kremlin's future strategy and cited Uganda, Equatorial Guinea and Mali as 'countries where we plan to work'. Libya and Ethiopia were flagged as nations 'where cooperation is possible'. Egypt is described as 'traditionally supportive'.

The Company also listed its achievements. These included getting rid of a politician 'orientated to France' in the Central African Republic while Andry Rajoelina was elected president of Madagascar with 'the Company's support'. Rajoelina denied receiving assistance. Prigozhin provided spin doctors and staff for a Russian company mining chromium there.

In November 2018 the Libyan commander Khalifa Haftar travelled to Moscow and met the defence minister, Sergei Shoigu. Prigozhin, who had become an international person of interest as a result of the meticulous

Mueller investigation into Russia's 2016 election interference, was spotted at the talks. To put Prigozhin's significance into perspective, Bill Browder, once the largest foreign investor in Russia through his Hermitage Fund and now a human-rights campaigner, said that a lot of the malignant foreign policy that Putin had been running, either through mercenaries or disinformation operations, had been 'executed by this one man'.

'He is basically running black operations for Putin all over the world in different areas. He is performing a function that is highly valued by Putin', Browder said.

While the Kremlin continued to deny any official links to Wagner—or, indeed, that it even existed—Bellingcat revealed in August 2020 that Prigozhin had made 99 calls to Putin's chief of staff Anton Vayno in just eight months. In the same period Prigozhin had called and texted his spokesperson Dmitry Peskov 144 times. There were also 54 contacts with Putin's domestic politics chief and 25 calls with Alexey Dyumin, the deputy head of the GRU intelligence service. Emails also revealed at least two face-to-face meetings between Prigozhin and Russia's defence minister Sergey Shoigu. In addition, Prigozhin was found to have made at least 3 calls with Russia's former ambassador to the US, Yury Ushakov. Given Russia's kleptocracy, it was clear that all were involved in some way in making money off of Wagner Group PMC's African operations.

However, following the Mueller Inquiry's meticulous uncovering of Prigozhin's trolls, his growing public profile in the Western media was becoming a hindrance to Wagner's expansion plans and, in 2021, Prigozhin started court battles to defend his frayed reputation and suppress the stories that linked him, the Kremlin and Wagner PMC's digital and military operations.

He sued *Meduza.io*, an independent news website based in Latvia, and members of its editorial staff when it said that he had been convicted for 'involving minors in prostitution'. He produced Russian court papers that ostensibly proved that when he was arrested in his youth, he had only been convicted for involving minors in drunkenness and burglary. He won the case and the article was deleted with an award of 80,000 rubles (US$1,100) in compensation, having forced *Meduza* to spend a small fortune it didn't have on legal bills.

Prigozhin also gave his first interview to the Western press. Speaking to the *Sunday Telegraph* on 7 November 2021, he personally denied any connection between him and the Wagner Group. He strongly denied interfering in American elections and said: 'I have never served in the Russian government and, it bears repeating, I am not closely acquainted with President Putin.'

Asked why his name had been linked to the Wagner Group, he said: 'I "have been linked" by whom? By the US government? By the Russian opposition press which receives US funding? By academics who receive US grants? By a UN "panel of experts" in which the deputy spokesperson of the US State Department is a member?

'I do not know why I have become a minor character in America's geopolitical fairytales. Perhaps you will also ask me why the US government thought the kids they droned a few weeks ago in Afghanistan were terrorists. I have no idea. I am actually very surprised that anyone links me with Wagner Group because I am not connected with any groups.'

Emphasizing the point, he said: 'I can say with confidence that I have no connection whatsoever to Wagner Group or any other mercenary groups.' He added it 'worries me greatly that some people think I have such a connection'.

'I am a pacifist,' he insisted. It was all brazen lies as became clear a year later. In response to a request for information from the *Financial Times* about Wagner moving into Mali, his Concord company followed the usual Kremlin hymn sheet on Telegram: Wagner PMC did not exist, Prigozhin was not linked to mercenaries.

It all served to direct public attention away from Putin's neo-colonialism. Despite Russian denials as to its existence, the EU sanctioned the Wagner Group just over a year after it had imposed sanctions on Prigozhin himself, along with his wife and mother, for alleged business links to the Russian war from 2014 in Donbas and Crimea. Canada had added his two children Polina and Pavel.

Others were also subject to sanctions. On 13 December 2021, Wagner, three oil companies linked to the group in Syria and eight individuals had been banned from travelling to the EU and any assets held inside the bloc would be frozen.

The Wagner boss Dmityr Utkin was accused of extrajudicial killings, while Alexander Kuzen, a forty-four-year-old Russian believed to be a commander in Wagner's 1st Attack and Reconnaissance Company, was said to have destabilized Libya.

Another target, sixty-eight-year-old Andrei Roshev, said to be one of the group's co-founders, was cited as having led mercenary troops in Syria in support of Bashar al-Assad's regime. Former Russian state security agent Valery Zakharov, who was an advisor to the Central African Republic's president, was also on the EU list, along with Stanislav Dychko, Maxim Shugalei, Dmitry Sytii and Alexander Maloletko who the EU characterized as a 'close collaborator of Yevgeny Prigozhin'.

'The Wagner Group has recruited, trained and sent private military operatives to conflict zones around the world to fuel violence, loot natural resources and intimidate civilians in violation of international law, including international human rights law,' the EU said in a statement. 'The individuals listed by the

EU are involved in serious human rights abuses, including torture and extrajudicial, summary or arbitrary executions and killings, or in destabilising activities in some of the countries they operate in, including Libya, Syria, Ukraine (Donbas) and the Central African Republic.'

Wagner was also accused of having previously offered services to local leaders in sub-Saharan Africa, including Mali and the Central African Republic. The move was commended by the US. The sanctions were part of a wider retaliatory package being considered by EU ministers to deter any Russian invasion of Ukraine. By the middle of December, Russia has stationed about seventy-thousand troops on the Ukrainian border and had begun planning for a possible invasion early the following year, American intelligence said.

Russia's social-media army responded light-heartedly to the sanctions. 'That's original! I would like to see how these sanctions will be implemented, and if the Wagnerians impose sanctions against the EU in response,' *RIA Novosti* news agency commentator Vladimir Kornilov jeered on Twitter, adding an emoji of a winking face with its tongue sticking out.

Another pro-Kremlin troll, Yelena Pshenichnaya, tweeted: 'That's the end, let's disperse, the Wagnerians thought,' adding a rolling on the floor laughing emoji.

'That's funny... Considering that it was the French who could not cope with the instability in Mali. And sanctions against the private military company are caused by impotence,' offered Twitter troll @kompolk.

Prigozhin's family appealed against the EU sanctions and his wife Violetta won her appeal against EU sanctions. However, her granddaughters Polina and eighteen-year-old Veronika were no longer able to enjoy show-jumping holidays in the Mediterranean in any case. The horses they competed on have not appeared in international show jumping events since the February Ukraine invasion as they fell under a blanket ban on Russian registration.

Prigozhin himself filed a libel suit in the High Court in London in December 2021. Like Latvia, Britain's legal system had a bias towards protecting rich claimants. A whole industry of London libel lawyers existed to exploit procedure in English common law to ringfence from criticism those who could afford it. Prigozhin's lawsuit showed to what extent British law was a helping hand in indirectly suppressing facts from coming out into the open.

Prigozhin's lawsuit was against Eliot Higgins, founder of Bellingcat, for saying in five tweets and three articles that Prigozhin was bankrolling the Wagner Group. Bellingcat, which was responsible for unmasking the two Salisbury poisoners in 2018, also published reports uncovering Wagner's operations in Africa and the Middle East, and revealed Prigozhin's links to the Kremlin.

The suit against Higgins claimed the British journalist had defamed

Prigozhin by linking him to the activities of Wagner and the murder of the three Russian journalists in the Central African Republic. Higgins has suggested that Prigozhin was 'centrally involved in the Russian state's unlawful, clandestine and deadly military and paramilitary operations in countries around the world' had resulted in Prigozhin being 'gravely damaged in his character and reputation and [suffering] great distress' for which he was seeking aggravated damages.

In the end, the defamation case was thrown out on the grounds that it was an abuse of process aimed to shut Higgins up or exhaust him financially. This itself was no surprise given that Prigozhin was an internationally sanctioned individual.

But what was clear that a sanctioned individual had been given access to British courts to file a vexatious case, racking up fees for his lawyers and forcing Bellingcat merely to defend itself at vast expense against the bias in Britain's legal system.

Even more extraordinary was that Prigozhin's lawyer had to apply for a special licence from the UK Treasury to sue someone on behalf of a sanctioned individual. It had been granted so he could use frozen funds to pay for the case. To pass anti-money-laundering regulations, he was asked for a copy of his passport and a utility bill. He provided a gas bill from his eight-one-year-old mother Violetta Prigozhina home in St Petersburg. In Britain this was all thought to be acceptable under the rule of law. It was a shocking moment that showed that in some cases the British legal system shared suppressive characteristics with countries that had no freedom of expression.

'It was very clear that this was an act of revenge by Prigozhin,' Higgins said of the libel action against him. 'He was given relief from sanctions to sue me, and I find that particularly aggravating. All the evidence since then has shown this was a clear abuse of the English legal system.' Higgins says he was left £70,000 out of pocket for costs he will not be able to recover. 'His lawyers knew what they were doing, and we have had to bear the financial cost.'

On 12 February 2022, two weeks before Russia's invasion of Ukraine, Prigozhin also appealed to the EU's Court of Justice demanding the removal of wording justifying his inclusion on a European sanctions lists for his alleged sponsorship of the Wagner private military company. Prigozhin filed a similar suit in a Moscow court where his application would likely be rubber stamped.

Still maintaining the fiction that he was merely a caterer rather than the chief executive of the Kremlin's robber company Wagner PMC, his catering company Concord said: 'Yevgeny Viktorovich [Prigozhin] has filed an application with the General Court of the European Union with a request to remove the text of the unfounded claim about him which the Council of the European Union cited as justification for the sanctions measures imposed on 13

December 2021 against the non-existent "Wagner Group".'

The company added Prigozhin 'has always denied and continues to deny the existence of any ties between him and whatever paramilitary or quasi-military structures. And, as has been repeatedly proven in Russian courts, any accusations of such ties are slander.'

The EU's Court of Justice rejected the appeal on Prigozhin's personal sanctions. When the *Financial Times* requested a response from one of Prigozhin's employees, Prigozhin himself replied on Telegram: 'If [the *FT*] thinks that my employee will respond to this endless chewing of shit in his mouth, in turn I would like to respond to the *Financial Times*... Spit that shit out, breathe some fresh air.'

Prigozhin's legal moves came on the heels of Marat Gabidullin's *In the Same River Twice,* newly published memoirs of when he commanded 95 *Wagnerovcis* in Syria, told an interviewer in an upmarket Moscow suburb that he suspected Prigozhin would react. The memoirs painted Wagner PMC in a relatively positive light compared to the negative headlines and news of brutality.

'I wrote this because I realised it's time for our country to face the truth— mercenaries exist,' he said.

A Russian airborne forces veteran and former bodyguard, Gabidullin had joined Wagner in 2015 and was soon sent to Syria, quickly rising to command one of Wagner's five units there. He was proud of his service.

'Mercenary groups are nothing to be ashamed of,' he said. 'We have specialized skills that a normal army lacks.'

The memoir followed three years of Wagner's Syrian campaign and described some of the mercenaries' big battles, including two operations to liberate the ancient city of Palmyra.

'The Russian army's achievements in Syria were largely because of the mercenaries' sacrifices. That fact is completely ignored by the military establishment and not known to the wider public,' he said, grumbling that 'mediocre' Russian army generals received promotions based on Wagner's successes. He was a harbinger of what Prigozhin himself would say not much later.

Gabidullin said he participated in the Battle of Khasham in 2018, where hundreds of Russian mercenaries were killed in US airstrikes, after the Kremlin disowned the presence of Wagner PMC on the Cold War disconflict line before the attack.

'We should never have been there; our leadership messed up. The Americans knew exactly where we were,' he said.

He said he had 'vaguely heard' of mercenary deployments in Ukraine, then already a fact, quickly adding that a Russian invasion would be a fatal mistake.

'I believe that war between Ukraine and Russia will be a complete disaster for Russia,' he said. 'Under no circumstances should this be allowed. Ukraine is our brother.'

He first wanted to publish the memoir in 2020 but quickly withdrew his book after pressure from 'certain people'. But in 2022, he claimed he would no longer hold back and found a brave publisher in the city of Yekaterinburg. He said the ban on private military companies in Russia pressured family members of deceased mercenaries to remain quiet about their loved ones, and hoped his book will help lift the veil of secrecy.

'This current situation does not suit many of my comrades,' he said. 'More importantly, it does not suit the dead mercenaries' parents and relatives, who cannot even talk openly about how their son or brother died. They can only whisper it.'

By now, Russian state television channels had begun screening numerous patriotic action movies, including *Touriste*, produced by Prigozhin-linked firms, depicting unnamed Russian volunteers fighting in eastern Ukraine, Central African Republic and Mozambique—places where Wagner fighters had been active.

Gabidullin dismissed the films as 'trash' that portrayed heroic Russians saving local people from violent rebels, while Wagner soldiers had been accused of raping, torturing and killing civilians. Gabidullin said he never saw his comrades engaged in such acts but added that such crimes were to be expected given the group's current shadowy status.

'The state puts mercenaries in a situation where they can act outside the law, and a soldier is forced to establish his own moral norms,' he said. 'But, of course, we should investigate that messed-up stuff.'

He realized that coming out of the shadows would have consequences. 'I suspect that there will be attempts by [Prigozhin] to discredit me. I am walking on a tightrope here,' he said. He later sought asylum in France after finding a publisher there for his memoirs.

Prigozhin kept up the swagger well into 2023. In July, UK-based human rights lawyer Jason McCue, head of the UK civil lawfare programme, sought to turn the tables on Prigozhin. He launched his own offensive to bring the billionaire to book with a case before the High Court in London, seeking compensation for tens of thousands of Wagner's victims. McCue hoped to seize the group's international assets as compensation for Ukrainians as part of a wider 'lawfare' campaign around the world against Prigozhin's war machine.

Prigozhin responded to the lawsuit by cheekily offered to finance the prosecution himself, saying: 'McCue doesn't have any money.'

McCue fired back an email: ' No, we won't take your money.' And he quoted those Ukrainian soldier on Snake Island who refused to surrender to Russian forces 'Go f*** yourself.'

Nine months earlier, Prigozhin had at last been caught. In September,

2022, a video emerged online of a squat, bald man delivering a pitch to prisoners standing in a courtyard in Russia. 'I represent a private military company,' he tells the inmates in black uniforms surrounding him in a circle. 'You must have heard of Wagner?' The speaker in the video was quickly identified as Yevgeny Prigozhin himself—the man who had spent the past four years pursuing every legal avenue to hide his mercenary operations.

Within days of the video appearing, Prigozhin made another stunning statement—he admitted to founding the mercenary group. 'I cleaned the old weapons myself, sorted out the bulletproof vests myself and found specialists who could help me with this. From that moment, on 1 May 2014, a group of patriots was born, which later came to be called the Wagner Battalion,' he said.

With his association with Wagner PMC's purveyors of Russian war-crimes and underhand deception on social media now beyond doubt, he said when asked why he kept denying it: 'In any issue there should be room for sport.'

It is not clear whether Prigozhin himself realised it, but the fact that his connection to Wagner PMC was now a matter of public record changed the winning formula of the past decade. Neither Wagner PMC, nor his link to the organisation, could no longer be denied by him. He may have thought that *Wagnerovci* successes in Ukraine during the second invasion in 2022 would prove even more compelling advertising for his skills than the stealth success in 2014. Or that, after the war, he could claim he had just lied about Wagner's existence in order to do his patriotic duty, and return to denying involvement. Either way, from an efficient backstage fixer, he was becoming an acknowledged character in the drama. The public exposure put him at a new risk.

PART 2

NEMESIS
THE INVASION OF UKRAINE 2022

I

LUKASHENKO

While *Wagnerovcis* and Wagner trolls continued to be active for Russia in eastern Ukraine in the Donbas, in July 2020, Prigozhin picked up a specialist job at one of the Kremlin's neighbours. President Alexander Lukashenko was facing his toughest re-election contest in his twenty-six years running the former Soviet state. Strictly speaking, he needn't have worried, as he was considered to be the last dictator in Europe. However, even dictators organise elections for optical reasons and they can be a vehicle for powerful rivals to stage protests and oust the leading man without (too much) bloodshed with a lost election.

Lukashenko had refused to shut down the country during the pandemic. Providing homespun remedies, he said Covid could be cured by drinking vodka, riding a tractor, or visiting a sauna. He jailed other presidential candidates, claiming that 'foreign puppet masters' were backing his opponents and said this week that protesters against him were being led by 'professional soldiers, bandits who are specially trained in mercenary companies all over the world and make lots of money doing provocations'.

Russian media said they had learned two-hundred fighters had been sent to Belarus and that thirty-two of them had checked into a hotel in Minsk with only small hand luggage before moving to a sanatorium outside the capital. The men gave themselves away to sanatorium staff with their three heavy suitcases for the entire group, which required several of them to carry, as well as their military fatigues and 'atypical behaviour for Russian tourists,' according to the state news agency Belta.

'They did not drink alcohol or visit entertainment facilities and kept to themselves in an attempt to keep a low profile,' the agency said. Another man was arrested in southern Belarus, it added. In the run up to the elections, thirty-three Russian mercenaries were arrested outside Minsk. Video footage of the detained men's possessions showed Sudanese currency and a Sudanese phone card. It was also reported that they had Russian passports, badges with 'Death is our business' on them, dollar bills and leaflets in Arabic.

The Russian tabloid *Komsomolskaya Pravda* said they were handcuffed but not charged.

Russia's embassy said it had been given no information about the arrested men while the head of the Belarusian Committee for State Security (still called

KGB like the good old Soviet days, the Russian Federation had restyled their KGB as FSB/SVR) Valeryy Vakulchyk confirmed that the detainees were from Wagner. The state secretary of the Belarusian Security Council, Andrey Rawkow, said that fourteen of them had fought in Ukraine's breakaway Donbas region, describing their presence in Belarus as a 'very unpleasant situation'. They did not seem to like Russia's presence very much.

Zakhar Prilepin, a Russian novelist and ultra-nationalist who previously led a mercenary battalion fighting for the Kremlin-run breakaway regions in eastern Ukraine, told website *Ura.ru* that 'two or three' of the arrested men had previously served in his unit, but were using Minsk as a base for travel to conflict zones due to Belarus's porous border regime with Russia and lack of coronavirus-related flight restrictions. (In May 2023, his Audi would be blown up with a car bomb in Nizhny Novgorod, deep inside Russia.)

Prilepin suggested that the Wagner detainees were merely using Belarus as a transit hub en route to other destinations, presumably Sudan.

'No proof has been presented that these jolly fellows were planning to stir up trouble here. It is not ruled out at all that they were travelling for a job in Africa,' political scientist Alexander Klaskowski suggested.

But it seemed clear their presence was part of a plot cooked up between Lukashenko and Putin to scare Belarusians and put on a show for the West.

The results of the elections were contested and Lukashenko was not recognized as the legitimate president of Belarus by the UK, US or the EU.

Once the election was over Belarus extradited the suspected Wagner members to Russia. The secretary of the National Security and Defence Council of Ukraine Oleksiy Danilov said this was an 'unfriendly step with regard to Ukraine'. Kyiv had already made an extradition request of its own given their fighting on Ukraine soil.

'There is proof that twenty-eight mercenaries of the Wagner PMC, who were detained in Belarus, were involved in terrorist activities,' the Ukrainian foreign ministry said, however. 'It was described in detail in the extradition request the Ukrainian side had sent to Minsk in order for the criminals to face fair punishment.' The Prosecutor-General's Office of Ukraine stated that it would further investigate and try the Wagner group *in absentia*.

While the Ukraine did not recognize the results of the Belarus election either, Putin immediately congratulated Lukashenko on his victory.

Controversial Ukrainian journalist Yuriy Butusov said that the mercenaries had been lured out of Russia by the Ukrainian special services. Nine of them were, in fact, Ukrainian citizens. Two were involved in the downing of Malaysian flight MH17 over Donbas in July 2014. Others were involved in military actions in eastern Ukraine, including the downing of the Il-76 transport and the death of seventy Ukrainian soldiers. He said they were on their way to

Venezuela where they had been offered lucrative contracts to guard facilities belonging to Rosneft, the Russian oil company.

Ukraine's sly plot had begun with online advertisements on Russian employment websites had called for men with experience in 'handling weapons' and offered a monthly salary of 225,000 rubles (£2,290), far above the average wage in Russia. It aimed to attract mercenaries that Ukraine accused of committing crimes in the country's Donbas region. A former mid-ranking officer with Russia's GRU military intelligence service who had been compromised was recruited by the Ukraine to be used as an 'inside man' during the operation.

Although many of the applicants were of no interest to Ukraine, dozens of those seeking work were Wagner veterans who had fought in Donbas. As part of their job applications, the mercenaries supplied photos of medals they had been awarded by the Kremlin, as well as a wealth of information about crimes they had committed in eastern Ukraine.

Ukrainian intelligence also tricked one candidate into recruiting fellow fighters. Thirty-three mercenaries were approved and told to assemble in Minsk in July. From there, they were told they would be flown to Venezuela, via Istanbul. The passenger plane they were on would have been over Ukraine for about thirty minutes when a bomb hoax would have diverted it to Boryspil airport, Kyiv. There the mercenaries would have been arrested.

However, the operation was delayed because of a proposed ceasefire in Donbas. So the mercenaries were checked into the health resort near Minsk to wait for a new flight.

Details were then leaked to Belarus by pro-Russian factions within the administration, Butusov said. It was then scuppered by Belarus arrested the men and returned them to Russia. The head of the Ukrainian Defence Ministry's main intelligence directorate, Kyrylo Budanov dismissed this as a fairy tale.

However, the story was confirmed by Petro Poroshenko, who had been president of Ukraine until May 2019, and said that he had authorized the operation before being voted out of office. Then in a TV interview in June 2021, President Volodymyr Zelensky admitted that there had been such an operation, but he thwarted it in a telephone conversation with Lukashenko in the hope of a negotiated settlement in the Donbas, which had been one of his campaign promises when he was elected in 2019. Opposition activists accused him of high treason.

However, Wagner PMC's brief excursion and the help he had given to Lukashenko would stand Prigozhin in good stead in 2023 when he needed his own Minsk Accord with the Russian President, Vladimir Putin after having attacked Moscow.

With Russia massing over 100,000 troops and military hardware on

Ukraine's borders by mid-January 2022, British military intelligence expert Philip Ingram warned that Vladimir Putin might be planning a 'false flag' operation to give it an excuse to invade. He explained that elite members from Russia's paramilitary Wagner Group, Spetsnaz operatives and GRU special forces units, who had been sent in as 'advance forces' into warzones, could be ordered to open fire on the Russian army and ethnic Russians in eastern Ukraine as a pretext to send troops forward.

'It would not surprise me if we saw terrorist-style attacks inside Ukraine, false flag, and even terrorist-style attacks inside Russia itself, false flag, carried out by Wagner or GRU to give him an excuse to go across the border,' he said.

2

BOTCHED INVASION

On 24 February 2022, Russia began its invasion of the Ukraine. President Putin expected his 'special military operation' to be over in a few days, but the Russian army faced unexpectedly stiff resistance. Putin ordered Russia's nuclear deterrent forces on high alert, greatly escalating tensions even as President Zelensky of Ukraine agreed to peace talks on the Belarus border. The US had warned him of the imminent attack, but Zelensky initially thought it was no more than Russian sabre-rattling.

Fierce fighting continued on the fifth day of the invasion as defence forces searched for infiltrators who were believed to have entered Kyiv to assassinate Zelensky and prepare the way for a Russian ground force. Special units included mercenaries from the Wagner Group who had been instructed to use the cover of peace negotiations to 'decapitate' the Ukrainian government.

The assassination team the Kremlin had sent in was made up of some four-hundred hardened mercenaries, already linked to a string of robberies, murders, rapes and alleged war crimes. They were thought to have a hit list of another twenty-three key figures including Zelensky, his family, the prime minister Denys Shmyhal, the entire cabinet and mayor of Kyiv Vitali Klitschko and his brother Wladimir—both heavy-weight boxing champions who had taken up arms on the front lines of the capital and were important domestic public figures.

Like the Russian army, however, the assassins made little progress on their kill list. Ukraine MP Dymtro Gurin laughed off the danger, calling being on Putin's kill list 'an honour'.

'Of course, we think about our safety. Because I know our intelligence proved that I'm on Putin's shoot list, and of course, everybody understands that it's pretty dangerous. So for example we don't disclose all locations, but to be on these lists is kind of honourable.... I mean of course, we see risks but we don't fear them, we are just practical about them.'

Between two- and four thousand *Wagnerovcis* had been on the ground in the Ukraine since January. Some were sent to the Russian-puppet regions Donetsk and Luhansk in the east of the country, while four hundred were sent to infiltrate Kyiv, crossing the nearby border from Belarus. They had been flown in from Africa five weeks earlier before first regrouping at a base some sixty miles from Moscow for their departure to Belarus.

The Ukrainian government imposed a thirty-six-hour hard curfew so that special forces could sweep the empty streets in search of assassins and saboteurs. Citizens were warned that they risked being 'liquidated' if they were spotted outside during the curfew hours as they would be assumed to be the enemy.

The Wagner Group mercenaries were in contact with the Kremlin and were awaiting a signal before unleashing bloodshed on the streets. A Moscow Telegram channel with links to the security establishment reported that they had been issued with a special 'deck of cards'—like those issued by the US during the invasion of Iraq—detailing targets and had been promised large bonuses.

Western military analysts reported spotting three-hundred Wagner mercenaries in the Donbas breakaway region a few weeks earlier. They were using Russian military aircraft to move in and out of conflict zones. But they didn't wear uniforms and were not officially employed by the state, so Russia could deny all knowledge of them. Along with the Alpha Group, set up by a former KGB boss, and GRU's *Spetsnaz* uniformed special forces, Wagner were spearheading the ground forces.

GCHQ Director Jeremy Fleming said: 'We understand that the group is now prepared to send large numbers of personnel into Ukraine to fight alongside Russians. They are looking at relocating forces from other conflicts and recruiting new fighters to bolster numbers. These soldiers are likely to be used as cannon fodder to try to limit Russian military losses.'

Some sources have said Prigozhin had even been told to prepare for the invasion in December, long before the Russian military was told of Putin's plans. Their numbers included former and active-duty Russian, Ukrainian, Belarusian and Serbian soldiers, and their presence was confirmed in news reports and hinted at in cryptic social media posts by accounts associated with the mercenary group.

The Wagner fighters were to engage in scouting operations deep inside Ukrainian territory as part of an effort to minimize the regular Russian military death toll, as well as false flag operations to boost morale among Russians and sabotage operations to dampen the spirits of Ukrainians.

'The combination of Prigozhin's acumen in launching disinformation operations and his control over PMC Wagner creates a unique asymmetric Molotov cocktail,' US-based think tank Soufan noted. Ukraine was where Prigozhin had achieved his first success with Wagner fighters and trolls in Russia's bloodless occupation of parts of the country, and his teams now had honed their specialist skills in over 8 years of experience in the world's civil-war zones.

They were also being positioned for the dirty war that was anticipated to commence after the Kremlin victory, as pockets of Ukrainian government guerrillas would fight Moscow consolidating its power and installing a puppet regime. Capturing, interrogating and torturing rebels or deserters to extract information was Prigozhin's team's speciality. On 16 January more than thirty civilians were killed at the hands of alleged Wagner mercenaries and forces of the Central African Republic in an operation targeting a rebel group.

General Sir Richard Barrons, a former commander of Joint Forces Command, said: 'They are very effective because they are hard to pin down. They can appear from the shadows, do very violent things and then disappear again, without it being obvious who was responsible. They are not directly linked to the Russian government and therefore they are plausibly deniable.'

Russia expert Professor Galeotti said Wagner recruits included many discharged from the military on disciplinary grounds, who won't hesitate to burn down villages, terrorize civilians or kill women and children as they recently did in Mozambique. They were supplied by the Kremlin with cutting-edge military equipment, including tracking devices.

'About two months ago, around five-hundred Wagner operatives left their various postings around Africa 'on leave',' he said, 'and headed for Ukraine to undertake 'false-flag' operations, such as committing atrocities while wearing stolen Ukrainian uniforms, then blaming them on Ukrainian forces.'

With the Wagner Group now a key player in the first major war in Europe since World War II, information about who made up their troops became ever clearer as scrutiny intensified. Many officers had been in the *Spetsnaz*, the special forces, others in military intelligence, the GRU, the foreign intelligence service, the SVR, or the FSO, which guards the Kremlin and Vladimir Putin. Others were thugs who had served long prison sentences.

Another source said, 'There are violent offenders who have done time inside among the Wagner Group, who are extremely well-trained. It is run by intelligence operatives, special forces and some extremely blood-soaked people who have done very bad things.'

By 3 March, Zelensky had survived three assassination attempts and Wagner mercenaries in Kyiv had sustained losses during these failed operations. Unlike their operations elsewhere, they were not able to kill with impunity as the Ukrainians had anticipated their moves. A source close to the group said it was 'eerie' how well-briefed Zelensky's security team appeared to be. A cadre of Chechen assassins had also been 'eliminated' before they got to Zelensky. Apparently, the Wagner Group had not known they were there.

Given that many Ukrainians native tongue is Russian, Ukrainian special forces were able to spy on Russia with relative ease. Oleksiy Danilov, the secretary of Ukraine's National Security and Defence Council, told Ukrainian TV channels that Russian spies had tipped the Ukrainians off. He said: 'I can say that we have received information from the FSB, who do not want to take part in this bloody war.'

Veteran BBC foreign correspondent Paul Wood said: 'A gang of several hundred super assassins being secretly airlifted into Ukraine does sound like something dreamt up by a propagandist in the Kremlin. It could suit Russia's war aims to scare the Ukrainian public with stories like these: the Kremlin certainly has a long history of *dezinformatsiya* and *provokatsiya*, lies told to confuse and demoralize—or 'provoke'—the enemy.' But he had known the source for a long time and his stories had always checked out.

'This source went on to say that it was true as well that Zelensky had survived, thanks to a leak from within Russia's main security service, the FSB,' Wood said. 'The Ukrainians had been told not only that an operation to kill Zelensky was underway, but also the exact locations of the assassins, leading to their capture. The source said that Putin's anger over these extraordinary leaks lay behind the arrests, reported last week, of the head of the FSB's foreign intelligence branch and his deputy.'

Having been in Kyiv for six weeks, the *Wagnerovcis* had been told to await the arrival of the *Spetsnaz*. They believed the storming of Kyiv would provide a distraction and give them an opportunity to complete their mission. However, with the Russian convoy of tanks stalled outside the city, the pace of the attack has been slower than expected. Nevertheless, the mercenaries were under intense pressure from Prigozhin to get on with the assassination list.

Despite the loss of some of the group in botched operations, the mercenaries in Kyiv still believed that numbers were still on their side. 'It only takes one of them to get lucky and everyone goes home with a bonus,' a source close to the mercenaries said. They were already drawing up plans for another attempt that weekend.

It was a first sign of Kremlin desperation at the misfiring of their plan to replicate the Crimean strategy of a (relatively) bloodless occupation. The *Spetsnaz* were better equipped and better home-trained for assassination than the private Wagner Group, but assassinations carried out by mercenaries would be more difficult to trace back to the Kremlin. Particularly, the assassination of Zelensky required attention.

'They would be going in there with a very high-profile mission, something that the Russians would want to be deniable—a decapitation of a head of state is a huge mission. In terms of the impact on Russian sovereign policy, this would be perhaps their biggest mission so far. It would have a major impact on the war,' a diplomat said. 'It would not be unreasonable that Wagner were used on some form of operation to try and take out the president and do a decapitation job on the Ukrainian government as they are deniable. They have a lot more combat experience than the regular Russian *Spetsnaz* and they are lunatic enough to do it.'

Killing Zelensky was not far off from a *kamikaze* mission and it was a prize that suited the money-motivated *Wagnerovcis* more than Russia's professional spies. 'The risks of trying to get close to the president would be very high so that they would take significant casualties even if they could pin him down. One mission they could do, is if they could infiltrate and take in a laser guidance system and they could locate the president and put laser target marker on him then Russian air force could bomb very quickly', the diplomat said.

Roving Russian death squads opened fire on a Sky News crew on their way to Bucha, eighteen miles from Kyiv, where fierce fighting was taking place. Three volunteers were killed on the road to Bucha to take dog food to the canine refuge there. Their car was deliberately targeted at close range by Russian forces using heavy weaponry to instil fear.

Wagner troops were also seen in the thick of it all along the frontline, especially in the entrenched positions around the old Donbas mining town of Bakhmut, seen as a crucial strategic target by Moscow. They were also being lined up for a renewed assault on Kyiv. Meanwhile, Russian state TV was pumping out fake news to the Russian population about Zelensky, saying he was a cocaine addict of the puppet of MI6.

Vladimir Putin meanwhile claimed that the Kremlin's 'special military operation' was aimed at the 'denazification' of Ukraine. This was an oblique reference to the fact that during World War II tens of millions of Soviet citizens had died as they fought Nazi Germany. Ironically, up to half of this number had been Ukrainians.

In fact, however, the invasion was part of the same neo-colonial drive that the Kremlin had unleashed from 2014 in Africa and the Middle East. Apart from money, extremist Russian national pride was a key motivator for the military branch of Wagner PMC. One post on the messaging app Telegram, dated 15 March 2022, shows the flag of the Russian Imperial Movement (RIM), a white-supremacist paramilitary organization which the US lists as terrorist, allegedly flown by Moscow-backed separatists in Donetsk. The post was shared by a pro-Putin channel. RIM has long called for the capture of 'Novorossiya', the Tsarist term for southern and eastern Ukraine. Its leader, Denis Gariyev, posted a message on his Telegram channel saying: 'Without a doubt, we are in favour of the liquidation of the separatist entity Ukraine.'

Much of the extremist content, posted on Telegram and the Russian social media platform *VKontakte* (VK), relates to a far-right unit within the Wagner Group called Rusich with others linked to pro-Kremlin online communities, some bearing the name and logo of Wagner Group.

Psychopaths and serial killers on the loose might be another way of describing some of them. One account on VK was dedicated to the Rusich 'sabotage and assault reconnaissance group' which appeared to be operating in Ukraine, according to a post on 17 March 2022. The Rusich logo featured a Slavic Swastika known as a *kolovrat*. Rusich, whose name is a reference to a mythical fortress in ancient Russia, was founded in St Petersburg in 2014 by thirty-year-old former paratrooper Aleksei Milchakov and thirty-three-year-old Yan Petrovsky. They met at a RIM meeting. It was thought that there were a few hundred of them.

Milchakov openly bragged about photographing the bodies of mutilated and burnt Ukrainian bodies from the pro-Kyiv paramilitary Aidar Battalion in 2014. The following year, he posted pictures that showed him removing the ears of Ukrainian soldiers in Donbas and carving the *kolovrat* into their fore-heads.

He admitted to being a neo-Nazi and said he 'got high from the smell of burning human flesh'. His *VKontakte* page once featured a photograph of him cutting the head off a puppy when he was a teenager and allegedly eating it. In a video published on a Russian nationalist YouTube channel. 'I'm not going to go deep and say, I'm a nationalist, a patriot, an imperialist, and so forth. I'll say it outright: I'm a Nazi.'

He added: 'You have to understand that when you kill a person, you feel the excitement of the hunt. If you've never been hunting, you should try it. It's interesting.' Rusich mercenaries have been photographed doing Nazi salutes around a campfire.

Photographs and videos posted to social media in 2020-2021 indicated that Rusich fighters had been in Syria where they were accused of crimes including the dismemberment of a prisoner. They fought alongside pro-Russian sepa-ratists in 2014 and 2015 in Donbas where they became notorious for its 'par-ticular brutality' and for 'never taking prisoners', according to the BND, Germany's foreign intelligence service. They were filmed mutilating and setting fire to corpses, and Ukrainian human rights groups accused them of torturing prisoners of war.

The Rusich fought mostly in the Luhansk region but, in one photograph, Denis Pushilin, the president of the Russian-run Donetsk People's Republic, was shown presenting an award to a fighter wearing the unit's *valknut* emblem. The soldier was also wearing a Totenkopf, the skull-and-crossbones emblem of the Nazi SS. Wagner also adopted the skull as its emblem.

Rusich recently published a cartoon of a Russian soldier returning home with blood-covered looted gifts for his wife and son Its caption read: 'If you are a real man and a Russian, join our ranks. You will spill litres of blood from vile Russophobes, and become rich and cool.'

The group has been investigated for war crimes by the International

Criminal Court in the Hague, and Michalkov and Petrovsky have both been charged with terrorism in Ukraine. Petrovsky denied war crimes in a 2017 interview with the independent Russian outlet *Meduza.io*.

Another VK posting listed Rusich as part of a coalition of separatist groups and militias including the extreme far-right group, Russian National Unity. An image shared on VK by a Rusich-affiliated account shows fighters, seemingly in Ukraine, holding a valknut flag, a symbol also commonly appropriated by white supremacists.

It was also being reported that mercenary units recruited to Wagner were being given names like 'The Hawks', possibly to shield the group's reputation from further damage after repeated accusations of human rights abuses in its operations in Syria and Libya.

The Tech Against Terrorism analysis found a prominent Wagner Group-affiliated Telegram channel sharing an image in May 2021 of the *kolovrat* allegedly daubed on a cliff in Palmyra. It also found Wagner Telegram channels continued sharing footage and memes as recently as 4 March relating to the torture and beheading of Mohammad Taha al-Ismail Abdallah by Wagner mercenaries in 2017.

Fighters from the Wagner group also used Telegram to post death threats to twenty-seven-year-old Aiden Aslin, a former care worker from Newark, Nottinghamshire, who had survived the fighting in Mariupol. In a video update on social media, Aslin said he had documented war crimes.

'Russian forces have continued to target the civilian areas where we're not located,' he said. 'I know this first hand because I've watched it, I've watched multiple Grad vehicles launch their missiles into the civilian areas behind us.'

Later Aslin was captured by Russian forces. A video was released of his interrogation. He was shown with a swollen eyelid and a gash on his forehead. He was later seen with forty-eight-year-old Shaun Pinner, another British expatriate who had settled in the Ukraine with his Ukrainian wife.

A pro-Russian Telegram channel called Rybar with almost 400,000 subscribers claimed that a hundred British mercenaries were fighting in Ukraine. It said it had a list of their names, dates of birth and ID numbers. Prigozhin's troll factory was working overtime alongside the *Wagnerovcis*.

In areas under Russian control, Wagner mercenaries formed up into 'special commandos' of four soldiers. The first man in each group was a sniper. They were equipped with a variety of weapons for the task. Some were given a Hungarian Gepard M1, powerful enough to stop a truck with its large, .50 calibre bullet. Others had the German SIG Sauer bolt-action sniper rifle, or the Austrian Steyr 'sharpshooter', with its distinctive folding stock. The second man in the commando was designated as a spotter for the sniper. Two others were to guard them while they worked. That work would be, their orders said, to 'eliminate high-priority targets'. In other words, they were assassins. In this, they would be honouring the motto of the Wagner Group's soldiers: 'Death is our business—and business is good.' Though in polite company, their motto was the more vapid: 'Blood, honour, Motherland, courage.'

A source with connections at the highest levels of the '*mafiya*' confirmed that there were 'many psychos' in the Wagner Group, but also some of the most trusted and experienced men the Kremlin can call on. As for the assassins sent to Ukraine, 'these are professionals who know what they are doing. You can see how serious they are; with these Gepard M1 rifles, you can easily shoot a target a mile away. It will cripple any—and I mean any—vehicle. So they are making sure they can stop anyone and anything, and kill anyone and anything. They make sure they get their target. They are not playing around. They don't make mistakes.'

While the Wagner Group were being issued these high-powered weapons, demoralized teenage Russian conscripts were given 1940s-vintage rifles. A video shared on pro-Ukrainian Telegram channels shows a group of ten soldiers travelling in the back of a lorry near Sumy, just twenty miles inside Ukraine from the Russian border where intense fighting had been going on. In the video, the young men, who describe themselves as 'ordinary students', complain of heavy losses.

'Know the truth! The Russian Ministry of Defence has no idea about us, or what we're doing here. We've been thrown into the shit,' said one. Another said: 'Our rifles are from the 1940s! They don't f***ing fire! They're sending f***ing ordinary students into war.'

One boy, wearing a helmet that appeared too big for his head, looks at the camera and points to himself saying: 'I'm eighteen years old.'

Given that most of the *Wagnerovcis* in Kyiv were more interested in getting rich than killing Ukrainian government leaders or enlarging Russia's borders. Being sent to Ukraine meant they could get a hundred times what they were making, but that was just one benefit. There were important additional benefits, such as opportunities to extort Ukrainian oligarchs.

A black Cadillac Escalade—a luxury SUV—belonging to one of Ukraine's richest men was brought to a halt with a 0.50 calibre bullet fired into the engine block. The oligarch didn't just have bodyguards for protection, he had his own militia. Two black pick-ups packed with heavily armed men followed the Escalade, but they could do nothing but look on. In fact, the oligarch wasn't in the vehicle, just one of his employees. But the message to him was clear: 'You think you're untouchable. We can get you any time.'

A number of the oligarchs were already paying up. They supported the Ukrainian government, but they were more afraid of Wagner than of what President Zelensky would do if he found out. A source close to the mafia said,

'Maybe squeezing the oligarchs helps *Vova*—as some Russians nickname Putin—Wagner mercenaries have no loyalty to a country or an ideology, or even to Putin. They just want to make money.'

'Like the men who join the French Foreign Legion, Wagner's soldiers of fortune believe '*La Légion est notre mère*'. They will help the man next to them, but little more than that.'

3

BEATING THE RUSSIAN ARMY

A former colonel in the FSB explained that if Putin wants something done members of the royal court at the Kremlin—oligarchs, generals, lawyers, secret policemen—fight each other to do it, because when Putin smiles, you get rich. And over the last twenty years, Putin's smile fell upon Prigozhin, who put together businesses, and in close cooperation, the Wagner Group—though Prigozhin still vehemently denied it. Putin like Russian Tsars before him had a fear of being poisoned. This is particularly acute in the says of Polonium-210 and Novichok. The fact that 'Putin's chef' was allowed to provide his food shows how much Putin trusted him, perhaps more than anyone else in his inner circle.

It seemed that Prigozhin was one of the few people who got to see Putin and one of the very few Putin consulted over the invasion of Ukraine when career soldiers and intelligence officers were excluded. Short of threatening the use of nuclear weapons, military consultant General Sir Richard Barrons believed that the Wagner Group were seen by the Kremlin as a key to victory.

'We are going to see a resort to astonishing violence directed against the civil population,' he said, 'the widespread, indiscriminate application of fire-power and the unleashing of the sort of gratuitous violence the Wagner Group is capable of inflicting.' This would 'create an environment of terror designed to make Ukrainians sue for peace'.

These tactics were used during the Second Chechen war 1999-2009. Then, *contractniki*—'contract soldiers'—were told they could do what they wanted with any place they captured. They would kill indiscriminately and steal anything of value they found. For the Wagner Group the pickings would be good. Ukraine was far richer than Chechnya.

Britain's Ministry of Defence also thought that the Wagner Group were being deployed because of the heavy losses regular Russian forces were suffering. By 28 March 2022, it was thought that more than ten thousand Russians had been killed. That's when Wagner moved in.

In an intelligence briefing the British MoD said: 'Russian Private Military Company the Wagner Group has deployed to eastern Ukraine. They are expected to deploy more than a thousand mercenaries, including senior leaders of the organization, to undertake combat operations.'

The defence chiefs added: 'Due to heavy losses and a largely stalled invasion, Russia has highly likely been forced to reprioritize Wagner personnel for Ukraine at the expense of operations in Africa and Syria.'

Edward Arnold, a research fellow at the Royal United Services Institute, said: 'Wagner mercenaries have joined the war in larger numbers, alongside Syrian forces and reportedly other armed groupings from African states such as the Central African Republic. Russia is in dire need of well-led troops with combat experience, especially battle-hardened junior non-commissioned officers.'

On 4 April, a photograph of a Wagner mercenary in military fatigues and carrying an AK-15 assault rifle used by Russian special forces outside the Park Inn in Donetsk appeared on the pro-Kremlin *Wargonzo* Telegram channel confirming, for the first time, that they were there. He wore the grinning skull of the Wagner insignia on his uniform. The photograph was posted by Semyon Pegov, a pro-Kremlin war correspondent, who has been embedded with Russian forces in Ukraine.

'The GRU use Wagner as their deniable dirty operations troops,' said former British intelligence officer Philip Ingram. 'The fact that they are using AK-15s, the *Spetsnaz*'s new assault rifle, is a clear indication that they are being contracted and commanded by Russian special forces.'

Other mercenaries, thought to be neo-Nazi Rusich fighters with the Wagner Group, were photographed near the border between Russia and Ukraine on 6 April 2022. They appeared, crossing into the Kharkiv region near the village of Pletenivka in Z-marked vehicles. Pletenivka was roughly forty miles from Kharkiv, the country's second city, where Ukrainian defence officials were bracing themselves for a renewed assault by Russian forces. Rusich reported casualties as soon as it entered Ukraine this week. Milchakov was receiving treatment and the militia was under the command of Petrovsky, the group said on the messaging app Telegram on the 6th.

Photographs showed Russian soldiers advancing towards Kharkiv, probably from the Russian city of Belgorod. A sign for Vovchansk, the name of a town near Kharkiv, was defaced and changed to Volchansk, the imperial Russian name.

At the beginning of April 2022, the Russians withdrew from Bucha leaving the streets littered with bodies. Some 458 were recovered from the town, including nine children under eighteen.

The UN High Commissioner for Human Rights documented the unlawful killings, including summary executions, of at least seventy-three civilians in Bucha. Photos showed corpses of civilians, lined up with their hands bound behind their backs, shot at point-blank range, which ostensibly gave proof that summary executions had taken place. An inquiry by Radio Free Europe reported the use of a basement beneath a campground as a torture chamber Many bodies were found mutilated and burnt, and girls as young as fourteen reported being raped. Bodies were found in mass graves. More bodies of civilians were found in other towns around Kyiv.

'Not many bodies have been found in Hostomel, but shot bodies, killed residents, were found further in the villages of our community,' said Taras Dumenko, head of the local military administration. 'Several residents were also found in Bucha. It is necessary to understand that the occupiers removed people. People from [the village of] Hlibivka came to Hostomel and then the contact with them was lost. But we need to understand that the occupiers also covered the traces of their crimes.'

They were checking basements for further bodies, but the remains of the local mayor Yuriy Prylypko. along with volunteers Ruslan Karpenko and Ivan Zoria, had been found.

Radio messages which prove Russian forces deliberately murdered Ukrainian civilians in Bucha were intercepted by Germany's BND, according to details leaked to *Der Spiegel* magazine. They showed that the Wagner Group was in the city and had played a central role in the killings.

This was confirmed by Dmitry Peskov, Vladimir Putin's spokesman, in a backhanded sort of way. He told Sky News: 'Those dead bodies were not victims of Russian military personnel.' Of course, *Wagnerovcis* were not considered Russian military personnel.

In a recording obtained by German intelligence, a Russian can be heard ordering: 'First question the soldiers, then kill them'.

Separately Ukrainian intelligence released what it said was an intercept of Russian communications in which soldiers are ordered to kill civilians. Several of them can be directly matched to locations and objects shown in photos that document the aftermath of the killings, the magazine reported.

In one recording a Russian soldier can be heard reporting there are civilians in the area and is ordered: 'Kill them all.'

'What are you waiting for, you arse-f***kers?' the officer asked.

'This is a whole village of civilians,' the soldier replied.

'Shoot the civilian cars,' the officer said.

In another recording, a Russian soldier said he had just shot a cyclist. The description matches pictures and video from the town, and a video recorded during the fighting shows two armoured vehicles opening fire on a cyclist. A second video shot after Russian forces withdrew shows the dead body of a cyclist wearing the same clothes.

'Radio intercepts by German intelligence show that the massacre of civilians in Bucha was not accidental or actions of rogue soldiers. Russian occupiers talk about atrocities in their daily routine,' the Ukrainian ministry of defence tweeted. 'Almost 90% of the murdered civilians in Bucha were found to have bullet wounds, not shrapnel ones... They are not random collateral casualties of war. They were killed deliberately, on purpose.'

It was said that the BND had more disturbing recordings of intercepted radio messages which appeared to indicate further Russian atrocities in other locations that had yet to emerge. Ukrainian officials have warned the horrors in the town of Borodyanka will be 'worse than Bucha'. Ukraine's foreign minister Dmytro Kuleba said Bucha was 'the tip of the iceberg'.

Further horror stories yesterday emerged from there and nearby Irpin, also devastated by Putin's invasion. Locals said Russians shot civilians without provocation. Eighty-four-year-old retired engineer Hryhoriy Zamohylnyi, who was born and raised in Bucha, said: 'I saw the war with the Germans and now this war with the Russians. What you see here is animal cruelty.'

As relief teams and volunteers ventured further into territory around Kyiv, retaken from Russian troops, evidence of more atrocities committed against Ukrainian civilians by the occupying force continued to emerge. Residents returned home to find their homes looted or destroyed, neighbours missing, bodies decomposing in basements, and hastily dug graves in gardens.

More than four hundred people are missing from Hostomel, eight miles north of Bucha. Officials said they vanished after Russian forces captured it early on in the war and held it for thirty-five days.

Taras Dumenko, head of the local military administration, said: 'We are checking the basements of Hostomel together with the State Emergency Service and patrol police officers. We have about 1,200 residents with whom the contact has been established.'

He said Russian troops killed local mayor Yuriy Prylypko along with volunteers Ruslan Karpenko and Ivan Zoria, whose remains had been found.

'Not many bodies have been found in Hostomel, but shot bodies, killed residents, were found further in the villages of our community,' said Dumenko. 'Several residents were also found in Bucha. It is necessary to understand that the occupiers removed people. People from [the village of] Hlibivka came to Hostomel and then the contact with them was lost. But we need to understand that the occupiers also covered the traces of their crimes.'

The Kyiv regime claims Bucha, Irpin, Hostomel and the region around the capital have been retaken but mass killings of civilians by Russian soldiers have been recorded in liberated towns and villages.

Amnesty International published a report detailing apparent war crimes in the Kyiv region, based on interviews with twenty people who witnessed or had direct knowledge of horrifying violence. A woman in a village east of the capital told Amnesty's investigators that on 9 March two Russian soldiers entered her house, killed her husband in front of her and repeatedly raped her at gunpoint while her young son hid nearby. She later managed to escape to Ukrainian-controlled territory.

In the village of Vorzel, Nataliya and Valeryi Tkachova left their basement on 3 March to check whether Russian tanks were coming, telling their eighteen-year-old daughter Kateryna to stay hidden. After hearing gunshots, Kateryna left the cellar to find her parents lying dead in the street, her father was shot six times in the back, and her mother once in the chest. She was assisted in leaving Vorzel on 10 March.

Up to a thousand people were massacred in the area and the Wagner Group were accused of war crimes in Bucha.

It was also reported that in Donbas, one member of the Wagner Group was suspected of transferring local citizens to a police station where they were being tortured and killed. The fighters then hung the mutilated corpses of their tortured prisoners in public view as a warning, it was reported.

Not long after Prigozhin was photographed in military fatigues alongside Vitaly Milonov, an ultra-conservative member of the Russian Duma and Kremlin loyalist who shared images of himself in eastern Ukraine.

Sources from inside the group reportedly told Meduza that Prigozhin had been ordered to the front line by the Kremlin and that he was under instruction to capture a prominent Ukrainian politician or commander.

The Institute for War Studies (ISW), an American think tank, said his appearance in Ukraine was unlikely to mean he was overseeing military manoeuvres.

'Prigozhin, who has no military experience and is the financier and organizer of Wagner Group rather than its military commander, is likely in Donbas to co-ordinate recruitment and financing of Wagner Group operations rather than to command combat operations,' the institute said.

Giving evidence to the House of Commons Foreign Affairs Committee, Christo Grozev, executive director of the Bellingcat, said that 8000 Wagner mercenaries had been deployed in the Ukraine and that 3000 were thought to have been killed on the battlefield. He said sources within the group had told them that the numbers fighting alongside Russian forces had been much higher than had been expected.

They included two hundred who had been sent to Kyiv before the conflict in a failed attempt to scout out and assassinate political figures, while a large number had been deployed with convoys which advanced on the capital from Belarus. He said they had also been present in Bucha, where some of the worst evidence of alleged war crimes had been discovered. Grozev said they had been told by one former group member that some chose to fight because they enjoyed killing.

'He said that about ten to fifteen per cent are sociopaths, people who go there just because they want to kill. They are bloodthirsty, they are not just adrenalin junkies,' he told the committee.

Dr Sean McFate, a senior fellow at the Atlantic Council thinktank and professor at the US National Defence University, said the group's brutality in conflicts such as the Syrian civil war was 'part of their selling point' as far as Russian president Vladimir Putin was concerned. He thought that it meant Prigozhin got things done where others prevaricated, forgetting that Prigozhin's successes were of a different order from conquering a whole country the size of France.

'If you look at Bucha and others, there is the same pattern you saw in Syria, where they would interrogate, torture and behead people,' he said.

Dr McFate said that western countries had not taken the threat of the group very seriously, and had not tracked the movements of its members.

'This has emboldened Russia to use this as a stratagem for national expansion, national interests,' he said. 'We have not done a good enough job in tracking them. We see them as cheap Hollywood villains, but in fact they are not.'

The point was made by a pro-Russian blogger who posted drone footage from the town of Popasna in the Luhansk Oblast. It showed Russian mercenaries advanced in single file, picking their way over rubble as they approached a cluster of houses containing Ukrainian defenders.

One fighter, purportedly from the Wagner Group, broke away from the formation and approached the house from the left. Another, from the right. A volley of grenades was thrown into a house with a green door. Moments later around a dozen Ukrainian troops were seen lying on their bellies, prisoners of war.

After four days of fighting the Wagners took Popasna. In another video, Wagner fighters with their faces blurred were pictures standing on the Ukrainian flag outside the bombed-out civic offices. A pro-Russian Donbas news outlet said the clip showed that 'a stealth infantry from the assault detachments of the Wagner Group' had 'defeated opponents' in the town. The pro-Putin Reverse Side of the Medal Telegram channel added a Wagner Group logo to the bombed building online.

In August, a video and photos of the head and hands of a Ukrainian prisoner of war stuck on poles appeared. The video showed the mutilated body of the captured soldier and then his head stuck on a wooden pole with his hands on metal spikes on either side of it, in front of the garden of a house. The footage appeared to have been taken in late July near the centre of Popasna. A sign saying '21 Nahirna Street' was seen on a wall in one of the photos. The video and photos were published by Serhiy Haidai, head of the Luhansk Regional Military Administration until the Russian invasion, in his Telegram channel along with the comments 'They really are orcs. Twenty-first century, occupied Popasna, human skull on the fence' and 'We are at war with non-humans'.

A source said, 'The presence of the Wagner Group in large numbers in east Ukraine is a worrying development because they are so unaccountable. Even though they almost certainly have financial links to Putin and others in his Kremlin inner circle they can be sent on plausible deniability operations. They are not regular troops but they will be executing the wishes and ambitions of Moscow as an extension of Russia's military, albeit at arm's length. The only possible reason they are there is to be used as a force that can do what it likes and with impunity and it won't be seen as the responsibility of the Russian regime.'

But they could not win on their own. A Telegram statement from the Wagner Group said Russia would need '600,000 to 800,000 men' to defeat Ukraine. At the time Russia only had some 100,000 troops deployed in the Ukraine.

Ex-mercenary Marat Gabidullin, who quit the Wagner Group in 2019 said that the Russian military's failure to seize the Ukrainian capital was inevitable because in the preceding years, they had never directly faced a powerful enemy, despite its successes in Syria. Several months before Russia launched its invasion of Ukraine he said he received a call from a recruiter who invited him to go back to fighting as a mercenary in Ukraine. He refused, in part because, he said, he knew Russian forces were not up to the job, even though they trumpeted their arsenal of new weapons.

'They were caught completely by surprise that the Ukrainian army resisted so fiercely and that they faced the actual army,' Gabidullin said. Russians he had spoken to told him they expected to face rag-tag militias, not well-drilled regular troops. 'I told them: "Guys, that's a mistake".' Unlike the African failed states where Prigozhin had become powerful, Ukraine had systematically beefed up and trained its military since 2014 for another conflict with one enemy in mind—Russia.

4

DROPPING LIKE FLIES

On 24 February 2022, the first day of the invasions, Russians had taken Snake Island, or Zmiinyi Island, in the Black Sea. After the Ukrainians sank the Russian-guided missile cruiser *Moskva* on 14 April, they began a campaign to take it back. Wagner fighters were sent as reinforcements and found themselves being bombed and strafed by the Ukrainian air force.

The Wagner Group said on its Telegram channel: 'In just a few days, according to conservative estimates, the enemy destroyed an Mi-8 [helicopter] with crew and special forces evacuation group, several Tor-M2 air defence systems, two high-speed 'Raptor' boats, inflicted missile and bomb attacks on deployment areas and destroyed a seaborne weapons convoy.'

The Ukrainians recaptured the island on 30 June, though the Russians claimed their withdrawal was a 'goodwill gesture' to allow the export of Ukrainian grain.

On 24 May 2022, two alleged Wagner Group fighters from Belarus gained the dubious distinction of becoming the first foreign mercenaries to face war crimes charges in Ukraine. They were accused of murdering civilians near Kyiv. Ukrainian prosecutors the names and photographs of eight men wanted for alleged war crimes—including murder and torture—in the village of Motyzhyn twenty miles west of the capital. Along with two Belarusians, there were a Russian Wagner fighter and five regular Russian soldiers. Several were believed to have fought in Syria.

They were accused of over fourteen war crimes including the systematic torture and murder of civilians in Ukraine including the head of the village council and her husband and son. A survivor told how the invaders perpetrated a sadistic killing spree lasting days in the village and described Ukraine as a 'fairytale' compared with Syria.

These were the first charges against allegedly serving mercenaries, and the first non-Russians charged. Prosecutors said that fifty-one-year-old Sergey Vladimirovich Sazanov, born in the town of Rechitsa in Belarus, was one of Wagner mercenaries who participated in a February 2018 offensive in the Syrian province of Deir ez-Zor. They cited the open-source research group *InformNapalm*.

Thirty-two-year-old Alexander Alexandrovich Stupnitsky, a native of

Orsha in Belarus, was identified as a liaison officer for the assault platoon of the Wagner Group's 1st reconnaissance and assault company. The third Wagner member, thirty-three-year-old Sergey Sergeevich Sazonov, was born in Kaliningrad and was allegedly the driver of the Wagner Group command vehicle.

Denis Korotkov, an expert on the Wagner Group, confirmed that two of the suspects had previously worked for the mercenary company. 'Sazonov and Stupnitsky are in my files,' Korotkov said. It was unusual for Belarusian citizens to fight with the group because they could face jail sentences for it.

'It is likely that Sazonov and Stupnitsky fought in Syria,' Korotkov added. 'They don't have a particular reputation, just regular Wagner soldiers.'

None of the accused were in custody, and prosecutors believed they had been relocated to the frontline in the Donbas following the retreat from Kyiv.

'There is a possibility that these men are still fighting in Ukraine, or that they will be killed during the fighting,' said Oleh Tkalenko, a senior prosecutor in the Kyiv oblast. 'We are still working on it and we will do everything possible to arrest them.'

Tkalenko said the investigation was based on photographic evidence, CCTV footage and reports of survivors who confirmed the identities of their torturers. Only three men survived the torture camp in Motyzhyn. According to neighbours, when Russian troops occupied Motyzhyn, they tried to win the support of local officials and butchered them when they refused to collaborate.

After killing the civilians, the soldiers buried them in mass graves around the camp. In one, investigators found the corpse of Olha Petrivna Sukhenko, the head of the village council of Motyzhyn, together with her husband Igor and son professional footballer Alexander, buried in a shallow grave. Petrivna had chosen to stay in the town and coordinate aid and territorial defence when the Russians arrived. A fourth body was also found but had yet to be identified.

According to Ukraine's Prosecutor General Iryna Venediktova, Olha and her family were tortured at a Russian base as Russian soldiers tried to find out information about the Armed Forces of Ukraine and territorial defence forces.

'First, they shot at the son's leg right before his mother's eyes, then they killed him by shooting him in the head,' Venediktova said. 'The entire family died from multiple gunshot wounds.'

They were not the only victims of seemingly random killings.

'Consider the reason for another murder: one of their victims was shot in the head just because she was wearing black,' Venediktova said. 'Her father was taken prisoner and held in an outbuilding blindfolded and with his hands tied behind his back, practically without water or food.'

The investigation also discovered that two volunteers who were trying to bring humanitarian aid to the residents of Motyzhyn were also captured. After they were interrogated and tortured, they were taken to the forest nearby and shot, though one of them managed to survive the ordeal.

The accused were also said to have tortured to death two members of the Patriot civil society organization. Their bodies were riddled with multiple gunshot wounds. One of the suspects tied another of their victims to a quad bike and forced him to run after the vehicle for almost a kilometre. He was also interrogated, beaten up and threatened with being killed, before being forced to spend several days in a sewer pit. Venediktova also said the suspects had also shelled and set fire to civilian houses and stolen people's mobile phones.

The Wagner Group were suffering other reverses. Along with estimates 30,000 Russian deaths in the first hundred days of the war, the Wagner Group had suffered losses in their hundreds which had sent morale among Moscow's invasion forces plummeting, according to the Ukraine's SBU intelligence agency.

The SBU had intercepted a phone call homemade by a Russian soldier. In the recording the man was heard telling his wife that the 'elite unit' had been smashed, leaving 'ordinary' troops scared to fight.

'Even well-trained mercenaries cannot succeed in performing their tasks,' he said. 'Just miserable remnants are left.'

Bellingcat put Wagner losses at nearly three thousand—nearly forty per cent of their whole force in the Ukraine.

One of those killed was forty-four-year-old Vladimir Andonov from the Buryatia region of Russia's Far East. Andonov earned himself the nickname 'The Executioner' because of the brutal warmongering tactics he used fighting while with the Wagner Group in Ukraine and on previous missions in Syria and Libya. It was thought he had been shot dead by a sniper in the Kharkiv region of eastern Ukraine.

His death was first reported by the Russian publication *Moskovsky Komsomolets*, which lamented: 'The death in Ukraine of Vladimir Andonov, better known as Vaha, has become known. He died last night during a reconnaissance of the area together with his friend.' Vaha is an exclamation of pain.

Moskovsky Komsomolets said Andonov had previously fought in the Donbas in 2014 with the special forces and had received a medal 'For Merit in Battle'. That same year, according to Ukrainian sources, he became notorious as a bloodthirsty butcher during the battle for Debaltsevo. His name was also included in the Ukrainian-run 'Peacemaker' database, the Ukrainian blacklist website with close ties to law enforcement agencies and hackers that listed the alleged crimes of the Russian military. Andonov was thought to have personally taken part in the shooting of Ukrainian prisoners of war in Logvinovo as well as the massacre of civilians in the Donbas.

After fighting the breakaway states in the Ukraine, he returned home to work as an instructor for Combat Brotherhood, which holds military drills around the former Soviet Union. Then he travelled to Syria with the Wagner Group, also fighting missions in Libya. He was first spotted back in Ukraine shortly after the start of the war.

Andonov's death was also to be confirmed by Russian military sources based in his home of Buryatia on the messaging app Telegram. Another military channel on Telegram said he died with Bair Mitupov, another fighter from Buryatia.

One user on a Buryatia Telegram channel wrote: 'He died at night, during the reconnaissance of the area, together with his companion, probably killed by a sniper.'

Born in the remote village of Kusoci, in the Mogoituiski district on the Mongolian border in 1978, Andonov enlisted in the Russian army in 1997.

'I was in Donbas in September 2014, volunteering,' he said in an interview in the Buryat publication *Gazeta Nomer Odin* in 2017. I was urged by the events of 2 May in Odessa, where people were burned alive. For ideological reasons, my grandfather fought in Ukraine, in Vinita, he led Bandera until 1946.'

Gazeta Nomer Odin called him 'perhaps the most famous volunteer in Buryatia'. Another newspaper, the *Baikal Daily*, wrote: 'In Ukraine, the legendary volunteer from Buryatia Vladimir Andonov, known as Vaha, has died. Information about his death was confirmed by the head of the Buryat branch of the public organisation of Combat Brotherhood veterans, Jambal-Jamso Janaev. He said the funeral would take place in Ulan-Ude'—the capital of Buryatia.

There were more setbacks for the Wagner Group when regional governor Serhiy Haidai shared a video of a burning building which he said showed the remains of the base set up by the Wagner Group at a local stadium in the city of Kadiivka in the Luhansk Oblast.

'The Armed Forces of Ukraine launched a well-aimed attack on it. Only one survived,' Haidai tweeted. Ukrainian news outlet *Hromadske* said that twenty-two had died and four others were injured in the strike. Others reported hundreds dead after an ammunition dump was hit.

By way of answer, the Wagner Group set up its own air force—the poor effectiveness of the Russian airforce was one of the surprises to come out of the invasion—and was hiring pilots. A social media recruitment advert stated the outfit 'has everything—from shooting weapons, to aviation and anti-aircraft systems'. It was hiring for the 'near abroad', it said, meaning operations in ex-Soviet countries.

'We need absolutely everyone who fits the general work description. We will find a way to use everyone. Some will be taught extra skills, some will be trained from zero level... There are vacancies in the front and in the rear...'

The mention of aviation confirmed a UK Ministry of Defence intelligence report that Wagner was supplying pilots using Soviet-era planes. The report came after a former Russian air force major was captured on video after being shot down over Ukraine in a Sukhoi Su-25 Grach, a Soviet-made single-seater jet which first flew in 1975. Wearing just his pants and a blindfold the wounded pilot was said to have ejected from his plane before it crashed. The MoD said he later explained he was employed by Wagner and had flown several missions during the war.

'The use of retired personnel, now working as Wagner contractors, to conduct close air support missions indicates that the Russian air force likely is struggling to support the invasion of Ukraine with sufficient aircrew,' the MoD said. 'This is likely due to a combination of Russia 's insufficient numbers of suitably trained personnel and its combat losses. Whilst conducting his missions, the Russian pilot reportedly used commercial GPS devices rather than Russian military navigation equipment. This likely indicates that Wagner aircraft are older models of the Su-25 and that the Russian air force is not providing Wagner with up-to-date avionics equipment.'

In May, another retired Russian airman was killed after the same model of plane was blasted out of the sky over Luhansk with a Stinger missile. Former general Kanamat Botashev, then sixty-three, was evidently fighting with Wagner. Russia also lost two Su-25s on its own territory on what it called 'training' flights close to the border. The invasion was stalling.

5

PRISONER DECEPTION

By the late Spring, it was clear to the Kremlin that an additional tactic was needed to force Ukraine to the negotiation table before NATO and other nations were able to strengthen Ukraine. Again Putin turned to Prigozhin for answers. The answer was to grow the non-official army of mercenaries, presumably because they had, on balance, achieved the most impressive results as far as the Kremlin was concerned. Putin was between a rock and a hard place. A legion of random maniacal criminals would not have the cohesion that Wagner PMC had created over almost a decade with its mercenaries. At the same, time, an army of conscripts reluctant to fight was unlikely going to be very effective however large.

Soon, the Wagner Group began its recruitment drive in Russian prisons to create a legion of *Wagnerovcis* well above 2021 staffing levels as Moscow pumped extraordinary amounts of money into Prigozhin's operation. Relatives of inmates at two prisons outside St Petersburg, IK-7 Yablonevka and IK-6 Obukhovo, told *iStories*, an investigative journalism website outlawed by the Kremlin, on 25 July that prisoners have been promised 200,000 rubles (£2,800) a month and an amnesty if they survive six months of 'voluntary' service. The inmates were told they would serve with Wagner to 'defend the Motherland'.

In mid-July Wagner recruiters visited three prison colonies outside St Petersburg, which is where the military contractor is based. According to one relative, prison officials told the inmates they would be transported out of prison with official papers showing they were being transferred to another prison. From there, they would be under guard all the way until they crossed over into Ukraine.

'He was told not everyone will come back alive,' the relative said. 'If they die, the family will be paid five million rubles (£72,000). All of this is just words. It's not written anywhere.'

Also, the exact nature of the assignment was not made clear. Some were told they would be involved in reconstruction work in Russia-occupied areas of Ukraine. Others were told they would serve alongside the Wagners in the fighting or doing dangerous reconnaissance work where the chances of survival were low.

'At first, they were told that they would only consider those who had served or fought [in the military]. But after a few hours it became clear that they were putting absolutely anyone who wanted to go on the list,' a relative said. 'Initially, they said that just twenty per cent would return [alive]. Then, that "almost no one will return".'

There was little a prisoner do once they'd signed on the dotted line and found out the truth. One Yablonevka inmate had already signed a contract to go to Ukraine.

'He told me two days after the meeting that he signed the contract and that there's no going back,' his relative said. 'He says they're going there to fight. Why did he agree? He was tempted by a promise that he would be back home in six months and his conviction would be invalidated.'

Another forty followed. One told a relative: 'If the worst happens, I will earn you an apartment.'

iStories was dubbed a 'foreign agent' and promptly blocked by the Kremlin.

The opposition *Verstka* website quoted a spokesman for Prigozhin as saying that he had not been involved in the recruitment drive.

'Firstly, recruiters show interest in those convicted for murder and robbery,' *Verstka* reported, quoting prisoners. 'Those inmates in prison for drug and sex offences are normally not selected.'

Physical condition and allegiance to the Motherland were Wagner recruiters' top criteria. After volunteering, the potential criminal recruits were given an immediate physical test to see if they could cope with the strains of life as a mercenary.

'Wagner recruiters refuse elderly people and those with serious illnesses. To check, they are asked to do push-ups on the floor, sit-ups and perform other physical exercises,' inmates told *Verstka*. Only then are they sent from their prison to basic training and then the front line in Donbas, eastern Ukraine.

By 7 August, *Verstka* said that the Wagner Group had persuaded up to a thousand Russian criminals from seventeen prisons to sign up to fight in Ukraine in return for a salary and a presidential pardon.

'Three prisoners told human rights activists that businessman Yevgeny Prigozhin was allegedly coming to the colony,' the website also reported. He reportedly told inmates: 'I was jailed, too. Now I am a Hero of Russia. We need your skills.'

The charity Russian Sitting which supports families of convicts warned inmates and their families that this was not the easy way out of a prison sentence that they may be looking for. On its website, it said that all the promises made by Wagner and other Russian mercenary groups such as Shield, Slavic Corps, Patriot and Redut were legally impossible to enforce and that they should not be trusted.

Nevertheless, the opposition news outlet *Mediazona* said that Prigozhin took another 373 conscripts from three brutal penal colonies after they spoke to a prisoner at one of them. He was quoted as saying: 'They are interested in robbers and murderers. They said: "You will like it with us".'

It was now that Prigozhin was secretly filmed recruiting in a penal colony in Mordovia, five hundred miles east of Moscow, and was finally directly linked to Wagner PMC.

'I am a representative of a private war company, perhaps you heard the name—Wagner Group,' he told the crowd comprising hundreds of convicts.

'He's one of us,' a recruit was quoted as saying, noting that the Wagner boss had served nine years in prison. Prigozhin, for his part, has made clear why he's interested in them: 'I need your criminal talents,' he said.

He promised them amnesty on their sentences if they signed up to fight in Ukraine and a bullet in the head if they desert when they get there.

'In six months you will go home, having been pardoned,' Prigozhin said. 'There is no chance of returning to prison.' Those who refuse to fight after arriving in Ukraine would be classified as deserters, he said. 'And then they will be shot.' But if they died in action, they will be buried 'as heroes'.

Then he told them the odds.

'In the first attack in Ukraine using forty prisoners,' he said, 'three died and seven were wounded.' They had 'stormed the enemy trenches and cut them up with knives. One of the dead was fifty-two years old. He'd been serving thirty years but died a heroic death.'

'This war is tough. It isn't like any Chechen wars or anything,' he said: 'My ammunition consumption is two-and-a-half times higher than in the Battle of Stalingrad,' he adds, referring to the Second World War battle which saw almost two million casualties.

He explained the rules: 'No alcohol, and no sex with local women, flora, fauna, men, whoever. No desertions or surrender—troops will be issued two hand grenades to blow themselves up if needed.' One was for the enemy, the other for themselves.

'No one is retreating. No one backs down. No one is being taken prisoner,' he said. 'The minimum age we are taking is twenty-two years old, if younger, you need a paper from close relatives that they are not against it. The maximum age, roughly, is fifty years old, but if you're strong right here at the interview we do basic tests to see how strong you are. Good physical shape is essential.'

He admitted that he had sent rapists to the front line if they passed the necessary tests.

'We take great care about those jailed for sex offences [but] we understand people make mistakes,' he said. The inmates were given five minutes to decide whether they wanted to come.

'Only two other people can get you out of here, God and Allah, and they'll do it in a wooden coffin,' he said. 'I can get you out alive. Nobody goes back behind bars. If you serve six months, you're free. If you arrive in Ukraine and decide it's not for you, we will execute you.'

For those serving ten years or longer in the bleak conditions of a penal colony, it was an attractive offer.

'Any questions?' Prigozhin asked at the end of his speech. 'You have five minutes to think things over.'

The inmates of penal colony No 8, in the Tambov region three hundred miles south of Moscow, rushed to their cell windows when they heard the sound of a helicopter approaching on a late afternoon in July.

'No one ever uses a chopper to get down here. We were curious what the big occasion was,' recalled one of the inmates who called himself Ivan. Half an hour later, the men were ordered to report to the prison's main square where two heavily guarded men were waiting.

'We couldn't believe our eyes, he would really come all the way to visit us,' said Ivan, who was halfway through a 23-year sentence for murder. 'But there he was standing in front of us: Prigozhin, in the flesh, urging us to join the Wagner private military group and fight in Ukraine.'

Prigozhin liked to dress in a pseudo-military uniform with the Hero of Russia medal pinned to his chest. Ivan was impressed.

'Prigozhin spoke with a lot of confidence,' he said Ivan. 'We all listened when he spoke, and trust me that is not easy to shut up a good [number] of prisoners. He is one of us in the end, a former inmate. I think many who signed up did so because they trusted Prigozhin. They don't trust the authorities, but they believe Prigozhin when he tells them that they will be let free.'

The video offering freedom for six months of service in Wagner had gone viral.

'When I saw that video, I thought Prigozhin must be on a very busy schedule because it was exactly what he told us as well,' Ivan said. 'He promised we would be free if we fought for six months. But he warned that few would come back.'

Four prisoners and three close family members of inmates across different penal colonies in Russia all gave similar accounts of how Prigozhin was personally conducting recruitment in prisons.

Ivan declined the job offer but he said roughly 120 inmates signed up and were then fighting in Ukraine after a one-week training course. He said he would join up if Prigozhin came calling again though.

'I have eleven more years to spend in jail,' he said. 'Either I die in this shithole or I die there, it doesn't matter that much. At least I'll have a chance to fight for my freedom. We all compare it to Russian roulette. Besides, right now, signing up is voluntary. Soon we might have no choice and be forced to go.'

This thought was echoed by others.

'The truth is,' said Ivan, the inmate from Tambov, 'we, thieves and killers, are now fighting Russia's war.'

Marat Gabidullin had been a convicted killer jailed in 1994 for shooting a criminal before he joined the mercenaries. A former paratrooper, he was unable to rejoin the Russian army because of his criminal record. Before being accepted as a mercenary he had to pass a routine lie-detector test designed to weed out crooks seeking access to weaponry.

An inmate calling himself Vladimir, at prison colony No 2 in Russia's isolated northern Komi region, described a similar visit by Prigozhin in mid-July. He said prisoners were shown footage during Prigozhin's visit of Russian soldiers 'bravely fighting' in Ukraine and were promised that their actions in the country would not be punished.

'Prisoners will know they can act with complete impunity there,' said Vladimir, who had since left jail. 'Prison turns you into an animal, and there is a lot of hate growing inside you. Their hands will be untied there.'

However, Vladimir said Prigozhin repeated that they were recruiting 'prisoners of all backgrounds, as long as they were healthy,' but warned that drinking, drug use, looting and desertion in Ukraine would be punishable by execution.

As Vladimir had only three weeks left of a sentence for theft when Prigozhin arrived, he decided to not sign up, but he said his cousin, who had fifteen years left behind bars, was one of 104 inmates there who agreed to fight in Ukraine.

Inmates said Prigozhin appeared comfortable inside the walls of Russia's notorious prisons. 'You could see he was commanding the respect of the inmates,' said Mikhail, a prisoner, from the Ivanovo region, whose penal colony Prigozhin visited in August. 'He wasn't trying to sweet talk us. He said we were going to enter hell, but that it could be our lucky ticket out.'

He said Prigozhin's speech made a 'great impression' on the prisoners, with 170 fellow inmates signing up to fight.

A US official said that Wagner was by now trying to recruit more than 1,500 convicted felons. But Olga Romanova, the head of Russia Behind Bars, a prisoners' rights NGO, believed the number was much higher. According to Romanova's estimate, about eleven thousand Russian prisoners had already signed up to go to Ukraine by September 2022, a number that she said was growing rapidly.

'The process is accelerating. Just this morning alone, we got reports of six hundred prisoners being transported from Nizhny Novgorod,' she said. In a country that has the world's fifth-largest prison population per capita, Prigozhin's helicopter is likely to keep on flying. 'They are covering more ground every day,' she said.

Prigozhin was no longer the elephant in the room in Russia. Although Concord had previously been circumspect when it came to Prigozhin's links to Wagner, when asked about the recruitment video and the man in the footage, they said he 'looked and spoke like Mr Prigozhin'.

Indeed not all prisoners going to Ukraine were raring to fight for Russia. Ukrainian journalist Yury Butusov published an interview with fifty-five-year-old murderer Yevgeny Nuzhin who had been serving twenty-four years before he was recruited to fight in Ukraine. He said he had signed up so he would have the opportunity to hand himself over to Ukraine where some of his family lived.

'I told myself that when I came, I would do whatever it took to surrender,' he said, citing his anti-war stance and adding that he hoped to fight for Ukraine against Russia. He said he defected because the training was poor and he had relatives in the Ukraine.

'As far as I understood, [we were] cannon fodder. If you didn't follow instructions, they would shoot you,' Nuzhin said. 'It was not Ukraine that attacked Russia, it was Putin who attacked Ukraine. I have relatives who live here. My uncle lives in the Ivano-Frankivsk region, and my sister lives in Lviv.'

Another recruited prisoner who might be a problem was 23-year-old Yegor Komarov who had been arrested after a headless body with multiple stab wounds fell out of a stolen car he was driving when the Mitsubishi crashed into a fence on a motorway near St Petersburg. Leaked court footage showed him admitting to killing an unnamed 38-year-old male victim 'without any reason'. He confessed to cutting off a part of the man's body, cooking and eating it at home.

'I nibbled to just take a taste,' he said.

He also admitted to scouring parks at night looking for victims and murdering the owner of the Mitsubishi, fifty-year-old Arkad Kazyanin.

When police took his handcuffs off during questioning he screamed: 'What are you doing, I can bite you to death!' His interrogator then asked: 'Are you ready to eat a human again?' To which Komarov replied: 'Do you have some?'

Russia Behind Bars Director Olga Romanova confirmed that Wagner had recruited a killer who had cannibalism 'in his portfolio'.

Another recruit was notorious Russian mobster Zaur Aliyev who was serving eighteen years in a penal colony. Aliyev was previously the leader of one of the most powerful Azerbaijani criminal clans in Moscow, before being arrested in November 2014. At forty-seven, he was a third of the way through his sentence for extortion, kidnapping and robbery when he signed up to fight in Ukraine. But the Telegram messaging channel VChK-OGPU, reported that Aliyev—nicknamed *Zaika* or rabbit—'decided to run away'. It went on:

'According to our source, private military company fighters quickly caught Aliyev and he was shot.'

Stanislav Bogdanov only lost a leg but was rewarded for it. At twenty-five he was sentenced to twenty-three years in prison in 2012 for 'murder with particular cruelty' after he used an iron poker and dumbbells to beat to death Sergei Zhiganov, a magistrate in Veliky Novgorod, a city in northern Russia. He had thirteen years left to serve when he signed up. Critics said, like the rest of the amnestied recruits, there were no legal grounds for his release.

In a video published by Prigozhin's RIA FAN media outlet, Bogdanov and three other former convicts were handed military awards and pardons by an unseen official. All the men had lost limbs during the war. Bogdanov's right leg was severed from the knee down.

'You have earned this pardon with your blood and sweat and your heroism,' the official told them. The video was filmed in Luhansk, eastern Ukraine, then under the control of Kremlin-backed separatists.

Bogdanov said he did not regret joining Wagner. He had taken up Prigozhin's offer of freedom in return for military service because 'you only get one offer like this in your life'. And Wagner was especially keen to recruit convicts serving long sentences for violent crimes.

In August 2022, a convicted murderer who was serving a twenty-five-year sentence before he was freed to be deployed in Ukraine was posthumously awarded Russia's medal of honour by President Putin. Ivan Neparatov, the head of a criminal gang near Moscow, was found guilty of killing five people in 2013. He was praised by the Kremlin for his 'courage and heroism' after being killed in action.

A posthumous bravery medal was given by pro-Russian officials in Luhansk to forty-one-year-old Sergei Kadatsky who had served nine years of his fifteen-year sentence for killing his ex-wife, thirty-six-year-old Yulia Donchik, the mother of a fifteen-year-old son from a previous relationship. Ex-cop Kadatsky, who had been fired from the police, shot her using a hunting rifle with special optical sights as she drove along the Rostov-Taganrog highway in southern Russia after a bitter divorce. Recruiters were impressed with his sniping skills.

Once the car came to a halt, Kadatsky finished his ex-wife off with a pistol. Her father in the car with her was also shot, resulting in the amputation of his left arm and shoulder. Her mother died of grief. Despite the posthumous medal, Kadatsky's father-in-law said he did not believe that he died. He could find no record of a funeral and no compensation had been paid to the family. Kadatsky had served his six months. Yulia's father thought that he had changed his name and walked free.

Another multiple murderer also received a medal for courage. According to investigators thirty-year-old Konstantine Kiselev had been to visit an acquaintance who took too long to open the door for him. When Kiselev finally got inside, he attacked the man who let him in and beat the hostess who tried to stop the fight with a wooden stick. Then he stabbed her in the head, chest and other body parts with a knife no less than twenty-nine times. He strangled a second woman who witnessed the killing. In 2017 Kiselev was jailed for nine-and-a-half years for one count of murder and one of manslaughter.

Kiselev had the Russian state Order of Courage pinned on his chest personally by Prigozhin. Russian reports claimed: 'Kiselev's wife has told his cell-mates that her husband received an order [of courage] and the position of group commander because he was the only one from the [of fifteen] unit who survived a shelling.'

In truth, it started to smack of desperation as Prigozhin's sales pitch to prisoners was in part becoming a confidence trick. Some former GULAG inmates recruited by Prigozhin captured by the Ukrainians told a very different story. No wonder President Putin's sidekick Medvedev started to up the nuclear rhetoric as well from the Kremlin when speaking to foreign media. One complained: 'We are being used as cannon fodder. Our commander sent us forward, at first we were walking alongside, but when we looked back, they were very far behind. Usual cannon fodder: They wanted us to scout their positions, to see who's where… We're like cannon fodder….'

The man claimed they had been given a 'completely different story' when they were personally recruited from prison by Prigozhin. He had told the recruits they would be fighting alongside the more 'experienced' and established soldiers, who would train them, the prisoner of war claimed. They were also told they wouldn't be headed to the front lines.

'Wagner has gone from a band of brothers to a group of combat serfs,' said Gabidullin.

Several Ukrainian soldiers in Bakhmut told AFP these alleged ex-convicts are used as a type of 'human bait'.

'It starts at around 6pm, when it's getting dark,' said Anton, a fifty-year-old Ukrainian soldier from the 93rd brigade. 'These soldiers—with no experience—are sent towards our guns and stay there for a few minutes.'

He estimated seven or eight were sent every night.

'Their job is to advance towards us, forcing us to fire on them, to reveal our positions,' said Sergiy, a major in the 53rd brigade. 'After that, they fire artillery or send more experienced commandos towards our positions.'

Prigozhin slowly upped the ante for his prison legions as tangible results for the Kremlin remained elusive. As battle conditions grew harsher, so did the punishment for desertion—or even capture. It was reported that conscripted convict Yevgeny Nuzhin had been returned to the Wagner Group in a prisoner exchange, or he may have been recaptured. In a video, Nuzhin claimed that he was kidnapped on 11 November 2022, while walking in the streets of Kyiv, Ukraine, although it is possible that, now he was back in the hands of the Wagner Group, he had been forced to say that.

Fifty-five-year-old Nuzhin had been serving twenty-four years for murder when he was recruited in July and sent to the Ukraine. In the video, he was shown looking tired and dirty. After giving his name, his head was taped to a concrete block as he confessed to desertion. An unidentified man in combat gear then smashed his face in with a sledgehammer which had become the unofficial emblem of the outfit.

One of the Wagner Group's official Telegram channels *Grey Zone* called the video of Nuzhin's 'execution for treachery', *The Hammer of Vengeance*. It got more than a billion views on TikTok.

'It seems to me that this film should be called: 'A dog dies a dog's death,"' said Prigozhin. 'It was an excellent directional piece of work and can be watched in a single sitting. I hope no animals were harmed during filming.'

Prigozhin called Nuzhin a 'traitor'.

'Nuzhin betrayed his people, betrayed his comrades, betrayed consciously,' he said.

Nuzhin's family were horrified. His son said: 'Our whole family was in tears watching the video… he was murdered like an animal.'

Prigozhin also treated European officials to the kind of campaign of threats Wagner PMC used to intimidate African governments. In November 2022, when the European Parliament adopted a resolution designating Russia as a state sponsor of terrorism, Prigozhin sent a sledgehammer engraved with the Wagner logo and smeared with fake blood to the European Parliament in a violin case. Then a group of masked men threw sledgehammers at the Finnish Embassy in Moscow after Finland applied to become a member of NATO and Sergei Mironov, a Russian parliamentarian, posted a photo of himself posing with a sledgehammer branded with Wagner's logo atop an engraving of a pile of skulls. Mass-produced sledgehammers with the name 'Wagner' engraved on its head have gone on sale across Russia, along with other Wagner merchandize including carved wooden backgammon sets, keyrings, mugs, T-shirts and car stickers.

Politicians looking to attract support ahead of regional elections in Russia posed for photos in their offices with Wagner sledgehammers and bragged about taking courses in combat at Wagner training centres. In another video, Prigozhin addressed 'traitors' and wealthy Russians abroad, saying: 'The Wagner sledgehammer will be waiting for you.' He called for 'urgent Stalinist repressions' against tycoons seen to be insufficiently enthusiastic about the war.

Prigozhin was on a high. Asked by a journalist whether Russia was interfering in the US midterms on 8 November 2022, Putin's digital and offline warlord suddenly gloated: 'Gentlemen, we interfered, we interfere and we will interfere. Carefully, precisely, surgically and in our own way, as we know how.'

6

EXPANDING THE EMPIRE OF DEATH

As fighting intensified, the recruitment of convicts was stepped up. In November 2022, Russia's prison colony population fell by 23,000 in just two months as Moscow sought to beef up Prigozhin's army of savage butchers. To boost numbers, any pretence of subtlety or choice was shelved. While inmates had previously been given freedom deals if they joined the invasion, the Wagner Group had switched to more brutal recruitment tactics. All communications had been blocked, stopping any contact with anyone in the outside world. Some families were lied to by officials claiming they had to impose a sudden quarantine to explain their absence from the prison and absorption in a Wagner death squad.

In just two months more than five hundred ex-jailbirds had been killed in Ukraine after being forcibly recruited or having 'volunteered' in exchange for freedom. The Kremlin-sanctioned recruitment drive was pushed in extremely remote detention centres in Siberia and Russia's Far East including in Novosibirsk, Krasnoyarsk, Norilsk inside the Arctic Circle and Yakutia, though Rostov Oblast seemed to have been the group's main recruiting hub as it was near to the front. However, isolated camps in the Far East were out of reach for relatives living in European Russia, making it easier for prisoners simply to be wiped from records. Many prisoners were thought to suffer from tuberculosis, but their poor health didn't matter. Wagner PMC was interested in their survival instinct.

Foreign convicts in prisons across Russia, including citizens from the five central African nations were now also pushed into Wagner PMC. To boost its numbers, the Wagner Group then began to recruit Afghan special forces soldiers who fought alongside American troops. They had been trained by the US Navy SEALs and the Green Berets.

'They don't want to go fight—but they have no choice,' said General Abdul Raof Arghandiwal, former commander of Afghanistan's elite 207 Zafar Army Corps. "What should we do? If we go back to Afghanistan, the Taliban will kill us".'

On 14 November, Zambia's foreign affairs minister said Nathan Lemekhani Nyirenda, a twenty-three-year-old national from that country, who was serving a jail sentence for drug possession at a prison on the outskirts of Moscow, ended up fighting in Ukraine, where he was killed.

He had been a scholarship student at the Moscow Engineering Physics Institute when he was jailed for nine years in 2020 and sent to a medium-security prison on the edge of the capital. His father, Edwin Nyirenda, told Reuters that at the time of his arrest, his son had been working as a part-time courier when an unknown customer handed him a package containing drugs.

Edwin Nyirenda said he would travel to Russia after the family 'received a message from a man we do not know in Russia who told us that there was a will, which our son left'.

Thirty-three-year-old Nemes Tarimo, a Tanzanian, was also killed fighting for the Wagner Group. He had been studying at a Moscow university but was subsequently imprisoned for what was described as drug-related offences. His family told the BBC they warned him against joining Russian mercenaries last October.

'Nemes informed me and some other family members about joining Wagner, and we advised him not to,' a family member said. 'He said he would join to free himself.' Tarimo's family has learned that he died at the end of October while on a combat mission in Ukraine with Wagner.

And in a video shot in the Ukraine, Prigozhin was seen with a former bus driver from west Africa who had ended up in a Russian jail before being recruited and sent to the front in the Ukraine. Singing the praises of the man from Abidjan in the Ivory Coast named only as Aboya, Prigozhin later posted on social media: 'I think he will make a great president of the Ivory Coast... I will discuss these plans with him later.'

Recruiters aimed to take 150 to two hundred from each jail, targeting those who had committed the most serious crimes. A source told the *Daily Mirror*: 'According to information gathered from what is being said by relatives it is impossible to refuse, as, if prisoners do, they might disappear. Some prisoners have been beaten so badly they are unable to walk and are likely to then be given extended sentences and face a terrible choice. On the front line, many are simply cannon fodder—shot if they retreat and likely killed if they advance. So they are done for, whatever they choose.'

Like World War I trench warfare, generals dispatched their troops to a certain death—except that Russian prisoners hadn't volunteered for glory. When 109 recruits from prisons arrived in Belogorivka, Luhansk, they were ordered to take a nearby forest. When they refused, 19 were summarily shot after an attempt was first made to poison their breakfast. The rest launched the attack where most of them died.

There were other problems with conscripted convicts. Some simply went mad. After deserting his post, thirty-eight-year-old Pavel Nikolin emerged from the forest and shot up a customs point in the border town of Novoshakhtinsk with a machine gun or Kalashnikov assault rifle, injuring one officer. Authorities quickly shut down roads going in and out of the city, schools and kindergartens, and ordered people to stay at home while they searched for him. He was found in a deserted building and arrested. Others shot up aid workers travelling to the Ukraine to help.

Now Wagner was out of the shadows, it started a new recruitment drive for Russian volunteers with advertising on roadside billboards and the sides of busses, as well as social media to entice fresh fighters to join its ranks. One billboard seen outside Yekaterinburg read simply: 'Motherland, Honour, Blood, Bravery. WAGNER.' Another showed three men in military uniform next to the recruiting site wagner2022.org. The Russian population had been plied since 2014 by a bloodthirsty died of nationalism that painted its peaceful neighbour Ukraine as an incarnation of the devil that had to be exorcised.

'It looks like they have decided that they will no longer try to hide their existence. By now, everyone knows who they are,' said Denis Korotkov, a former *Novaya Gazeta* journalist and long-time observer of Wagner.

Indeed, Wagner were making no attempt to hide their existence when the story of their storming of Ukraine's second biggest power plant at Vuhlehirsk in the Donetsk Oblast appeared on the front page of *Komsomolskaya Pravda*, Russia's most widely-read tabloid.

Prigozhin himself leapt out of the shadows with gusto, sanctioned by the Kremlin. His photograph began to appear on Wagner posters. On social media, he criticized those who opposed the recruitment of prisoners. 'It is either private military contractors and prisoners [fighting in Ukraine] or your children—decide for yourself,' he said. Telegram groups with links to Prigozhin also share videos of prisoners turned Wagner soldiers who encourage other inmates to join their ranks.

Using the Reverse Side of the Medal Telegram channel, which had 290,000 subscribers, Wagner posted photos and videos set to rock music showing its fighters carrying modern rifles and promising travel and adventure. They look rugged and burly, compared to the often spindly Russian army conscripts. Part of the pitch was distancing itself from the corrupt and incompetent Russian Army. Instead, Wagner portrayed its fighters as rebel bad boys. Some photos showed Wagner mercenaries posing with hammers akin to the brutal 2017 murder of Syrian deserter Mohammad Taha al-Ismail Abdallah circulating on YouTube.

Wagner also played up to its name by referring to itself as an 'orchestra' and saying it was looking for 'musicians'. One recruitment photo showed five Wagner mercenaries posing in the destroyed town of Severodonetsk in Donbas, holding guitars, a trumpet and a saxophone.

After signing up, Wagner recruits were given a 200,000-ruble (£2,900) bonus—three times the average monthly salary in Russia. Training took another fortnight and then the mercenaries were sent to Ukraine to fight. Despite the high casualty rate and tough battles in Ukraine, this is a potentially attractive option for young Russian men looking for adventure and a way out of their life in provincial Russia with its low job prospects and endemic alcoholism.

Fatalities were played down on the wagner2022.org website with propaganda that promised potential mercenaries that Wagner 'is winning' in Ukraine.

'The orchestra needs musicians in Ukraine!' the website says. 'Embark on your first combat campaign with living industry legends!'

Wagner publicly boasted of its involvement in the war with a message on its website stating: 'They have already liberated Popasna, join us to liberate the entire Donbas! Go on your first combat campaign with living industry legends!'

An individual claiming to represent the Wagner group said that it had started its recruitment campaign because 'we saw that the support for our company is colossal, and there are many who want to join'. However, the person in the email exchange added: 'But nothing changes, there is no Wagner and never was, it's just a legend. There are only Robin Hoods who protect the poor who are oppressed by the rich.'

Wagner established regional recruitment centres in over twenty cities, posting the phone numbers of recruiters on popular social media channels linked to the group. Ads upped the salary to over 240,000 rubles (£3,370) a month, several times regular soldiers' typical wages. Unless they had signed off on this parallel army of volunteers, regular chiefs of the Russian Army and their political chief, minister of defence Shoigu, must have felt irked by the Kremlin's favouritism of Prigozhin's Wagner.

Some recruiters used the mercenary group's symbols as their profile pictures on WhatsApp and Telegram, and none denied their association with Wagner. A recruiter from the Nizhny Novgorod region in central Russia sent a list of the documents needed to join up, which included a passport from any country that 'wasn't NATO or Ukraine' and several medical certificates. He also sent a list of items to bring once accepted by Wagner, ranging from shower gel to tourniquets and other medical equipment. 'See you in Molkino', referring to the military base where Wagner was headquartered, was the battle cry.

Britain's Ministry of Defence observed: 'Wagner has almost certainly played a central role in recent fighting, including the capture of Popasna and Lysyschansk. This fighting has inflicted heavy casualties on the group.' This was a result of lowering 'recruitment standards, hiring convicts and formerly blacklisted individuals' who received limited training.

'This will highly likely impact on the future operational effectiveness of the group and will reduce its value as a prop to the regular Russian forces,' the MoD said.

'Even before the conflict, less than thirty per cent of the soldiers in Wagner were actual professionals,' said Marat Gabidullin. 'Now, the group will mostly consist of a bunch of amateurs.'

Wagner got involved in Russia's dirty war of intimidation where the Kremlin wanted deniability towards other governments. The PMC bombed prison Molodizhne near Olenivka, Donetsk Oblast, killing fifty-three Ukrainian prisoners of war and leaving seventy-five wounded. The prisoners were mainly Azov fighters from the Azovstal steelworks, the last Ukrainian stronghold in the siege of Mariupol, who surrendered on 20 May.

The General Staff of the Ukrainian Armed Forces said that the Russians blew up the barracks in order to cover up the torture and murder of Ukrainian PoWs that had been taking place there, and Ukrainian authorities provided what they said were satellite images of pre-dug graves and intercepted communications indicating Russian culpability, while Moscow suggested that a HIMARS (High Mobility Artillery Rocket System) rocket was shot from Ukrainian territory. According to a CNN investigation based on the work of forensic and weapons experts, the Russian version of events was very likely a fabrication, as there was virtually no chance that the damage was caused by a HIMARS rocket.

The Security Service of Ukraine (SBU) released a statement on its website that said: 'Judging by the militants' conversations, Russians could have staged a tragedy having placed the explosives in the premises of the prison. In particular, none of the eyewitnesses heard any missile flying towards the correctional facility.

'Moreover, judging by the videos available on the Internet, the windows have remained intact in some rooms of the facility. This indicates that the epicentre of the explosion was inside the destroyed building and its walls took the hit from the blast waves, protecting some of the neighbouring rooms.'

A spokeswoman for the breakaway Donetsk People's Republic confirmed to Russian war reporters that no Russian guards were killed or injured in the strike.

Footage released on Russian state TV appeared to show a prison compartment with charred bunk beds and other belongings scattered around. Body parts and shoes were seen strewn on the floor. Moscow said the attack was a 'bloody provocation of the Kyiv regime' designed to discourage Ukrainian troops from surrendering on the battlefield. This egregious provocation was carried out to intimidate Ukrainian servicemen,' the Russian defence ministry said.

On the day of the explosion, the Russian Embassy in London posted a video said to be of a man and his wife they claimed to have been shelled during the fighting for Mariupol. Quoting the man in the clip, it tweeted: '#Azov militants deserve execution, but death not by firing squad but by hanging, because they're not real soldiers. They deserve a humiliating death.'

Russian commentators claimed a wafer-thin justification for the carnage. In August 2021, the Russian Supreme Court had declared the Azov Regiment a terrorist organization. State media had repeatedly shown what it claimed to be Nazi insignias, literature and tattoos associated with Azov, though AP said no evidence had surfaced to back up the assertions about their mistreatment of civilians.

Acting Head of the SBU Vasyl Malyuk said: 'No matter what nonsense the enemies invent to justify themselves, it is obvious to everyone that Russia is guilty of the deliberate killing of Ukrainian prisoners. This is confirmed by the first available evidence. I am confident that later there will be more evidence. SSU investigators have already started investigating this crime as part of the relevant criminal proceedings.'

On 3 August the intelligence arm of the Ukrainian defence ministry issued a statement claiming they had evidence that local Kremlin-backed separatists colluded with the Russian FSB and Wagner to mine the barrack before 'using a flammable substance, which led to the rapid spread of fire in the room'. It had already concluded that the block had been blown up from the inside, citing the nature of the damage, which it said was inconsistent with Russian claims that Ukraine armed forces had shelled the building.

Meanwhile Prigozhin also organized Russia's efforts to destabilize the EU and stop it backing Ukraine, using mass immigration. Moscow paid him for trafficking immigrants and to Prigozhin it was simply another profit centre for his expanding empire of death. Refugees, mainly from Iraq, were flown to Minsk and then bussed to Belarus's heavily forested border with Poland and told to walk across. Meanwhile, the Wagner Group encouraged thousands of migrants to set sail across the Mediterranean from areas in Libya it controlled in the run-up to elections in Italy.

'It shouldn't surprise anyone that Wagner should get involved in the electoral contest in Italy,' said Enrico Borghi, a member of Italy's parliamentary intelligence committee. 'Putin's Russia is trying to influence elections in our country. [He] has fired up a furnace—Libya, Africa. To place Italy in difficulty means keeping in check the whole of Europe.'

When the allegations were repeated the following year by Italy's defence minister Guido Crosetto after a surge in immigration, Prigozhin responded in a typically expletive-laden voice message posted on his Telegram channel: 'We have no idea what's happening with the migrant crisis, we don't concern ourselves with it.' He then used a series of obscenities to describe Crosetto—calling him a *mudak* which means 'shithead' or 'arsehole'—and urged him to pay attention to his own country.

Later it was reported that the Wagner Group had put a bounty of €15 million (£13.1 million) on Crosetto's head taking a leaf from Italy's mafia. The order to assassinate the minister could be carried out by Wagner based in Serbia or Estonia.

7

ASSASSINATION ATTEMPT

On 15 August, it was reported that Prigozhin himself was a casualty after the frontline Wagner base he was visiting in Popasna was hit. One account said he was wounded and immediately evacuated to Burdenko hospital in Moscow.

'He is alive, even swearing,' a witness from Popasna told the VCHK-OGPU Telegram channel.

Initially it was reported the Prigozhin was among the estimated hundred dead. A pro-Kremlin war reporter known only as Kotenok wrote on Telegram: 'A strike was carried out on one of the Wagner PMC locations in Popasna. Sources in Donbas confirm that. Probably 'HIMARS'. Ukrainian sources report the death of Prigozhin. We don't confirm that.'

But a source close to Wagner denied Prigozhin had been killed, saying: 'This is not the first time they have buried him,' noting earlier Ukrainian reports had wrongly reported his death in a previous incidents. 'So there will probably be no official denials this time either. They are simply not needed.'

However, there were reports of 'mild panic', as Prigozhin has not been seen since the strike. There was confirmation that Wagner's headquarters had been targeted by a HIMARS missile—possibly with knowledge that Prigozhin was visiting.

Video footage and pictures show the scene after the missile strike in Popasna. One grainy clip shows one of the men leaving a building. Another, filmed in between some shrubs, shows three Wagner mercenaries by a truck. They were crouching to the ground, but it is unclear whether they were picking something up.

That Prigozhin was at the site is beyond doubt. Pro-Kremlin journalist Sergei Sreda had shared pictures following a visit to the hidden site, with one showing him alongside Russian mercenaries by a street sign giving the address of the nearest air-raid shelter. He said: 'I arrived in Popsana. Went to Wagner's HQ. They greeted me like family, told me a few funny stories.' In another picture he is seen shaking hands with Prigozhin. According to Sreda's footage Prigozhin had been visiting to hand out medals to Wagner fighters for the role in taking Popasna.

Pro-Russia Telegram channel HS Kharkiv shared photos and footage showing a bombed-out building believed to be the headquarters. A man was seen being carried on a stretcher amid the rubble, with the video captioned: 'We're digging out our guys in Popasna.'

Later Prigozhin boasted he had 'cheated death', suggesting the strike was intended to kill him but he had survived. Serhiy Haidai said: 'Unfortunately, there will most likely not be such wonderful news about the "chef" but there will be about his deputies.'

Russian die-hard, pro-war voices expressed outrage with Russian state-television posting pictures that would make the Wagner PMC base easy to locate. Popular pro-Kremlin Telegram channel Voenny Osvedomitel wrote: 'It's sad that this missile strike that the enemy was able to launch thanks to a thoughtless publication of the current military positions was not the first time it happened. There's a long list I can already publish.'

However, the security blunder was so glaring that some open-source investigators wondered whether it wasn't part of the usual Prigozhin misinformation, given the Kremlin's vice-like grip over mass media. Ruslan Leviev, head of the Conflict Intelligence Team, said: 'When those photos first surfaced and we discussed them at a planning meeting, I said they look too staged… as if [the Russians] were trying to invite a strike at that location. Knowing how much Prigozhin likes trolling and how much money he is willing to spend on it, I still have my doubts whether this really happened.'

Leviev suggested that Prigozhin might have set out to get the Ukrainian army to hit the base so that they could prepare an anti-missile defence ready to shoot down US-provided HIMARS missiles. Unofficial reports claimed that the Kremlin was so rattled by the HIMARS firepower that it promised its soldiers the Hero of Russia medal for taking out a HIMARS launcher.

Nevertheless, there was some cause for celebration. Ukrainian MP Oleksiy Honcharenko wrote on Facebook: 'There is no more Wagner HQ in Popasna. Thank you, HIMARS and the Armed Forces of Ukraine!'

A former Wagner contractor, who had deployed to Syria and Libya, said that friends serving in Ukraine told him that things were going badly there.

'It's common knowledge that the situation is very poor, and a lot of people don't want to go. I was told of all kinds of problems, lack of coordination, planning, untrained soldiers who were a danger to everyone else. I thought about Ukraine, went to have a look in Donetsk, but didn't go at the end and certainly won't go now', said Murat Usmanov from a central Asian republic.

'Their [Wagner's] quality also deteriorated, the people they are sending are substandard. The Russians underestimated the Ukrainians who are better trained and better armed. With winter coming a lot of people on the Russian side won't have proper clothing, proper equipment, proper weapons, It's going to get even more bad for them.'

All Russian security forces were ordered to support Prigozhin. On 1

January 2023, six former convicts were on the run from police in Russia after deserting from a training centre in Ukraine run by the Wagner Group. Three are from Uzbekistan, one from Belarus, one from Russia and one from Kazakhstan. They were armed, but Prigozhin played down the danger to Russian citizens. 'The National Guard, the police and the Wagner security services are always catching various kinds of armed people,' he said. 'Many villains are being detained whom you don't even need to know about. So sleep well.'

There was, however, now a growing sense of resentment with Russia's regular army among Wagner members and other volunteers as they fought in Ukraine while the 'state didn't fully mobilize'. A short video shared on the Telegram messaging app showed the pictures of at least five young officers in military uniforms hanging above urinals in an attempt to shame them. Another video emerged online apparently of a fighter from the Wagner group of mercenaries brawling with Rosgvardia national guards at a hotel in Voronezh, Russia, after telling them he served his country in Ukraine.

Prigozhin's digital army made sure to create slick hero stories around its fallen mercenaries. On 20 September 2022 Alexei Nagin, the 41-year-old commander of one of the Wagner Group's assault detachments, was found dead near Bakhmut. After studying at technical school, he was drafted into the army to fight in Chechnya. After completing his compulsory military service, he signed a contract to stay on to fight in the Russo-Georgian War.

Then he joined the FSB special forces in Volgograd as a reconnaissance sniper. From 2014 to 2016, he was an instructor training scouts in Crimea. He then quit the FSB and joined the Wagner Group, fighting in Syria and Libya. He then participated in the invasion of the Ukraine. On 12 May he was seriously wounded. After a long treatment in August, he returned to the service, only to be killed in action in the Battle of Bakhmut. He was awarded the 'Hero of the Russian Federation' posthumously and Prigozhin attended his funeral.

The Russian public's bloodthirst was fed amply by the exploits of the Wagner Group's Rusich detachment. A message on Rusich's Telegram channel on 22 September advocated the 'destruction of prisoners on the spot'. It also incited atrocities against prisoners of war and explicitly advocated the torture of captives including 'removing body parts'.

The Rusich Telegram post contained specific and detailed instructions for the 'disposal of prisoners of war from the armed forces of Ukraine'. Its key points included the explicit instruction to murder captives after interrogation and encouraged forcing the families of murdered captives to pay Rusich for the co-ordinates of their loved ones' bodies. It also stated the capture of Ukrainians should not be reported to the pro-Kremlin command, and if a report had to be made, it should say that the captive was already injured or dying.

As the fighting around Bakhmut intensified Prigozhin began to join in with his mercenaries and criticize the commanders of the Russian army for their ineptitude. He issued a statement saying: 'Send all these pieces of garbage bare-foot with machine guns straight to the front.'

Former Wagner commander Marat Gabidullin highlighted the preferential treatment Prigozhin was receiving compared to the regular Russian army: 'I am convinced that if Russia did not use mercenary groups on such a massive scale, there would be no question of the success that the Russian army has achieved so far.'

He added, 'The Russian army cannot handle [the war] without mercenaries,' he said, adding that there was 'a very big myth, a very big obfuscation about a strong Russian army'. It seemed the yawning divide between the high-earning Wagner Group and the low-paid Army was growing.

At least 5000 mercenaries tied to the Wagner group were operating with Russian forces in Ukraine, Andrii Yusov, a spokesperson for Ukraine's defence intelligence agency said. Wagner was increasingly being used to patch holes in the Russian front line. That led to significant logistical challenges with the need for a separate supply chain to Wagner troops with ammunition, food and support for extended operations, while Ukraine has upped its attacks on Russia's logistics.

Bodycam footage from Wagner fighters showed mercenaries complaining of a lack of body armour and helmets. In another video, a fighter complained about orders to attack Ukrainian positions when his unit was out of ammunition. Wagner Group was plummeting and Gabidullin wasn't 'surprised to see Prigozhin stepping into the spotlight'.

'On the current wave of patriotism, he wants to position himself as a fierce defender of the motherland who created a professional military organisation. He wants to show that he can fight better than the regular army. We always had tensions with the ministry of defence, we really didn't like each other,' said Gabidullin.

According to a former senior defence official who worked with Defence Minister Sergei Shoigu and Prigozhin, the rivalry between the two men was a longstanding feud that went back to the founding of Wagner in 2014 after the annexation of Crimea, pre-dating even before the Palmyra offensive in 2016. It was exacerbated when Shoigu fired deputy defence minister Dmitry Bulgakov, through whom Prigozhin arranged lucrative catering contracts supplying the army.

'Prigozhin will now be out for revenge against Shoigu,' the source said. He described Prigozhin as a person with 'no morals, no conscience, and no hobbies… He is a machine in the bad sense of the word.'

Prigozhin found an unlikely ally in Ramzan Kadyrov, the volatile leader of

Chechnya who had established the North Caucasus republic as a personal fiefdom in exchange for pledging its loyalty to Russia. As to Ukraine, he emerged as one of the harshest critics of the Russian defence ministry, claiming his own fighters could have taken Kyiv within days even after the Russian army had been repulsed.

Shortly after the Russian defeat at Lyman, a crucial railway hub in the Donetsk region, Kadyrov unleashed a withering attack on the Russian General Staff and the central military district commander Colonel-General Alexander Lapin responsible for the city's defence.

'The shame isn't that Lapin is incompetent,' Kadyrov wrote on Telegram. 'It's that he's being shielded from above by the leadership in the General Staff. If it was up to me, I would bust him down to a private, take away his medals and send him with a rifle to the front in order to cleanse his shame in blood.'

'Beautiful, Ramzan, keep it up,' Prigozhin chimed in. 'These punks should be shipped to the front barefoot with machine guns.'

In October, General Lapin was sacked. Meanwhile, Prigozhin applauded the appointment of General Sergei Surovikin to lead the war effort. He was nicknamed 'General Armageddon' for his hardline and unorthodox approach to waging war, particularly the destruction of Aleppo in 2016. The fifty-six-year-old was also known as the 'Butcher of Syria' and had a shaven head and a stern scowl to match his hard-man image. Mikhail Khodorkovsky told the House of Common's foreign affairs committee that Yevgeny Prigozhin was behind the appointment and was working in close conjunction with him in Ukraine.

'Surovikin is absolutely ruthless with little disregard for human life,' a former defence ministry official said. 'I am afraid his hands will be completely covered in Ukrainian blood.'

Gleb Irisov, a former air force lieutenant who worked with Surovikin up to 2020, said: 'He is very cruel but also a competent commander.' According to Irisov, Surovikin maintained a good working relationship with the Wagner group. Prigozhin called him 'the most competent commander in the Russian army' and a 'legendary figure' who 'was born to serve his motherland faithfully'.

The Russian Anti-Corruption Foundation pointed out that, as well as killing thousands of civilians with gas, barrel bombs and other horror weapons in Syria, it was there that Surovikin made his fortune like Prigozhin. Behind his image as a hard-nosed general was a 'crook and a hustler' who has lined his bulging pockets with 'blood-soaked' money—living life large along with his glamorous wife Anna. He and his wife bought a £2.7 million mansion on a gaudy fake 'English estate' in Russia. The money he made from a phosphate concession near Palmyra after the Wagner Group had driven ISIL out also allegedly helped pay for a giant palace built for Putin, complete with a lap dancing den, casino and tunnel leading to a private beach.

It was noted that, by then, Prigozhin had as much influence as Sergey Lavrov, the foreign minister, or Sergei Shoigu, the defence minister. 'He has a lot of personal meetings with Putin,' said Khodorkovsky.

'He confronted Putin about the war and how it is being 'mismanaged by top generals'. Prigozhin preferred a more aggressive approach and called on Russian lawmakers to fund their own private armies to fight in Ukraine or head to the frontlines themselves.

'Those people who have been shouting slogans from the rostrum have to start doing something,' Prigozhin said in a statement. 'I'm calling on the talking heads to get together and lead units like Wagner while those who lack managerial skills can pick up automatic rifles or at least sapper's shovels. This will be a true service to the Motherland.'

8

BAKHMUT'S MEAT GRINDER

By 19 October, Prigozhin was boasting of creating a fortified line of defence in Ukraine's eastern Lugansk region—the 'Wagner Line'. He posted on social media of his company Concord that: 'A complex of fortifications is being built on the contact line, commonly known as the 'Wagner line'. It is a multi-level and layered defence.' There was no real need for it, he bragged somewhat unconvincingly, as 'the presence of a Wagner unit at the front line is already an impregnable wall' in itself. Imagery confirmed a section of newly constructed anti-tank defences and trench systems south-east of Kreminna in the Luhansk oblast in Ukraine's eastern province.

Fearing that all was not going as well as he hoped, Prigozhin, said, 'Wagner is helping and will keep helping the population in border areas to learn how to build engineering structures, to train and to organize a militia,' Prigozhin was quoted as saying by the press service of his catering company Concord. He said 'a huge number of people are already ready to defend their land'. Wagner's main aim was to start building fortifications and training schools in the Belgorod and Kursk regions, which have come under fire regularly in recent months in attacks blamed by Moscow on the Ukrainian army.

'If you want peace, prepare for war,' he said.

At Bakhmut in Donetsk, progress was painfully slow. It took months for Wagner to inch their way across several miles of fields to the east of the city and into the outer suburbs. Their situation was all the more perilous when a high-ranking mercenary defected from the Wagner Group along with a Russian intelligence officer. They managed to reach France where they were debriefed and sought political asylum. Wagner-led Russian forces penetrated the southern suburbs of Ivanhrad and Opytne, but these were retaken by the Ukrainian 93rd Brigade, which rushed to this front, though some of the area has slipped back into enemy hands.

'The situation near Bakhmut is difficult,' Prigozhin said on Telegram. 'The Ukrainian troops are putting up decent resistance, and the legend of the fleeing Ukrainians is just a legend. Ukrainians are guys with the same iron balls as us.'

The Ukrainians returned the compliment. 'We have heard that Wagner is recruiting from prisons to serve in this country. They are desperate like all the Russian military,' says Ruslan, a sergeant in Ukraine's 57th Motorized Infantry

Brigade. 'But the ones we are seeing seem pretty experienced. We captured a guy who had been in Libya. Maybe they are on a special bonus to fight in Bakhmut. They are certainly trying really hard.'

Prigozhin had to be a winner and he needed to capture Bakhmut as a political prize, though he acknowledged the slow pace of advance. His troops were only making a hundred to two hundred metres a day, rather than the planned thirty kilometres. Prigozhin claimed this was 'normal in modern warfare'. Britain's MoD noted that Prigozhin 'is likely trying to burnish his credibility within the stressed Russian national security system.'

With the vasts amounts of money coming his way, he had even opened a Wagner Centre office in St Petersburg, Putin's hometown. It was a shiny glass-fronted twenty-three-storey building topped with a big white 'Wagner' sign and staffed people in combat gear. Its black and gold interiors housed a 'business incubator', offices for pro-Putin journalists and a 'war museum'.

Military drones were on display at the entrance and flat-screen TVs played video clips set to music, including one showcasing Wagner's battle victories in the Donbas and another with a woman singing about the glories of mercenary groups to hundreds of cheering men. It also hosted pro-war photo exhibitions.

Press officer Anastasia Vasilevskaya said that the new headquarters were 'a response to sanctions, an act of patriotism, a way to increase Russia's defence capabilities'. The top floor offices were dedicated to 'journalists' (trolls) providing content for blogs, news sites and Telegram channels.

'The objective is to offer them free offices if they adhere to Mr Prigozhin's points of view and wish to disseminate them', she told *Society* magazine.

On its new website, Wagner Group says that companies involved in strengthening the Russian defence sector will be able to rent office space in the building. 'We break stereotypes. We know how to be the best,' it said.

'The mission of the PMC Wagner Centre is to provide a comfortable environment for generating new ideas to improve Russia's defence capability,' Prigozhin said in a statement. At the same time, he rebranded the Wagner Group, ditching its skull and sniper crosshairs logo for an anodyne 'W'.

All this was done, apparently, with Moscow's approval. A Kremlin source told the website *Meduza.io*: 'He isn't just an errand boy charged with some unpleasant tasks. Prigozhin is considered an effective war manager, and a liberator of Luhansk.'

The ChVK Wagner Centre was officially registered. It listed 'management consulting' as its core activity. Secondary activities included a variety of business endeavours from book publishing to aircraft leasing. Registering as a PMC remained illegal in Russia, though they were clearly tolerated, if not encouraged. While the company's owner was not listed, the company's director is identified as Alexei Tensin who served as an executive at the Russian state-controlled arms maker Kalashnikov that makes AK-47 rifles.

Britain's MoD said the rebrand shows that 'the role of Wagner Group has evolved significantly since Russia's invasion of Ukraine'. While he was not at the opening of his plush new offices, Prigozhin flexed his political muscles by taking issue with Alexander Beglov, the governor of the St Petersburg in what was seen as a long-running feud. He later branded city officials as cowards when they would not allow one of his fighters to be buried in a Soviet-era military cemetery.

'He voluntarily went to Donbas to defend his homeland,' Prigozhin said of one of his dead fighters. 'Unfortunately, no one from Smolny went to Donbas. They cowardly continue to sit in their offices.' Smolny is the collection of imperial-era buildings in St Petersburg that house the city government.

Prigozhin raised eyebrows in Russia when he described Zelensky—normally denounced by Moscow as a neo-Nazi drug addict—as a 'strong, confident, pragmatic leader', adding: 'Don't underestimate him.' He also chose the moment to admit to interfering in the American elections. Then, on the eve of the US midterm elections, he said: 'During our pinpoint operations, we will remove both kidneys and the liver at once.' He did not elaborate on this cryptic comment.

Meanwhile, on the battlefield, Wagner Group fighters were shown using Solntepek heavy flamethrower systems to hit Ukrainian forces in Bakhmut and its suburbs. Such thermobaric weapons are also known as vacuum bombs or the 'poor man's nuclear weapon'. Dr Marcus Hellyer, a senior analyst at the Australian Strategic Policy Institute, said: 'They are not illegal even though their effects can be pretty horrific, because of that effect of creating a vacuum and sucking the air out of the lungs of defenders.'

Footage recorded in the Bakhmut area showed the TOS-1A Multiple Launch Rocket Systems, which launch these weapons, hitting their targets. A comment on the video read: 'To be on the wrong side of TOS would have to be a terrifying experience. Ruptured lungs and GI [gastrointestinal] tract have gotta be a terrible way to go.'

The effects are, of course, indiscriminate. The bodies of four civilians were found, apparently killed by the Russians in Bakhmut and contested areas of Donetsk.

As winter drew on, Wagner Group mercenaries were reduced to fighting in heavy mud, rubble and sub-zero temperatures in what has become a savage war of attrition in the Donbas. By the end of November, the battlefield resembled Passchendaele. And while Ukrainian troops were warmly attired, for the most part, the Russian mercenaries had not been issued with winter clothing.

Despite his bravado, Wagner's advance on Bakhmut had stalled altogether under heavy Ukrainian artillery fire. Nevertheless, Mikhail Khodorkovsky told the House of Common's foreign affairs committee that the Wagner Group's popularity in Russia had surged in recent months since it was able to argue that its existence acted as an alternative to wider mobilization. And, with only some 7000 men, Wagner would not take the blame if the military operations failed in Ukraine, since the Russian forces were 150,000 to 200,000.

In these conditions, Prigozhin's objectives were curtailed. He said Wagner Group formations were not trying to take Bakhmut, but instead to wear down Ukrainian forces. 'Our task is not Bakhmut itself, but the destruction of the Ukrainian army and the reduction of its combat potential, which has an extremely positive effect on other areas, which is why this operation was dubbed the "Bakhmut meat grinder",' he said as an apology.

He now had a parallel force inside Russia's border, an unheard-of development. While it must have been given Putin's seal of approval, the Institute for the Study of War (ISW) did note on 24 October that 'Prigozhin continues to accrue power and is setting up a military structure parallel to the Russian Armed Forces, which may come to pose a threat to Putin's rule—at least within the information space.' Its report went on to say, 'Putin depends on Wagner forces in Bakhmut and is likely attempting to appease Prigozhin despite the fact that Prigozhin is undermining the conventional Russian military.'

Another problem with Prigozhin's Wagner mercenaries recruited from prison became clear during the Bakhmut meat grinder. It turned out tuberculosis was but one of the illnesses endemic in Russia's prison population. Many of them were ill with serious infectious diseases such as HIV and hepatitis C. Drugs were widespread in the GULAG and these diseases were often spread through sharing dirty needles. More than a hundred infected prisoners infected had been mobilized from one prison alone close to St Petersburg. There were as many as twenty-thousand altogether.

'In order to "mark" infected militants, the command of Wagners forces them to wear red bracelets on the arm in case of HIV, and white bracelets in case of hepatitis,' Ukraine's Ministry's Main Directorate of Intelligence said in a statement.

It did not do much to build whatever solidarity there was on the Russian side. Russian conscripts were said to be furious about having to serve alongside infected mercenaries. The report also claimed that Russian military doctors regularly refused to provide assistance to the infected soldiers if they got wounded on the battlefield. In Ukraine, a number of Wagner militants with HIV and hepatitis had already reportedly been detained.

Aid workers sent HIV drugs and abortion pills to Ukraine for women who had been raped by Russian soldiers. More than fifty cases of sexual violence by Russian troops were being investigated, according to Ukraine's human rights chief Lyudmila Denisova. She accused the Russian army of several instances of rape including the gang-rape of a fourteen-year-old girl who became pregnant; of twenty-five women and girls locked in a basement; and of an eleven-year-old boy in front of his mother.

International abortion providers said they had been inundated with requests from Ukrainian hospitals and volunteer organizations for emergency contraceptives. Kinga Jelinska, who heads the non-profit abortion provider Women Help Women, said: 'We have heard of sexual assaults and violence in Ukraine. We know this from the groups working on the front line where the Russian occupation is happening, from feminist groups who have contacted us and said that they are short on supplies that are related to sexual assault, so emergency contraception, abortion pills, prophylaxis of HIV, for the prevention of HIV transmission.'

A special British-led investigations unit set about hunting down and prosecuting Russian troops suspected of rape and other sex attacks on men, women and children in Ukraine. Many of the allegations were aimed at convicted sex attackers given pardons when they signed up for the Wagner Group.

The Ukrainian Ministry of Defence noted the change in tactics. It tweeted on 30 October: 'On 27 October 2022, Russian mogul Yevgeny Prigozhin posted online, apparently admitting allegations that his private military company, the Wagner Group, had altered its standards and was recruiting Russian convicts suffering from serious diseases including HIV and Hepatitis C.

'The role of Wagner Group has evolved significantly since Russia's invasion of Ukraine. In previous conflicts, it maintained relatively high recruitment standards, with many of its operators having previously served as professional Russian soldiers. The admission of prisoners with serious medical concerns highlights an approach which now prioritizes numbers over experience or quality.'

Later when 300 Wagner troops turned up at a hospital in Luhansk, the General Staff of the Armed Forces of Ukraine said: 'Due to the fact most of them are carriers of such diseases as HIV/Aids, syphilis, tuberculosis and pneumonia, local medics refuse to provide mercenaries with medical care.'

And the problem was growing. Convicts who had tested positive for HIV were choosing to be sent to the frontline in the hope of getting lifesaving medication. They preferred the battlefield rather than to rot in jail where they were denied treatment. Ukrainian officials estimate about twenty per cent of recruits in Russian prisoner units were HIV positive. A lot of them were so desperate for the anti-viral medications they couldn't get in jail, they opted to fight in Ukraine.

Speaking from a detention centre in Dnipro, an HIV-positive Russian soldier said doctors in prison changed the anti-viral medication to a different type that he suspected was not effective. Fearing he was not going to last his ten-year sentence behind bars, he had agreed to join the Wagner Group for six months in exchange for a pardon and supplies of effective anti-viral medication.

'I understood I would have a quick death or a slow death. I chose a quick death,' he said. He had no military experience and, after two weeks of training, was delivered to the front, where his unit's commanders 'repeated many times, "if you try to leave this field, we will shoot you".' While most of the recruits were killed on the first day, he was captured.

Another forty-two-year-old soldier said he welcomed Wagner's acceptance of HIV-positive inmates and joined the frontline for a chance at medication and freedom.

'If you have a long sentence, it gives you a chance to begin life again,' he said.

Another HIV prisoner who suffered a gunshot wound before he was captured, said that, although he did receive treatment, he felt medics were careless about infecting other patients around him.

'There were no conditions for the HIV infected,' he said. 'We were all treated together, the healthy and the unhealthy.'

But things did not always go smoothly. 'What percentage of our guys who went [to Ukraine] are still alive?' one prisoner asked a Wagner recruiter in December, according to a report by the independent *Mediazona* outlet. 'At that point, [the recruiter] started to stammer; he couldn't give an answer, and he ended his speech there.'

9

ARMY OF CONVICTS

Meanwhile, having escaped to the French Riviera Marat Gabidullin said: 'Prigozhin is a very dangerous man who should not be underestimated. He is unique. He is very ruthless, very bright and thinks on a much larger scale than other people. He can be charming, he can be rude.'

The problem with Prigozhin, he said, 'is absolutely sure that he is always right. There can be no objections. Fear was in the atmosphere inside the office.'

He based this on the three months at Wagner headquarters giving Prigozhin daily updates on the military situation in Syria at the end of 2017.

'He ruled through fear,' Gabidullin recalled. 'The office atmosphere was extremely strict, Prigozhin would often cross the line with his workers. He was very rude to his staff. He would curse people, and embarrass them in public.'

Putin will not hesitate to destroy Wagner the moment it threatens him, Gabidullin said. 'The action which is needed to erase this Wagner Group would take only two days. For Putin, it is enough just to click and they will not exist anymore.'

Asked whether Prigozhin could replace Putin, Gabidullin told the National Security News website: 'He is not going to be able to become president because he doesn't have the power base to become a president. So he is in active search of people to create a political union. Probably he is going to try to take the place of Zhirinovsky. He definitely has political ambitions.'

Vladimir Zhirinovsky was a veteran ultra-nationalist and showman of Russian politics who predicted the invasion of Ukraine almost to the day. He died of Covid-19 in April 2022 aged seventy-five. The leader of the far-right Liberal Democratic Party for thirty years had been described as 'Russia's Trump'.

Gabidullin compared Wagner to the Oprichnik, the secret police of Ivan the Terrible, who ruled from 1547. The Oprichnik dressed in black robes with the insignia of a severed dog's head and rode black horses. They quelled dissent through intimidation, beating and ritual executions, boiling the Tsar's opponents to death and tearing them limb from limb with horses.

He said that Prigozhin's public delight at Nuzhin's murder video was an attempt to reinforce his authority. Gabidullin said it was 'to show that they have their own laws that are higher than any laws. It's a kind of message sent to everybody, to traitors, advertising the possibilities of how they can do things.'

Gabidullin believes: 'Wagner is a symptom of the disease infecting Russia. Other countries need to be aware that this is what happens when democracy breaks down. You end up with Wagner—a private military company which has become a tool of the Russian state.'

Wagner was enlisting prisoners to go to war in Ukraine because its best men are required for overseas operations, Gabidullin claimed. It was clearly more lucrative not to sacrifice talented mercenaries in trench warfare.

'Prigozhin is not going to put into the war people who are veterans who are staying with him,' he said. 'Wagner needs them in Africa or Syria. The Russian state mindset is that you can put criminals at your power, at your service. Their life is not worth anything.'

Nevertheless, the Battle for Bakhmut was vital for Prigozhin. Ben Barry, of the International Institute for Strategic Studies, said that Bakhmut had no more military significance than other similar-sized towns along hundreds of miles of front line.

'But it has political significance as a town the Russian leadership wants to be seen to capture. It may also be that any role Wagner has in capturing it would amplify the political position of its owner,' Barry said.

But it seemed that there were other targets. At the beginning of December, the official Telegram channel for 'Task Force Rusich' asked its members to submit intelligence on border and military activity in Latvia, Lithuania and Estonia, which were formerly part of the Soviet Union, raising concerns over whether far-right Russian groups are planning an attack on Nato countries.

There were more setbacks in the Ukraine. Serhiy Haidai said a hotel where the Wagner Group was based in Kadiivka, Luhansk Oblast, was hit. There had been major Russian losses and 'at least fifty per cent' of survivors would die due to a lack of medical treatment.

It was reported that HIMARS struck the building when there were members of PMC Wagner inside. Video uploaded from the scene showed that several men at least had been injured and were awaiting medical help. In another video, a number of men in camouflage stand around a rocket tail recovered from the site and discuss the attack.

In another twist, an old photo at the hotel showed Prigozhin's son in full camouflage holding a rifle. Pavel Prigozhin has previously been reported to be fighting for Wagner. Prigozhin denied that his son had been injured in the strike. Later Pavel was awarded Wagner's 'black cross', its own award for military service.

Although the Russians were throwing everything they had at Bakhmut, the Ukrainians held out. Ukrainian battalion commander Major Andrii Polukin said: 'Drones, jets, missiles, artillery—and Wagner's convicts too. It is true, we are taking losses, but we are killing more of them than they are us, and it's too early to say which way this battle is going. We will fight into the winter, hoping the snow will come to our aid.'

Britain's MoD said that Wagner mercenaries in Ukraine faced execution if they deviated from battlefield plans. They were issued with smartphones or tablets that outlined their routes and assault objectives, while commanders at platoon level and above used drone imagery to monitor the fighting from a distance, the MoD said.

'Individuals and sections are ordered to proceed on the preplanned route, often with fire support but less often alongside armoured vehicles. Wagner operatives who deviate from their assault routes without authorization are likely being threatened with summary execution,' the MoD said in a daily briefing. 'These brutal tactics aim to conserve Wagner's rare assets of experienced commanders and armoured vehicles, at the expense of the more readily available convict recruits, which the organization assesses as expendable.'

A spokesman for Ukraine's Eastern Military Command explained how the Russians operated in Bakhmut: 'The first people Wagner sends in [across No Man's Land] are the convicts and poorly trained men, and only behind them come the more professional soldiers.'

Prisoners' rights activist Olga Romanova said that at least forty convicts had been executed on Prigozhin's orders. 'And he will get away with this,' she said. 'When prison service officials are asked about the whereabouts of prisoners, they say this is a state secret.'

The stand-off with Russia's ministry of defence was increasing and Wagner was buying in weapons including infantry rockets and missiles directly from North Korea, White House national security spokesman John Kirby said on 22 December.

'We can confirm that North Korea has completed an initial arms delivery to Wagner, which paid for that equipment,' he said. Wagner group, which is independent of the Russian defence forces, is spending more than $100 million each month on its Ukraine operations.'

'Because of our sanctions and export controls, Wagner is searching around the world for arms suppliers to support its military operations in Ukraine,' Kirby said. The US estimated Wagner had by now about fifty-thousand personnel deployed to Ukraine, including ten-thousand contractors and forty-thousand convicts.

About a thousand Wagner fighters were killed in the fighting in weeks, ninety per cent of whom were convicts. 'He's literally throwing bodies into the meat grinder there in Bakhmut,' Kirby said.

The Chinese firm Changsha Tianyi Space Science and Technology Research Institute Co. Ltd., known as Spacety China, and its Luxembourg subsidiary were then sanctioned by the US for providing Wagner with satellite imagery which aided their combat operations.

'Prigozhin is behaving like a parallel government,' said Andrei Kolesnikov, an analyst at the Carnegie Endowment for International Peace. 'He may be able to compete for power, if not under Putin then after him.'

'In certain instances, Russian military officials are actually subordinate to Wagner's command,' said Kirby. 'It's pretty apparent to us that Wagner is emerging as a rival power centre to the Russian military and other Russian ministries.'

With his troll factory and the use of propaganda in Africa, Prigozhin had made himself master of counter-information. Now, as head of an army of convicts, he became vulnerable himself as he pitted himself against the Russian Federation Army chiefs.

Little was known about his time behind bars, but new information suddenly started to appear. In a new video, it was alleged that Prigozhin had been sexually abused by other inmates, an accusation that had the potential to undermine his authority.

According to the harsh code of Russian convicts, men who were forced into a passive role in sexual abuse were called *petukhi*, meaning roosters, and were the lowest of the castes within the prison system. Other inmates were forbidden to speak or to stand close to them, and they were assigned the dirtiest jobs, such as cleaning the latrines.

In an expletive-strewn online video, a man covered in prison tattoos who identified himself as a crime boss called Sasha Kurara said that in jail Prigozhin was his bitch and had performed oral sex on him and other inmates. 'He knew his place and he agreed to his place,' he said. 'He is a f***ing faggot, a *petukh*, and anyone who goes into Wagner is a faggot too.'

Pro-Kremlin bloggers said the video was a smear campaign against Prigozhin that had been orchestrated by Kyiv. Others suggested that it was an attempt by Prigozhin's enemies within the Russian military or security services to cut him down to size. Although Kurara described himself as a crime boss, he had served twenty-four years in prison and was likely to have exaggerated his importance within Russia's criminal hierarchy.

Some said the claims of sexual abuse were likely to be fabricated because Prigozhin would not have been able to win the respect of crime bosses in St Petersburg in the 1990s if they were true. 'Bandits wouldn't have sat at the same table as him,' prisoners' rights activist Olga Romanova said.

'Prigozhin, never a widely popular man within the elite, has been making even more enemies of late, including within a security apparatus that thinks he's getting a bit too big for his boots,' said Mark Galeotti. '"Sasha Kurara" doesn't seem to have any real authority or profile within the Russian underworld, so it is hard to think someone like that would pick a fight with Prigozhin on his own initiative. The suspicion must be that this was initiated or encouraged by one of Prigozhin's many enemies.'

Oleksiy Arestovich, a Ukrainian presidential adviser, said it was unclear if the accusations were genuine or if they were the result of a plot against Prigozhin. Either way, he said, the video had the potential to turn Prigozhin into a 'toxic' figure among Wagner fighters. 'A loss of credibility could cost him his influence, as well as the [Kremlin's] support and funding of his activities,' Arestovich wrote on Telegram.

His only response was another expletive-laden video where members of the Wagner Group said that the Russian armed force's chief of general staff General Valery Gerasimov a 'piece of shit'. Prigozhin offered no criticism of the comment.

Prigozhin was undeterred and returned to the GULAG on a second major recruitment drive. It was also reported that Wagner was recruiting in Serbia. A Serbian nationalist group called People Patrol had visited Wagner's corporate headquarters in St Petersburg in November, where they posed holding a flag which proclaimed that Ukraine's Donbas region was part of Russia just as Kosovo was part of Serbia. Wagner by now had an office in Belgrade as well and RT's Serbian channel carried Wagner recruitment ads which said the group offers 'more than attractive' incentives to come and fight with them. In exchange, the Wagner Group was helping Serbian paramilitaries to smuggle weapons and unmarked military uniforms into Kosovo.

'They bring in weapons and uniforms but they are not formally part of the Serbian army. Serbia wants to achieve its aims without it being called a military operation,' said Kosovo's President Vjosa Osmani. She feared they were laying the groundwork for a hybrid attack to seize Kosovan territory in an operation similar to Russia's annexation of Crimea.

'Increasingly Russia's military machine is being depleted and the country it serves is going rogue with Wagner Group commanding in parts,' observed a Western security source. 'Putin seems to have abandoned using Wagner fighters to distance the Kremlin from their horrific behaviour and they are becoming an integral part of his war machine. The fact that Prigozhin is now returning to jails he has recruited from previously means Russia commanders are becoming desperate for bodies to throw into the Ukraine war.'

10

PYRRHIC VICTORY

Mercenaries complained of scant training and poor living conditions. Then there was the attrition rate. According to reports on the Telegram channel of General SVR, which claimed to be run by former and current members of the Russian Foreign Intelligence Service, or SVR, as well as other state bodies, the losses in Russia's regular army alone amount to 104,186, with another 33,902 from private military companies such as the Wagner Group. The battlefield was strewn with corpses of peers over which Russian troops had to advance.

Having made Bakhmut symbolic of his military prowess, he was now counting the cost as success remained elusive. 'Everyone has a question,' he said in a video posted on social media, 'when are you taking Bakhmut?'

Explaining why his mercenaries, who took a prominent role in the assault, had so far failed, he said: 'Every house has become a fortress. The guys lock horns for every home, sometimes not just for one day. Sometimes for weeks over a single house. They take one home, they take a second, a third. What is breaking through the defences? It's taking one house. If we say there are five hundred lines of defence, probably we won't be wrong. A line of defence every ten metres.'

But the real problem was not the neophyte *Wagnerovcis*, or him, but the shortage of ammunition and armoured vehicles. Speaking to troops from what appeared to be an underground gym, he said: 'We are lacking vehicles, BMP-3, and 100mm shells, in order to move through Arymovsk [the Russian name for Bakhmut] quicker and with more confidence.'

In December, singling out Russian armed force's chief of general staff General Valery Gerasimov, he posted on Telegram: 'The guys have asked me to pass this on: When you're sitting in a warm office, it's hard to hear about the problems on the front line, but when you're dragging the dead bodies of your friends every day and seeing them for the last time—then supplies are very much needed.'

Video footage showed him visiting a makeshift morgue on New Year's Day, where he observed bodies on stretchers and a pile of body bags stuffed in the corner of an underground bunker. Prigozhin said: 'Their contract has finished, they will go home next week. These are getting ready to be sent. We all work during New Year's Eve. Here lie Wagner fighters who died at the front. They are now being put in zinc coffins and they will return home.'

Prigozhin could then be seen looking on as more bodies were loaded from a lorry onto stretchers. 'So long, guys. Happy New Year!' he said.

'That's how Prigozhin sends off his Wagner members,' Anton Gerashchenko, an adviser to the Ukrainian interior minister, wrote on Twitter. 'They are just thrown on top of each other in black bags, like garbage.'

A White House official now revealed that Prigozhin's obsession with taking Bakhmut had monetary motives. He wanted to take the salt and gypsum mines nearby for commercial reasons. This was Prigozhin's modus operandi in Africa and so it was in Ukraine. As part of Bakhmut, fighting intensified around nearby Soledar. Prigozhin claimed that mines in the area would prove vital for Russia's offensive. 'The system of Soledar and Bakhmut mines, which is actually a network of underground cities, cannot only [hold] a big group of people at a depth of eighty to a hundred metres, but also tanks and infantry fighting vehicles, which can move about there,' he defended himself on Telegram.

In the area, there is a labyrinth of caves and salt mines that consist of more than 180 miles of tunnels. They contain a vast underground room that in peaceful times hosted football matches and classical music concerts. The caves also housed art galleries and a winery that stopped production only after Putin ordered tanks into Ukraine. Both sides were concerned that the tunnels could be used to infiltrate troops behind their lines. The salt and gypsum that could be plundered from the historic mines of Soledar would represent a commercially lucrative asset to those who control them, while the subterranean caverns could be used as an underground weapons store, protected from aerial bombardments.

Late on 10 January, Prigozhin took to Telegram again to crow that Wagner units had taken the whole territory of Soledar under control, Moscow's first major battlefield success since the previous summer. Prigozhin also released a photograph of himself, surrounded by Wagner fighters, in what appeared to be one of Soledar's salt mines.

'I want to underline once more that no units took part in the storming of Soledar apart from Wagner,' said Prigozhin. But they also had praise for the Ukrainians.

'On the western outskirts of Soledar there are heavy, bloody battles,' he said on social media. 'The Ukrainian army is bravely fighting for Bakhmut and Soledar. Reports of their mass desertion are not true.' It made Wagner PMC look more impressive if the Ukrainians lost Soledar after tenacious fighting. The Ukrainian military analyst Oleh Zhdanov said fighting in Bakhmut and Soledar was 'the most intense on the entire frontline'.

'So many remain on the battlefield… either dead or wounded,' he said on YouTube. 'They attack our positions in waves, but the wounded as a rule die where they lie, either from exposure as it is very cold or from blood loss. No one is coming to help them or to collect the dead from the battlefield.'

One Western observer concluded: 'The proxy Wagner Group has moved from a niche sideshow of Russia's war to a major component of the conflict. There is a realistic possibility that Wagner personnel now make up a quarter or more of Russian combatants.'

A couple of hours earlier, another post in the Telegram group said: 'Once again I want to confirm the complete liberation and cleansing of the territory of Soledar from units of the Ukrainian army. Civilians were withdrawn, the fighters of the Armed Forces of Ukraine, who did not want to surrender, were destroyed. Killed about five hundred people. The whole city is littered with the corpses of Ukrainian soldiers. There can be no talk of any humanitarian corridor. Let's start clearing mines.'

The Ukrainians contested Prigozhin's claim. The strategic communications branch of the Ukrainian military said the pictures released by the Wagner Group had been taken elsewhere. And a Ukrainian soldier said: 'Positions are being taken and re-taken constantly. What was our house today, becomes Wagner's the next day.' Then footage was posted online from 'Magyar', a Ukrainian drone operator, which showed two-dozen Russian troops, apparently from Wagner, making the mistake of pouring into a house in Soledar in columns for shelter. Within minutes a shell, possibly from a HIMARS judging by its size and accuracy, followed co-ordinates sent in by the drone. It landed smack into the roof, destroying the house and presumably everyone inside.

The Russian ministry of defence, however, denied the battle was over and said its paratroopers were responsible for recent progress, in a rare slap down to the upstart warlord. It was an ominous change. The two branches of Putin's troops were now openly at each other's throats. 'Airborne units have blockaded Soledar from the north and south. The Russian air force strikes enemy strong points. Assault detachments are fighting in the town,' it said in a statement that made no mention of the Wagner Group.

The Kremlin itself added it was important not to declare victory in Soledar prematurely, in a first public intervention that undermined Prigozhin. 'Let's not rush. Let's wait for official announcements,' Kremlin spokesman Dmitry Peskov said, though he conceded that there had been a 'positive dynamic in advances' in Soledar and saluted the 'heroism of our fighters'. Playing down Prigozhin's announcement, he said: 'Tactical successes, of course, are very important.' After all, the Russian army should take its fair share of credit.

Prigozhin was livid. 'I read with surprise the statement from the Ministry of Defence,' said Prigozhin. 'Soledar was taken solely by the efforts of the fighters of the Wagner PMC and there is no need to offend the fighters by downplaying their contribution. You are demotivating them. It is necessary to fight instead of comparing each others' d**ks and stealing others' achievements.' He did not, however, comment on Peskov.

Tensions between Prigozhin and Russia's regular army had been growing for months, with the mercenary boss increasingly attacking the generals' handling of the war. Abbas Gallyamov, a former speechwriter for Putin said: 'He invested too much hope into Prigozhin… ignoring official structures to such a big extent is not good.'

More bad news followed. On 11 January 2023, Russian Defence Minister Sergei Shoigu demoted Sergey Surovikin after just three months in command and appointed Valery Gerasimov in his place. Surovikin would stay on as one of Gerasimov's deputies. The appointment appeared to be a direct rebuke to Prigozhin, an ally of General Surovikin. Prigozhin had also accused Gerasimov of incompetence and blamed him for a string of Russian military setbacks.

Eventually, on 13 January, the Russian ministry of defence had to admit that it was Wagner who took Soledar. 'This combat mission was successfully implemented by the courageous and selfless actions of the volunteers of the Wagner assault squads,' it said in a statement. Prigozhin insisted 'not a single paratrooper' was involved. Markov revealed there had been a meeting between Putin and Prigozhin in St Petersburg where Putin had 'recognized the heroism of the Wagner soldiers'.

Prigozhin was quoted on Telegram saying that Wagner faced a struggle against 'corruption, bureaucracy and officials who want to stay in their places,' calling this a 'more serious threat' to his company than the United States.

The battle of Soledar saw an estimated ten thousand Russian military deaths—mainly from the Wagner group. The death toll from private military companies—of which Wagner is the main one—by that point was estimated at over 38,000. More than three-quarters of the 38,244 Russian prisoners freed to fight with the Wagner group have been killed, wounded or captured, according to Ukrainian officials. All because of the salt mines Prigozhin wanted to capture.

After Soledar, Prigozhin was walking on air. He evidently reckoned the Soledar victory had proven the worth of Wagner PMC's privatised approach to war. His digital worked overtime to create the image of the Wagner hero in Ukraine. Earlier, in August 2022, a new cemetery had been opened dedicated to the Wagner dead just over the Sea of Azov from the Ukraine in the Krasnodar region which was then connected to the Crimea by the Kerch Bridge.

'There are graves of those who, for various reasons, wrote in their statement that in case of death, they wanted to be buried near the chapel of the Wagner PMC in Goryachiy Klyuch,' said Prigozhin. 'Since there are no burial places near the chapel itself, with the support of the administration of the

Krasnodar region, a plot was allocated in the nearby village of Bakinskaya.'

By January 2023, there were 120 graves there, some named, some not. Prigozhin visited the graveyard and laid flowers on the grave of soldier Denis Glazkov who died on 1 December 2022. A large monument to the fighters has been erected at Goryachiy Klyuch, with plates and personal numbers of fallen fighters.

In March the Wagner Group was given permission to expand the graveyard to take the bodies of seven hundred men whose relatives had not asked for them to be buried in their home region. A video was released with a commentary by a weeping woman who said: 'It's such a big graveyard, all graves are new... There is no end in sight... There are young men, and men of all ages. Rest in peace. You can't even walk to the other end of it.' It was 'impossible to count' the graves, she said. 'My soul is bleeding.' It underlined the exceptional efforts of the unknown convict *Wagnerovcis*.

In another video Prigozhin could be seen telling a group of injured fighters, some in wheelchairs, that they were expected to stay at the front even if they had lost limbs. 'The fact that they have been left without legs, without arms, without their eyesight doesn't mean they [can] go home,' he said. 'They can carry out duties that don't require both legs. They can work as sappers. If another mine explodes, their metal leg will be blown off and we'll weld another one on.'

By the New Year, some of the convict recruits had completed their six-month contracts with Wagner. They were urged on camera (rather than forced) 'to come back and finish off what we started'. One, who agreed to sign a second contract, claimed: 'It's no longer a job. It's a lifestyle. Of course, we're going back.'

Those being discharged were told that they deserved the nation's respect for doing their duty, but that they should 'behave'.

'Don't get too hammered, don't take drugs, don't rape women—[sex] only for love or for money as they say,' he said. They laughed when he added: 'The police should treat you with respect. If they are being unreasonable... I myself will call, and sort things out with the governors and so on. We will find a solution.'

On the bus leaving the base, Prigozhin told them: 'You have learned a great deal—first of all: how to kill the enemy. I really don't want you to practise that skill on forbidden territory... If you want to kill the enemy again you return.'

In a video published by Russia's *RIA Novosti* news agency, Prigozhin said to the newly-discharged mercenaries: 'You've worked through your contract. You worked honourably, with dignity.' He said that the men 'should be treated with deepest respect by society'.

However, there was bound to be trouble. Several violent incidents involving Wagner mercenaries had been reported when men on short leave in Russia got involved in drunken brawls or took issue with locals who were not showing enough respect for them.

The former convicts who survived were awarded medals for bravery. At the ceremony Prigozhin said. 'I hope the adrenaline you have used up over this past half a year will be enough for at least a month. Some of you I am seeing for the last time, some I will see again. Remember life has given you this chance: you didn't dodge the honour, you didn't arse it up: you defended the Motherland, all of you were ready to die in these past 180 days. Now we have to control ourselves.'

Again Putin stood by Prigozhin's side. Although there was no official way that Prigozhin could pardon those who served in the Wagner Group, 31-year-old Hayk Gasparyan was among a group of former prisoners honoured by Russia's president. Awarded the Order of Courage for bravery on the battle-field, he told Putin: 'I serve Russia and Wagner.'

He had been only a few months into a seven-year sentence in a Ryazan jail when he signed up. An armed robber, he had been convicted of stealing 375,000 rubles (£3,500) at gunpoint from a man outside a Moscow bank.

Another former prisoner hailed as a war hero was thirty-six-year-old Dmitry Karygin. He had served only six years of a fourteen-and-a-half-year sentence in the strict regime penal colony for killing his eighty-seven-year-old grandmother Zoya Anastasenko. He had beaten her to death with a hammer in 2014 after forcing her to sell her flat. Taking home 885,000 rubles (£8,200), he left her remains stashed in the garage where he brutally murdered her. When her corpse was found a year later, he went on the run, but the police eventually caught up with him.

Sixty-six-year-old Alexander Tyutin was also released after serving for six months and was recommended for a medal for courage on the frontline. Known as 'The Black Realtor', he paid $10,000 for the contract killing of his business partner Dmitry Zeinalov, his wife, their ten-year-old son and fourteen-year-old daughter in 2005. The killer bludgeoned Zeinalov's daughter with an axe at the family's country house outside St Petersburg, and used a machine gun to murder the man's pregnant wife. He then used the axe and gun on her son before killing Tyutin's business partner. Tyutin then reportedly urinated on their graves after the funeral.

He was only caught years later after he was found organizing the contract killing of his late wife's niece in a dispute over his dead spouse's £93,500 inheritance. The contact killer he hired for just under $9,000 turned out to be an undercover cop and was detained in 2018, while Tyutin himself was jailed in Karelia, northern Russia, in 2021.

The following year Tyutin joined Wagner despite being of pensionable age.

Prigozhin hit back at furious criticism over Tyutin's discharge, comparing him to wimpy conscripts. Asked if he felt it was just that Tyutin was now a free man given the gravity of his crimes, Prigozhin said: 'Let me explain to you the philosophy of jail inmates taking part in the war. An inmate killed a family of four. You don't know and haven't seen that family, but you feel angry about it. That inmate went to the war, and was killed. Or he survived by a miracle. He is a murderer, and in the war he is worth three or four or even more dandelion boys, whose milk on their lips is still wet. Among those dandelion boys is your son, your father, your husband. Consider what you want more: for a murdering realtor to be sent to fight or for it to be your loved ones, who you'll likely end up receiving back in a zinc coffin.'

According to Prigozhin, Tyutin 'carried out the task of storming a fortified settlement of the Ukrainian armed forces. Thanks to his decisive and skilful actions, the assault team was able to occupy the enemy stronghold with minimal losses and fulfil the task.'

Once Tyutin was freed, he flew to Turkey to be reunited with his wife.

The release of former convicts did not go down well with residents of Moscow who were bombarded with calls from people purporting to be cops, telling them to lock up their children. Parents were warned that some of those now free to walk the streets had been locked up for paedophilia. Dozens of complaints have been made about a man who identified himself as 'Major Solovyov' and his colleagues.

One complainant told the *Agentstvo* news outlet: 'He asked me, 'Do you have kids?' I responded that we are not located in Russia. He continued, 'In connection with the [war], inmates who fought for Wagner have received pardons and will now be free'. [He] said it's dangerous to let children out after 7pm and said goodbye.'

Another Moscow resident said her husband received a similar call and initially thought it was a scam. He was then surprised when the caller simply warned 'about the return to Moscow of Wagner fighters'. Cops in Moscow were said to be trying to track down the rogue callers and work out if they had any links to law enforcement.

11

BAKHMUT PROPAGANDA

Things were not going so well in Bakhmut either. *Independent* journalist Kim Sengupta met a young Wagner fighter taken prisoner there. Talat Nazarbekov, an Uzbek, had been with a patrol trying to infiltrate Ukrainian positions when they were ambushed. He had been wounded. Two others had been killed. The others, though injured, had made it back to Russian lines.

Talat said that the Wagner contingent on the frontline was running short of ammunition, that supplies were not arriving, fire support they were promised had not materialized and morale was very low.

'We are going to be taking back the areas Wagner have occupied, they are in poor shape, we are ready,' said a captain of the 93rd Brigade that had captured him. 'A lot of them will not live, this man is lucky we got him really. He will be taken to hospital for treatment.'

The Wagner fighter told Sengupta: 'They will shoot me when you guys are gone.' He asked for a cigarette. Lighting him one, a Ukrainian soldier grinned. 'We should put you out of your misery, but don't worry, we are not going to,' he said. In the event, Talat was not executed. Sengupta saw him a few days later at a hospital in Dnipro. But the Ukrainian advance did not take place either with both sides were stalled in attritional street fighting and Talat spoke of the deep frustration and disenchantment at the losses being incurred for so little gain.

'We have had a hundred people killed and injured for a hundred metres. This does not make any sense,' he said. 'We began to realize that a long time ago. The quality of the *mobics* [newly-mobilised soldiers] was not acceptable, especially those from prisons. We don't understand the thinking of the senior people, what they are trying to do, where they are going with this.'

However, the Wagner Group could celebrate another small victory in January 2023—the collapse of the Mozart Group, a pro-Ukrainian mercenary outfit. It ceased operations after running out of money and its two founders— both ex-US Marine colonels—fell out.

Then there was a Russian Volunteer Corps, a bunch of pro-Ukrainian Russian nationalists who wanted to bring down Putin. They were led by Denis Nikitin, a notorious former football hooligan.

'One day you will see me riding a white Leopard 2 tank into Moscow,' he said. 'When I put the flag of the Russian Volunteer Corps over the Kremlin, we'll start rebuilding.'

Although the RVC's fighting strength is unclear, the Kremlin was spooked by a cross-border incursion which Nikitin said involved a gunfight with two Russian armoured personnel carriers that tried to cut off the fighters as they headed back into Ukraine. 'We used antitank weapons,' he said.

Wagner mercenaries captured by the Ukrainians said they had witnessed the public execution of men who did not carry out orders. One soldier: 'Those who disobey are eliminated—and it's done publicly.'

One incident occurred during the assault on Soledar, he said. 'There are squadrons of liquidators... shelling began. One of the prisoners laid down and didn't cover his own men. The shelling stopped, he went back, and the boss shouted: 'Why didn't you go forward' And they killed him. The boss is killed if his team deserts.'

More information of what went on within the Wagner Group came from former mercenary commander Andrei Medvedev who fled from Russia into Norway by creeping past border watchtowers, dodging rifle fire and scrambling away from tracker dogs. He claimed that at around 2am on 13 January, he climbed two barbed wire fences guarding the 123-mile-long Russia-Norway border in the Arctic, and then ran across the frozen Pasvik River.

'I heard dogs barking behind me, the spotlights came on and shots were fired at me,' the former Wagner unit commander who had fought in Bakhmut said. 'I just ran towards the forest.'

This frozen wasteland is where Russia and Nato face off and is one of the most heavily guarded areas in the world. Watchtowers equipped with search-lights stud the border, and armed guards with dogs mount regular patrols.

Medvedev said that Russian border guards tracked his footprints as far as they could go before setting a dog after him.

'I ran towards the first lights of houses that I could see, maybe two or two-and-a-half kilometres away. I just ran and ran and ran,' he said. 'I was afraid to look around and to see a dog but as I understand it got confused and lost.'

When Medvedev reached the houses, he banged on the first door he came to and begged for help.

'I am so grateful to be here, so grateful to all the people who helped me,' he said.

A petty thief, Medvedev signed up after he had left prison, so his contract was only for four months, but when it expired he was told that he had to stay on. There were threats of extrajudicial reprisals if he refused to fight.

With the help of fighters in his unit, Medvedev escaped in November. He went into hiding in Russia and released a video in December exposing Wagner's brutality. But Medvedev also knew his luck would run out. Wagner operated a special unit called *Myod*—'honey' in English—he said, whose job it is to track down deserters and then mete out Wagner-style justice.

'I was in great danger,' he said in an interview with the French human rights website *gulagu.net*, from a migrant detention centre in Oslo. 'If they had captured me, they would have killed me, or even worse.'

To travel in Russia, he needed documentation, so he got a passport from a man who looked like him which got him through the final checkpoint at Titovka in the Murmansk region of north-western Russia.

In a video, he detailed his dramatic escape from Russia: 'When I was on the ice, I heard dogs barking, I turned around, I saw people with torches, about 150 metres away, running in my direction. I heard two shots, the bullets whizzed by.'

He said Wagner's commanders were indifferent to whether its troops lived or died, claiming as many as fifteen to twenty could be killed in just one day of combat.

'There was a risk they would grab me and kill me, shoot me or do something worse—like they did to Nuzhin, just death by sledgehammer,' he said.

And Medvedev knew what he was talking about. One of the men under his command had been Yevgeny Nuzhin.

Even so, there was no shortage of volunteers. One potential recruit was Mikhail Popkov, aka the 'Angarsk Maniac'. A policeman and a security guard in Siberia and the Russian far east, he raped and killed around eighty-three women between 1998 and 2010.

'I would not hesitate to join,' he told Russian TV on 15 January. 'Even though I have been in prison for ten years now, I think it would be quite easy to pick up.'

He believed his speciality—he had radio-electronics experience from his time as a Red Army conscript—would be in demand.

After border guards escorted Medvedev to Oslo, he applied for political asylum, saying he was willing to talk about the extrajudicial killings he had witnessed and to testify against Yevgeny Prigozhin, who he said was involved in the murders of thousands of Ukrainians and Russians.

'I fought in Bakhmut, commanding the first squad of the 4th platoon of the 7th assault detachment,' Medvedev said. The casualty rate was appalling.

'The prisoners are used as cannon fodder, like meat. I was given a group of convicts. In my platoon, only three out of thirty men survived,' he said. 'We were then given more prisoners, and many of those died too.'

Medvedev, who grew up in a Siberian orphanage and spent at least four years in prison for robbery, also claimed he knew of at least ten killings of Wagner soldiers who had disobeyed orders, and had witnessed some executions personally.

'The commanders took them to a shooting field and they were shot in front of everyone. Sometimes one guy was shot, sometimes they would be shot in pairs,' he said. 'It shocked us to the core, it was so fucked-up.'

Medvedev said he grew disaffected with Wagner after witnessing this. the killing and mistreatment of Russian prisoners who were brought to the front by Wagner. He also said that Wagner mercenaries had killed captured Ukrainian servicemen.

Russian dissident Vladimir Osechkin who interviewed Medvedev on *gulagu.net* said the video had been viewed more than a million times on YouTube. 'It destroyed the myth about Wagner being this wonderful organization that pays great salaries and that everyone is trying to get into,' Osechkin said. 'Within two to three days, all the prisoners knew about the video. They started to realize the truth.'

Soon after, Prigozhin's press office released a statement saying the recruitment of prisoners had stopped completely. He added that 'all obligations to those currently working with us will be fulfilled'. Instead, the defence ministry started recruiting in the penal colonies.

'Wagner's just sending people out sometimes without even any weapons. It's like the Red Army in the second world war,' a western official said. 'They all get killed, then the regular forces come in and mop up.' They were told 'keep advancing or get shot when you turn back'.

Although Prigozhin brushed aside the suggestion that he had political ambitions of his own in 2022, he may have received some encouragement in January 2023 when a member of the Russian parliament's defence committee suggested that Wagner veterans—even ex-convicts—could serve their country well by going into politics. And Prigozhin did acknowledge the comparison of him to Rasputin made by the *Financial Times*.

'I am not very familiar with the history of Rasputin, but as far as I know, an important quality of Rasputin is that he staunched the blood flow of the young prince with incantations,' Prigozhin's press service quoted him as saying. 'Unfortunately, I do not staunch blood flow. I bleed the enemies of our motherland. And not by incantations, but by direct contact with them.'

Dr Huseyn Aliyev, an expert on Russia and the conflict in Ukraine from Glasgow University, also acknowledged the political rise of Prigozhin, saying: 'He has been moving up the ranks by criticizing senior generals and building up his own reputation.'

Kremlin spokesman Dmitry Peskov denied that there was any infighting on the Russian side, after the Warner Group posted another video boasting the superiority of its troops. In a veiled rebuke of Prigozhin, the Kremlin defended the regular army under minister of defence Shoigu. 'The country must know and knows its heroes, both those who serve in the armed forces and the Wagner Group,' Peskov said. 'Everyone is working for a common cause: everyone is fighting for the motherland.'

But Prigozhin could not resist banging his own drum. In the video, which was reportedly filmed close to the front lines near Soledar, he said: 'They are probably the most experienced army in the world. They have aircraft—the pilots are heroes who are not afraid to die. There is artillery of all calibres, tanks, infantry fighting vehicles and assault units that have no equal.'

In an implied criticism of the Russian army, he went on to say: 'The most important thing in Wagner is the control system. The commanders consult with the fighters, and the leadership of the PMC consults with the commanders. If a decision is made, then all tasks will be completed, no one can retreat.'

Russia's top generals have been repeatedly criticized for not listening to its soldiers on the ground in Ukraine and for staying in Russia, unlike Prigozhin, who has gone to great lengths to appear beside his forces on the front lines. General Gerasimov came under particular criticism for failing to provide the Wagners with ammunition while their comrades were dying in Ukraine.

There was cause for resentment between the Wagners and the army, when regular troops blew up a tank and killed Wagner mercenaries in friendly fire, according to an intercepted phone call from the front lines. Ukraine's military intelligence published what it said was a conversation between a Russian soldier and his father where the soldier described the incident on the battlefield in Ukraine.

'We were shooting at them. We blew up their tank and a Tiger [armoured vehicle] before we realized it's our guys,' the unidentified soldier was heard saying.

The man also claimed that Wagner had sustained heavy casualties in Ukraine but the defence ministry 'is not evening counting them'. The soldier also told his father about an accident with Wagner mercenaries where officers shot mobilized soldiers, and discussed rumours such as that two-thirds of the Ukrainian army were Polish or Black.

When General Gerasimov issued orders that troops were to be clean-shaven on the battlefield to improve their 'day-to-day discipline', the bearded Moscow-backed Chechen leader Ramzan Kadyrov hit back, calling the order an insult to his Muslim troops. Prigozhin supported him, openly mocking Gerasimov.

'Female war correspondents go into the absolute heat of [war],' said Prigozhin. 'Jail inmates fight better than units of the Guards. Servicemen with broken spines pass on their military experience at training camps, moving around like robots. And a bunch of clowns try to teach fighters exhausted with hard military labour how many times they ought to shave—and what kind of perfume they must use to greet high commanders.'

He suggested that there should be 'a jail term of up to fifty years for the glamorization of the army'. He added: 'I take this opportunity to ask you,

Ramzan, to grow your beard twice as long, for yourself and for me.'

This rant came as Prigozhin addressed another bunch of convicts in a propaganda video. They were ostensibly being discharged after serving six months in the war zone. They were apparently pardoned for their convictions under a secret decree from Putin. The Kremlin defended the practice, saying convicts were being given amnesty 'in strict adherence with Russian law'. Under the Russian constitution, only the president can issue pardons and critics pointed to the fact the Kremlin has not published such decrees since 2020.

'I have come to say thank you for what you have done, from myself... and from the Motherland,' said Prigozhin. 'You have gone through six months of hard warfare. Neither your grandfathers, nor great-grandfathers, were involved in such battles [in World War II]. Those who were at Soledar know that even Stalingrad pales in comparison, so thank you. The Motherland and our people are in debt to you. I treat the history of our ancestors with respect, but here are videos I made from a car window when approaching Soledar.'

Another propaganda opportunity came when war correspondent for the Russian online news site Readovka, Anastasia Yelsukova, suffered a knee injury after being hit by shell shrapnel, she was given first aid by members of the Wagner Group before being evacuated by helicopter and undergoing knee surgery.

'We believe that she will soon return to duty and will shoot more than one excellent report from the front line—she is a fearless person,' Readovka said in a statement.

Prigozhin wanted to show his caring side too when he was shown in the video watching one of his men with a spine injury use bionic legs to walk at one of Moscow's top private hospitals. 'Nobody gets left behind, no matter how badly injured,' he said. This seemed to be in response to reports from Bakhmut that said Wagner commanders were throwing their men forward with little care for their safety and were prepared to leave the dead and injured behind.

12

WAGNEROVCIS ON STEROIDS

On 29 January, Prigozhin said that Wagner had captured the strategic village of Blagodatnoe, this was denied by the Ukrainians who said the fighting there was ongoing. Meanwhile, it was reported that Wagner were developing 'swarm drones' with China. A swarm network is one in which large numbers of aerial robots directed by artificial intelligence storm one common goal together.

An intelligence report said: 'The group is attempting to develop a swarm platform for co-ordinated autonomous drone orchestration using the 2,500 delivered recently from China. The communications channel between the Wagnerites and the Chinese Communist Party is in two cloaked networks, one in Russia and one in China. That network is responsible for the clandestine shipments of war materials being used against Ukraine, regardless of how much the Chinese deny it.'

And deny it they did. Leaked US intelligence documents said that China 'had not sent [Wagner] any weapons, not even for testing, and had no contact with [Wagner] regarding weapons deliveries' after a request had been made in early 2023. However, China sent £2-million-worth of helmets and tried to evade sanctions by claiming they were for gaming.

Belarus and Syria had provided arms. The US report said Belarus 'already delivered 50 per cent of unspecified weapons promised' by early January and offered to send Wagner 300,000 VOG-17 grenade launcher rounds. Wagner also bought six SPG-9 grenade launchers and 180 grenades in Syria.

Wagner PMC now reached for drugs, copying Hitler whose Nazi troops had been high on methamphetamine when crossing the Ardennes to circumvent the Maginot Line in its Blitzkrieg on France.

In a Wagner video, shot at a special training ground for elite fighters, he could be heard boasting he is turning those criminals into bloodthirsty killing machines—or cannibals—before deploying them against Ukraine. He said: 'This is a supplementary training base for our fighters. The primary training is in Molkino, and here experienced fighters are given additional training in their specialities. 'So they raise young eagles there [in Molkino]. And here they make real cannibals.'

He slammed those who mock him for running a ragtag army of criminals, saying those who 'were once in the army' or 'once wore the shoulder straps of a general' were in the 'distant past'.

'Live in the present,' he said. '[This is] a war unlike anything that has happened, in the previous century or this one—except World War II.'

His scheme, he said, was a way that convicts could redeem themselves and he called on Russian lawmakers to slap a five-year prison sentence on anyone publishing 'negative information' about his Russian war volunteers. The Institute for the Study of War certainly had some 'negative information'. It reported that Wagner forces had sustained more than 4,100 dead and ten thousand wounded, including over one thousand killed between late November and early December near Bakhmut.

Ukrainian soldiers revealed the truth that Wagner mercenaries were pumped full of drugs before they went into battle. 'They're climbing above the corpse of their friends, stepping on them,' said one. 'It looks like it's very, very likely that they are getting some drugs before attack.'

He remembered one particularly horrendous battle in which he and nineteen comrades fought as two hundred Russians stormed their positions for ten hours in what was essentially a suicide mission.

'And it wasn't like just waves, it was uninterrupted. So it was just like they didn't stop coming'. Ukrainians' guns became so hot they had to keep changing them. The assault was all the more terrifying as, despite firing endless rounds of ammunition, the invaders wouldn't lie down and die.

He said: 'Our machine gunner was almost getting crazy, because he was shooting at them. And he said, I know I shot him, but he doesn't fall. And then after some time, when he maybe bleeds out, so he just falls down.' The soldier said it was like a scene from a zombie movie.

Prigozhin denied the allegations of drug abuse. Wagner, he claimed, demurely on this occasion, was an 'exemplary military organization that complies with all the necessary laws and rules of modern wars.' Ukrainian soldier Vitalii Ovcharenko said he'd seen 'syringes on Russian positions several times'.

On 4 February Igor Mangushev, Prigozhin's political strategist, was shot in the back of the head at a checkpoint in Kadiivka in the Luhansk Oblast. It was a symbolic hit. He claimed to have invented the Z symbol seen painted on Russian military vehicles. There is no Z in the Cyrillic alphabet. The equivalent is З (Ze).

A proponent of the war, he had given a speech justifying it while holding aloft a skull that he claimed belonged to a Ukrainian soldier killed during the siege of Mariupol. 'We're alive and this guy is already dead,' he said. 'Let him burn in hell. He wasn't lucky. We'll make a goblet out of his skull.... Ukraine must be de-Ukrainized. The Russian lands of Novorossiya must be returned back. He had gone on: 'We are not at war with people of blood and flesh. We are at war with an idea—Ukraine as an anti-Russian state. This is the tragedy of

Ukrainian soldiers. We don't care how many we have to kill.' Mangushev died of his wounds four days after the incident. Mark Galeotti drily noted: 'I think we can safely describe this as a hit.'

As Bakhmut remained elusive, Prigozhin tried to distract attention. Sitting in the cockpit of an SU-24 fighter-bomber, claiming he had just flown a night sortie over the town in the eastern Donbas region, Prigozhin challenged Zelensky to a dogfight.

'Volodymyr Oleksandrovych [Zelensky], we have landed. We have bombed Bakhmut,' he said. 'I will fly a MiG-29. If you so desire, let's meet in the skies. If you win, you take Artemovsk [Bakhmut's Soviet-era name]. If not, we advance till the [River] Dnipro.'

The Ukrainian response was to release a video of its own. Drone footage showed four Wagner dragging their badly wounded commander away from the battlefield through a landscape of bombed-out houses. They then dump him next to a barn. A second video appears to show three men then hitting him repeatedly with shovels. It was unclear whether the injured commander survived.

Meanwhile, the Wagner machine pumped out more information to suggest that no matter how bad the crime, however dangerous the individual, criminals would genuinely be released at the end of their contract and with disregard for the concern of the Russian population. Thus, after six-months service, convicted thief and murderer, Anatoly Salmin returned to the town of Pikalevo, 120 miles outside St Petersburg.

'We started seeing him in town a few weeks ago,' said one local resident who had known Salmin. 'He is a dangerous man, we all know what he did to his friend. I told my kids not to run around alone in the coming days. It wasn't just what he did to his friend, he stole from people, got in many fights and was harassing girls. He drank a lot, used drugs and was violent.

'What kind of hero is he?... We don't want such people back in Pikalevo.'

Salmin was recruited into Wagner while serving a sentence for theft. But in 2011 he was convicted of murder. In the court's description of the killing, Salmin and a friend got drunk while fishing at a local quarry and began to argue. Then Salmin grabbed a rock and hit his friend on the head twice. As the man continued to flail, Salmin held his friend's head underwater until he stopped moving.

'This is a small fraction of the crimes he committed,' another acquaintance said in an interview with BBC Russian shortly after Salmin's release was discovered. 'There are people who are still very afraid that he will return to our city. And I am very afraid that he will do something to these people. Salmin is a terrible person.'

Another who knew him said: 'We have known each other for many years.

He is not a pleasant person, in fact he is really dangerous. He is unpredictable. And he is back in town.' Many feared that those being discharged could be out to settle scores when they returned home.

In 2014, Kirill Neglin of Segezha in Karelia was sentenced to twelve years in prison on counts of drug dealing and domestic abuse. After a bout of heavy drinking, he repeatedly hit and kicked his wife, terrorizing her both at home and then followed her to their dacha where she said she silently endured another attack because she feared for their children's lives.

After she testified against him, Neglin issued a threat in court. 'She won't live long,' he said, according to a court transcript. 'Whatever sentence the court gives, that's how long she has left to live.'

Court records also showed that while he was in prison, he was sued by his own mother to return a loan for an apartment in Segezha. Social media from 2014, the year before Neglin was sentenced, showed he regularly posted ultra-patriotic memes, including some that suggested firing nuclear weapons at the US. In the video published by Wagner-affiliated media, Neglin offered bromides about patriotism and family values.

'You're not fighting here for just anything, you're fighting for your children,' he said. 'And naturally for your families, for money, and as for your homeland, that follows… So, guys, take care of yourselves, take care of those close to you.'

In Transbaikalia, in south-east Russia, relatives of one convicted murderer killed in Ukraine faced opposition in organizing his funeral, local media said. Village leader, Alena Kogodeeva, said: 'The young man was convicted of murder. It was only two or three years ago, people remember it… are we going to make heroes out of killers now?'

For others, the outcome was not quite so clear. In the video captioned 'video from the court for treason', published by the *Grey Zone* Telegram channel which was linked to Wagner, a man identifies himself as forty-four-year-old Dmitry Yakushchenko. Facing the camera in a seated position, Yakushchenko had his hands taped to a block.

'I am Dmitry Yakushchenko, born in 1978, in Crimea,' he said. 'I went to the front in the ranks of the Wagner PMC. At the front, I realized this was not my war…

'Today I was in the streets of the city of Dnipro where I got hit on the head and lost consciousness, I woke up in this room and was told I would be tried. I was planning on finding some loophole, just, as they say, to run away.'

Reports in Russia say that Yakushchenko had been convicted of murder and robbery in Crimea and sentenced to nineteen years. When Russia annexed Crimea he was transferred to a jail in Engels in Russia, where he had been released to fight in Ukraine.

After this, the person behind him wearing camouflage clothing raised the sledgehammer and appeared to swing it into his head. The video was blurred at this point, but a loud noise can be heard, and Yakushchenko collapsed to the floor. The man swung the sledgehammer twice more. A caption then appeared on the video, saying: 'The court session is declared closed.'

Later in a video on the popular news Telegram channel *Ostorozhno Novosti* linked to Wagner PMC, Yakushchenko appears alive, saying: 'In Wagner PMC everyone has the right to correct their mistakes. When I was captured, I said a lot of different shit and I'm still ashamed, but it was the only way to survive. Upon return from captivity, I brought lots of valuable information that saved the lives of many guys, so I was forgiven, for which I am very grateful.'

The same video was also posted on the official Telegram account of Prigozhin's press service with the accompanying text saying: 'Dmitry Yakushchenko is a good fellow.'

Prigozhin later confirmed that Dmitry Yakushchenko had been pardoned and the two men appeared together. 'This is to answer your question, whether he was actually killed with a sledgehammer,' Prigozhin said.

13

WINGS CLIPPED

Prigozhin himself admitted on 11 February that Bakhmut was proving harder to occupy than he had been promising.

'If we need to reach the Dnipro river, that'll take three years,' he said in an interview with Semyon Pegov, a pro-war military blogger.

'If we want to close down the whole of the DPR and LPR, then we need to work for at least one-and-a-half to two years,' he said, referring to the Donetsk and Luhansk regions of Donbas which Russia had annexed in 2022.

He still claimed that Wagner troops were making gradual progress in Bakhmut, but acknowledged that Russian soldiers had not yet been able to capture it in some of the fiercest fighting since the start of the war.

'It is probably too early to say that we are close. There are many roads out and fewer roads in. Ukrainian troops are well trained and, like any large city, it is impossible to capture it from head-on. We are managing very well. First, we have to quietly take [Bakhmut] and then we can say loud and clear that we have taken it,' Prigozhin said.

He went on to say that he didn't care if Wagner fighters 'like the Third Reich', or had 'gang tattoos', saying the only thing that mattered was 'how you treat your brothers in arms' and carry yourself in battle. In the interview, he also denied using prisoners as cannon fodder.

On 12 February, Prigozhin announced that Wagner had taken the village of Krasna Hora at the northern end of the city of Bakhmut. Although the Wagner Group were making progress, a turning point had been reached.

As he had failed to take Bakhmut, Moscow began to tighten the noose against the Wagner loudmouth, however. The Kremlin sent out an order to Russian propagandists to stop giving them a good press. Sergei Markov said he had received an order directly from 'the leadership' because the Wagner chief was not delivering.

The change in support for Prigozhin was picked up. Stories started to emerge from the middle of February that Putin was fearful that the Wagner Group was getting took powerful and ordered it to scale down its operations. Prigozhin had been openly critical, even abusive to senior military figures in the regular forces. This was beginning to be seen as a slight on Putin himself now that *Vagnerovci*-style fighting appeared to make no difference to Russia's invasion.

On the ground, things were going from bad to worse for Prigozhin. A unit of five thousand Wagner men was practically wiped out in an attempt to take the coal-mining town of Vuhledar in the Donetsk region in one of the heaviest losses since the start of the Ukraine invasion. Former FSB officer and DPR defence minister, Igor Girkin, said they were killed 'like turkeys in a shooting range', and added: 'Some of them are complete cretins—all the mistakes that were made before were repeated.'

On 14 February, after over six months of fighting, Prigozhin conceded: 'Bakhmut will not be taken tomorrow, because there is heavy resistance and grinding, the meat grinder is working. We will not be celebrating in the near future.' Ukraine, he said, was 'becoming more active, pulling up more and more new reserves'.

Two fighters captured by Ukraine confirmed the devastating losses Wagner had sustained. Recalling his first assault near the village of Bilohorivka in Luhansk, one said: 'There were ninety of us. Sixty died in that first assault, killed by mortar fire. A handful remained wounded.'

The other fighter said he was involved in a push for Lysychansk on the Luhansk-Donetsk border. 'The first steps into the forest were difficult because of all the landmines spread out. Out of ten guys, seven were killed immediately,' he said.

The fighting went on for five days. 'There is no feeling attached to it. Just wave after wave.' he said. 'Four hundred [Wagner fighters] were brought there, and then more and more, all the time.'

Using such tactics meant that some of Wagner's assault units had lost eighty per cent of their strength, according to Ukraine's deputy defence minister Hanna Maliar. The US Institute for the Study of War also said that Ukraine's defence had 'degraded significant Russian forces,' including units from the Wagner Group.

Prigozhin took to Telegram to warn Moscow of Wagner's shortage of ammunition and issued a plea for more resources after soldiers had been reduced to engaging in hand-to-hand combat with shovels due to the scarcity of weapons and bullets.

'If Wagner retreats from Bakhmut now, the whole front will collapse,' he said in a four-minute video. 'The situation will not be sweet for all military formations protecting Russian interests. If we retreat, then we will go down in history forever as people who have taken the main step towards losing the war. This is exactly the problem with ammunition hunger.'

But it started to look like an excuse. Significantly, the Kremlin issued a directive to local media not to praise General Surovikin, Prigozhin's ally in the Russian army, and only mention him in 'neutral' terms, a document leaked by former Russian MP Alexander Nevzorov showed. Prigozhin was not to be quoted and his recruitment of prisoners was not to be reported on, say the instructions.

Unable to recruit more convicts from the GULAG, Prigozhin's wings were being clipped by Ukraine forces and the Kremlin. The torrential attrition rate of the Wagner army of drugged convicts meant that the troops under his command were dwindling fast in Bakhmut. Shoigu's ministry of defence had taken over Wagner's role of recruiting inmates, effectively depriving the group of its main source of manpower in Ukraine.

'The number of Wagner units will decrease, and we will also not be able to carry out the scope of tasks that we would like to,' Prigozhin told a group of pro-war bloggers and state journalists gathered at an army barracks in eastern Ukraine on 15 February. In a thinly veiled criticism of the Russian ministry of defence, he said 'horrendous military bureaucracy' had prevented Wagner from taking Bakhmut by the New Year.

'Other units are not showing the activity that they should be. If there were three to five groups like Wagner, we would already be dipping our feet in the Dnipro river,' he said.

Wagner was permitted to recruit ordinary citizens to make up the deficit, however, and Prigozhin set up recruitment centres at sports clubs in forty-two cities across Russia: mercenaries apparently went to schools to give 'career talks' to kids. A photograph appeared on social media showing a burly man, masked in a black balaclava and clad in military apparel, addressing a room full of children.

The picture was posted by Jason Jay Smart, a special correspondent at *Kyiv Post*, who claimed Russian students were being encouraged to fight against Ukraine. The Twitter post read: 'Russian students' Spring Break. Now Russian high school students get visits from Wagner Group, where ski-masked, armed men regale them with stories of how they can "defend the Motherland" by joining up.' Questionnaires entitled 'Application for a Young Warrior' were given out to collect the contact details of interested pupils.'

Until YouTube removed some, Wagner-recruitment videos showed dancing balaclava-clad mercenaries chanting the lyrics: 'War is our element / Come on, Russia, get up / Come on Russia / Come on, Wagner play / It's the breath of Armageddon / This is the birth of a new country / Russia, rise under the holy banners / Holy banners of holy war.'

In another video, a former prisoner describes how joining the 'brotherhood' led to 'exciting games' on the battlefields of Ukraine: 'Right now, there is brotherhood. Their eyes are burning with excitement, they want to fight. They cleanse themselves through this and get complete absolution for themselves. No drugs, no alcohol, no violence against civilians or women. Not even to prisoners, just to hand them over. Excitement. It was interesting, like a game—life, death, walking on a razor's edge.'

The footage, viewed over 3.5 million times, was hosted on the YouTube channel of *Komsomolskaya Pravda* (KP), the biggest Russian tabloid newspaper owned by Sergei Rudnov, sanctioned by the UK government. Two 'war correspondents' who regularly post videos for KP, Alexander Kots and Dmitry Steshin, had also been sanctioned by the UK government, yet their content remained freely available on YouTube.

One of the most popular pro-Wagner music videos, 'Summer and Crossbows', was written by a war blogger and rapper, Akim Apachev. It has had 2.4 million views, while another version of the song has had more than four million. It began with a clipped English voice, taken from a western news report, saying: 'The Russian mercenary group Wagner is recruiting and is making it known.'

Then a beat rises as men brandishing weapons in the desert appear. 'Summer and Crossbows, Wagner are on their way,' the rap track blasts out over a map of the Central African Republic. The shoulder of a fighter bears a Wagner badge emblazoned with a red-and-black skull; its slogan: 'You can't kill the dead.' 'I danced in Donbas, Benghazi, Palmyra,' the song continued—sites of alleged atrocities committed by Wagner forces.

Russian singer Vika Tsyganova released a video clip for the song 'Wagner' on her YouTube channel, dedicating it to the 'defenders of our Fatherland'. In a new release called 'Give Them Shells', she implored the Russian public to donate towards the war effort, giving bank details for donations and promising the funds would only go to soldiers fighting in hotspots—largely Wagner troops currently dying in great numbers around Bakhmut.

In a lateral move, Wagner also put an ad on a Telegram porn channel, showing a blonde woman with red lipstick rolling a large lollipop around in her mouth.

'We're the most bad-ass private army in the world. We're hiring in all regions of Russia,' a woman's voice can be heard saying. 'Don't jerk off, go to work for PMC Wagner.' Then the Wagner's phone number popped up.

The ad was shown in regions outside Moscow. It was endorsed by Prigozhin who said in a statement: 'Placing Wagner's ads on porn websites is an excellent idea of our marketing specialists. I fully agree with them and what the ad says: "Go to war, stop jerking off." Who does not agree with this argument?'

Feeling the adverse wind from Moscow, Prigozhin tried to gain public support from Russia's right-wing commentariat. Backing his appeal for more ammunition, Prigozhin said he would risk arrest to get his fighters more shells and bullets. A graphic clip, posted by a Telegram account linked to Wagner, showed hundreds of dead bodies—allegedly of Wagner fighters—to show the human cost of the ammunition shortage.

'We're losing our fighters every day: it would be half as much if the military officials were to supply us with weapons and ammunition on time,' an unidentified man in a hazmat suit said in the video. 'Let us wage this war. Let us defend our country.'

The video showed men in camouflage who called themselves Wagner's artillery. They said: 'We're sure that you have ammunition somewhere at the warehouses. We badly need it,' the unidentified men said. 'We would greatly appreciate it if you could assist us and help deliver that ammunition.'

Notably, the tone of the video was far more respectful than a similar appeal last autumn in which alleged Wagner fighters were heard calling General Valery Gerasimov, head of the Russian general staff, a 'faggot' for chronic delays in supplies to the front.

Doors were closing one by one. Prigozhin said he had recently been able to secure some mortars and anti-tank rounds from unofficial sources, including a Chechen commander. 'As far as regular supplies go, I have knocked on the door of every office in Moscow I know and I will try to do that until the lads get all they need,' he said. He added he would continue 'even if they handcuff me at one of those offices and jail me for 'discrediting the armed forces',' in a reference to Russia's war censorship law that criminalizes criticism of the invasion. 'Despite the blockade of ammunition, despite heavy losses and bloody battles, the guys completely occupied the entire territory of Paraskoviivka,' he said. But they had paid a bloody price. The MoD estimated that there had been a casualty rate of fifty per cent among his prison recruits, while the White House said that Wagner had suffered more than thirty-thousand casualties in Ukraine, with ninety per cent of its recruits killed since December being convicts.

Former FSB officer Girkin supported Prigozhin. 'Unless supplies for Wagner improve, we can safely forget about seizing Bakhmut any time soon or ever,' he said on his Telegram channel.

Girkin mockingly asked his supporters to donate money to the Wagner boss so that he could buy shovels to dig trenches or graves: 'He can't afford them himself.'

For Prigozhin, the mines in Bakhmut and Soledar were only some of the European targets of Wagner. But there were rumblings that his African empire was under pressure. 'There are stories going around that the guys haven't been paid in Mali and won't leave barracks,' a British mercenary said. 'They feel exposed because of the concentration of effort on Ukraine—accommodation and flights have suffered.'

In response to an *FT* article about Wagner activities in Africa, including the killings and propaganda, he said the feature was largely correct but not where it said he was making large profits. 'The *Financial Times*, if you don't know, this is a British publication, published an article about the Wagner PMC, where much seems to be true,' he wrote. 'Except for the last part, where they talk about my financial enrichment.'

'I consider any sanctions against me, PMC Wagner, as well as any legal entities and individuals of the Russian Federation, to be absolutely illegal,' he ranted on Concord's Telegram channel. 'I spit and I will spit on any sanctions.'

He accused unnamed officials of 'directly working for the enemy' in an emotional and occasionally foul-mouthed tirade of threats. 'The shit is boiling, blood is churning but the question of ammunition supply is still not resolved,' he said. 'I know exactly where the warehouses are, the number of the store, the number of the boxes. But I'm unable to solve this problem despite all my connections and contacts.'

Astonishingly, he admitted candidly that people he asked for help 'raise their eyebrows and point upwards with a finger and say, "You know, Yevgeny Viktorovich, you have complicated relations there... so you have to go and apologize and obey, and then your fighters will get ammunition".'

'Apologize to who? Obey who?' he ranted. 'Those who interfere with us trying to win this war are absolutely, directly working for the enemy.'

The officials—that is minister of defence Shoigu—who were denying his men ammunition were 'eating breakfast, lunch and dinner off golden plates' and sending their relatives on holiday to Dubai, a popular destination for the Russian elite. However, this appeared to be a jab at Sergei Shoigu, the Russian ministry of defence, whose daughter Ksenia was photographed enjoying New Year celebrations there. He also said that there was never a problem with ammunition supply when General Surovikin commanded the Russian forces in Ukraine.

He had one more reliable ally left in the army, he thought. When General Apti Alaudinov, the commander of the Chechen Akhmat special forces unit, survived an assassination attempt, Prigozhin presented him with a Wagner sledgehammer. But the symbolic gift had lost some of its shine without military success.

'The chief of general staff and the defence minister give out orders left and right not only to not give ammunition to PMC Wagner, but also to not help it with air transport,' Prigozhin said in a voice message shared by his press service. 'There is just direct opposition going on, which is nothing less than an attempt to destroy Wagner. This can be equated to high treason in the very moment when Wagner is fighting for Bakhmut, losing hundreds of its fighters every day.'

14

EASTERN UKRAINE

Captured Wagner Group fighters continued to complain that they were thrown into battle as worthless cannon fodder ahead of the regular Russian army. In a secret location, the Ukrainian authorities allowed journalists to interview two men who wore balaclavas to protect their anonymity in case they were killed if they were ever released. The Ukrainians also asked the journalists to pixelate their eyes to avoid them being identified by Wagner Group hit squads in the future.

Thirty-two-year-old Viktor, a married father-of-two and former builder from the Stavropolsky region in Kavkaz, southeast Russia, was serving twenty years for murder when Prigozhin helicoptered into his penal colony.

'I met Yevgeny Prigozhin and in total two hundred of us agreed to join Wagner Group in exchange for a fresh start, money and I would be able to get a job after leaving Ukraine,' he said. 'With a criminal record, I would not get a job and I felt I had no choice, even though it took a week for me to decide to join Wagner. I had killed a man and was in the ninth year of my sentence. He was in a group of Muslims, Chechens, in a club and a fight with knives started. I killed him.'

But they were lied to.

'We were told other countries were involved in the war in Ukraine, including Britain and that we were defending Russia against foreign terrorists,' he said. 'We were told we would not be fighting civilians, but fascists and soldiers from other countries.'

After signing up in September last year he was taken by bus to Rostov, close to Ukraine and then to Luhansk, in Donbas, inside Ukraine, with two hundred others from his prison. They underwent six weeks of tough training with assault rifles, machine guns, mines, rocket-propelled grenades and some with sniper rifles. After training they were sent into battle in assault squads, quickly realising they were being lied to.

'I was nervous, yes. I did not know where I would be sent to and even now my family do not know I joined the Wagner Group,' he said. 'We'd be sent in groups of fifteen against what they said were just ten Ukrainian soldiers, then we'd discover there were up to forty Ukrainians. In the first battle a sniper was shooting, injuring our men, then he killed two. It was my first time and I saw someone lose a leg.'

Even Viktor's experience in one of Russia's strict regime penal colonies with their daily knife fights, beating and murders did not prepare him for war.

'It was very frightening,' he said. 'I saw arms and legs being shot off in battles. It was horrible and shocking. More than a thousand of us were killed.'

During his three-and-a-half months with the Wagner Group, he fought in four battles and said killed Ukrainian soldiers, but he did not know how many. Then he was injured in the back and the neck by shrapnel.

'I was not beaten and the Ukrainians treated me well. I have nothing against them,' he said. He had not been relieved to be captured, because when he joined the recruits were shown a video that said if they got captured they would be killed.

'But that did not happen. Now I don't know what will happen to me,' he said. 'Look, I did not start this war and I am sorry that Russia did. War is bad because civilians are killed but I didn't do that. Maybe I will be released back to Russia.'

Twenty-six-year-old car mechanic Anatoliy, married with a child from Samara, central Russia, had eighteen months left of his three-and-a-half-year sentence when Prigozhin flew in.

'I met him,' Anatoliy said. 'I signed up for Wagner and everyone makes his own decisions. I had no idea where I was going—but I understood we would fight in Ukraine.'

He was proud of being in the Wagner Group rather than the regular army.

'We were doing full-scale attacks and I was in five big battles and Wagner Group was always ahead of the Army,' he said, but he soon learnt that they were outclassed by the Ukrainian forces, especially in terms of tactics.

'First, a sniper killed ten of my fellow troops,' he said. 'Another guy was injured and I gave him first aid. Eventually, I was alone, pinned down by Ukrainian forces. Wagner Group sent in another detachment of ten men and the sniper killed five of them. Eventually, I was lying there with no more ammunition, a Ukrainian soldier standing above me with a machine gun. He fired into the ground near my legs as a warning. I was then taken prisoner unharmed.'

Prigozhin continued to complain about the shortage of ammunition. He appeared on the Telegram messaging app next to a pile of some fifty bodies, some wearing Russian red tactical armbands, stacked up in the snow outside Donetsk.

'These are the guys who died yesterday due to the so-called ammunition hunger,' he said, adding that Wagner losses outside Bakhmut were five times higher than they would have been with sufficient ammunition.

'I have placed a photograph below, it is one of the places for the bodies of those who were killed yesterday,' Prigozhin said in an audio clip shared alongside the picture. 'The reason was from so-called 'shell hunger'.'

He urged Russians to use social media to put pressure on the regular army to share its ammunition with Wagner.

'Who is to blame for the fact that they died?' Prigozhin continued. 'Those who should have decided to supply us with enough ammunition are to blame. The final signature must be put either by Gerasimov or Shoigu. Neither of them wants to make a decision.'

Prigozhin was not always so worried about the fate of his men. In one Telegram he sat on a bench in a darkened room, faced the camera and said: 'The war is only work, frontline work. When prisoners get an arm or a leg torn off in battle, they're still happy, they laugh quite merrily. Maybe they've discovered something in this hardship.'

Few of his men got the chance to say if they agreed. Western sources said that wounded Russians were three times more likely to die on the front line than Ukrainian troops and the losses in the mercenary outfit were thought to be high because their ill-equipped and ill-trained fighters have been used as 'human waves' in a bid to overwhelm defensive positions in and around Bakhmut simply mown down by Ukrainian troops, whose own life expectancy on the front line was just four hours. At Bakhmut and Marinka near Donetsk, the Russians were adopting the tactic of total destruction, deliberately razing the ruins, blasting walls that still stand, to 'destroy all cover, regardless of whether it is a civilian shelter or a military facility,' the chief of police said. 'They destroy everything because, with their tactics, they cannot defeat our troops, and resort to the destruction of all living things.'

Prigozhin also released a spreadsheet that he claimed showed that his units were receiving fewer shells than before.

In a rally on 22 February to mark the first anniversary of the 'special military operation' in the Ukraine, Putin called for unity in the fight against the West. But people livestreaming the 'festive event' at Luzhnini stadium, capacity of 200,000, began to share hashtag #GiveWagnerShells.

Russia's defence ministry issued a statement saying: 'All requests for ammunition for assault units are met as soon as possible.' It denounced as 'absolutely false' reports of shortages.

'Attempts to create a split within the close mechanism of interaction and support between units of the Russian [fighting] groups are counterproductive and work solely to the benefit of the enemy,' the statement read.

It was clear Prigozhin's star was falling, the more he asked the powerless Russian population to intervene on his behalf. Exiled Russian rights activist Vladimir Osechkin believed that Prigozhin's days were numbered.

'He has transformed into a monkey with a grenade from whom you can expect anything,' he said. 'He has lots of enemies and it is clear that he is at risk and in danger. There is no longer any safe place for Prigozhin in Russia. His life is worth nothing and he understands this.' Osechkin said Prigozhin's rows with defence officials were a desperate attempt to remain in the limelight and make himself too high-profile for assassination. About two dozen Russian officials and businessmen had died under mysterious circumstances since the start of the war, with some of the deaths believed to be linked to struggles for influence or power. 'Prigozhin will be liquidated according to the rules of the system just as soon as he fades from the public eye,' Osechkin said. 'He has ceased to become a solution and has become a problem.'

Bakhmut might have saved him. But he still could not conquer the town as the Ukrainians hung on. A Ukrainian soldier named Zhenya, the driver of a BMP-2 fighting vehicle, said: 'We were blasting out a Wagner position in houses at just eighty metres range with our 30mm three days ago. I could easily see them as we closed with them. It was a good job. They were flying everywhere.' He added: 'Wish me happy birthday. I am 21 today.'

Ukrainian soldiers told *The Times* how the mercenaries advanced regardless of casualties, unlike regular Russian forces.

'I can drop my mortar rounds straight into a concentration of Wagner fighters and still the rest keep coming,' said thirty-eight-year-old Riko, a team commander. 'If I drop rounds among regular Russian troops usually they scatter, then fall back dragging their casualties with them. Not so the convicts.'

At the end of February, US intelligence reports suggest the Wagner Group has suffered more than thirty-thousand casualties, most of them convicts, since the invasion began a year ago, with nine thousand of those killed in action. Half are believed to have died since mid-December when fighting intensified around Bakhmut and Prigozhin announced that they had taken the village of Yahidne on the outskirts and Berkhivka further to the north, though the Ukrainians said that the Russian offensives there were unsuccessful.

Ostensibly Moscow still gave Wagner some support, making it a criminal offence punishable by up to 15 years in prison to criticise paramilitary organizations such as the Wagner Group that are fighting for Russia in Ukraine. Before it was only illegal to discredit or spread 'fake news' about Russia's armed forces, not paramilitary groups—a loophole for the army's own trolls to take potshots at Wagner.

In desperation, Prigozhin started to lie about Bakhmut as Russian convicts were being slaughtered in the fight. On 2 March, Prigozhin posted a video on Telegram showing uniformed men lifting a Wagner banner on top of a heavily damaged building. One of the men was shown dancing and holding a guitar as he was, presumably, a 'musician'. Prigozhin was quoted by his press service as saying: 'The lads are mucking about, shooting home video. They brought this from Bakhmut this morning, practically the centre of the city.'

The video was geolocated to the east of Bakhmut, about 1.2 miles from the city centre, where Wagner fighters had been for a while.

The following day, Prigozhin could be seen standing on a rooftop, saying: 'Units of the private military company Wagner have practically surrounded Bakhmut. Only one route out is left. The pincers are closing.'

'If earlier we were fighting against the professional army, we now increasingly see old people and children,' Prigozhin said. 'They are fighting, but their life expectancy in Bakhmut is now very short, one day or two... give them a chance to leave the city,' he told Zelensky.

The video then showed an old man and two younger men who asked Zelensky to let them leave. But Zelensky had no intention of giving up despite the World War I-style slaughter that was going on in the city.

One injured Ukrainian who had been evacuated from the town after three days had seen four of his six-man squad killed. Only twenty-one of the fifty-two originally in his unit remained alive.

'When the Russian artillery was on us, it was hell,' he said. 'They are destroying us. I have seen more than fifty comrades killed with my own eyes. I have picked up the pieces of ten of my friends.'

A battalion of five hundred men was down to just 150. 'When you go out to the position, it's not even a fifty-fifty chance that you'll come out of there [alive],' said one Ukrainian soldier. 'It's more like thirty-seventy.'

Another video posted on Telegram by the Wagner Group showed Ukrainian soldiers trying to take aim from a trench before ducking for shelter.

'The video from the servants of the Kyiv regime clearly shows that they cannot even stick their heads out of the trench,' said the Wagner Group. 'The density of fire is high, our units are pressing from all sides.'

In the video, Prigozhin was shown clad in full military gear, saying: 'We are sending another shipment of Ukrainian army fighters home. They fought bravely and perished. That's why the latest truck will take them back to their Motherland.' The footage showed men in uniform nailing wooden coffins shut and loading them onto a truck.

Was there a shortage of ammunition. The Ukrainians noticed no shortage among their opponents. But Prigozhin continued to complain about an 'ammunition famine'.

'For now, we are trying to figure out the reason: Is it just ordinary bureaucracy or a betrayal,' he said on the Wagner Orchestra Telegram channel used for giving regular press updates. Prigozhin said his troops were worried Moscow wanted to set them up as possible scapegoats if Russia lost the war.

'If we step back, then we will go down in history forever as the people who took the main step to lose the war,' he said. 'And this is precisely the problem with that same shell hunger. This is not my opinion, but ordinary fighters'. What if they [the Russian authorities] want to set us up, saying that we are scoundrels, and that's why they don't give us ammunition, they don't give us weapons, and they don't let us replenish our personnel, including from among the imprisoned people?'

He also complained that the defence ministry wanted to exert more control over the Wagners, saying this was undermining morale. And he warned that if the Wagner Group was forced to retreat, the entire Russian attack would crumble.

'It will fall apart up to the Russian borders, and maybe even further,' he said, grumbling that his representative had been denied access to the headquarters of Russia's 'special military operation' in Ukraine.

15

BOMBING NOTICE

As a video of a Ukrainian prisoner of war being shot and killed in cold blood after saying 'glory to Ukraine' appeared on social media, Prigozhin was seen signing a case of the local champagne as it was being loaded onto a truck. Wagner had captured the Bakhmut Champagne Winery in the eastern part of the city in December and he was sending a truckload of Champagne made in Bakhmut to Ukrainian women to mark International Women's Day, he said, in a social media stunt on his personal press service on the Telegram messaging app.

Sergei Shoigu spoke up, ostensibly in a conciliatory gesture, saying that capturing Bakhmut 'will allow for further offensive operations deep into the defence lines of the Ukrainian armed forces'. In response, Prigozhin said he had 'not seen him in Bakhmut'. The Russian ministry of defence then released a video of a rare visit to Ukraine by Shoigu.

Prigozhin then backtracked in a rare sign of humility to say that 'Wagner units have taken all the eastern part of Bakhmut, all that's east of the Bakhmutka river' which bisects the town and continued to claim the key role.'

But the glossiness had come off the Wagner wunderkind. In the absence of success, the long leash he had been given by the Kremlin was shortening. Unlike campaigns in Africa, there was no foreign potentate to pick up the main bill, all Wagner costs were borne by Moscow. Furthermore, the failure to capture the salt mines meant that he was not likely going to enrich his Kremlin's backers with their proceeds as a return on investment. Like an unprofitable line of business, it seemed, that Wagner PMC's owners were shutting down its lead role in Ukraine behind the scenes and against the wishes of its CEO.

Prigozhin continued to fight his corner in the invasion, however, and hit back at Ukrainian reports that Wagner was suffering heavy losses in the battle for Bakhmut.

Suddenly there was conciliatory praise for the Russian army, 'We will conquer this frontier with dignity,' he said. 'The [Russian] Defence Minister has told you that after capturing Bakhmut, the operational space will open. And the world has not yet faced the Russian army, which is well prepared, with those units that have not yet entered into battle, with all possible modern weapons, intelligence, ideally prepared. They are waiting for their time. Right after the opening of the operational space by PMC Wagner after Bakhmut. Then the whole world will shudder.'

Prigozhin must now have understood that his opponent was not just Shoigu but someone more powerful, and he complained bitterly that he was being cut off. 'To get me to stop asking for ammunition, all the hotlines to offices, to departments etc have been cut off from me. But the real humdinger is that they've also blocked agencies from making decisions,' he said on Telegram. However, with a hint of sarcasm, he thanked the Russian government for a 'heroic' increase in the production of ammunition, but that he was still worried about shortages for his fighters and the Russian army as a whole.

He still wasn't sure and later he blamed the traditional Russian military again of thwarting him: 'Shells are being made, but we don't have any for some reason. But the global reason, I think, is the following. Wagner PMC is the most effective unit, and all the military know this.'

In March came another warning that Prigozhin might be out to unseat Putin. It came from Olga Lautman, Senior Fellow at the Centre for European Policy Analysis.

Surprisingly, given the fate of people like Khodorkovsky, Prigozhin now responded directly to questions about whether he harboured political ambitions. In a video posted on Telegram, he said: 'I'm making a political coming out. Looking at everything around me, I've got political ambitions. I decided to run for president in 2024. For President of Ukraine.' Explaining his thinking, he said: 'If I win the presidential elections of Ukraine, then everything will be fine, guys, the shells will not be needed.' He seemed entirely convinced that the Kremlin did not mistake his complaints as vying for power.

His militia required about $ 1 billion worth of ammunition each month to fight the war in Ukraine. Shrugging off the losses that the Wagner Group had already sustained, he said: 'Fighters die at war in any case, the war is so invented that one army kills another.'

His defiant accusations against his opponents dimmed however to mere hints as opposed to the crudely worded allegations of the past. 'I am not going anywhere. The question is—who took the money when we "made a gesture of goodwill" and [in 2022] surrendered Kherson, Kharkiv region and many other territories?' he asked. 'There are new fighters coming there who will go side by side with us to defend their country and their family. To make our common future and protect the memory of the past. In spite of the colossal resistance of the Ukrainian armed forces, we will go forward. Despite the sticks in the wheels that are thrown at us at every step, we will overcome this together.'

In fact, the *Wagnerovcis* were stuck in Bakhmut. The Ukrainians had blown the bridges across the Bakhmutka River, which runs through a strip of open ground two- to eight hundred meters wide. This had become a killing zone where life expectancy was just four hours.

The US Institute of War Studies thought that Shoigu finally had Prigozhin where he wanted him, dependent on the Russian military: 'The Russian MoD—specifically the Russian defence minister Sergei Shoigu and the chief of the Russian general staff General Valery Gerasimov—is currently prioritizing eliminating Wagner on the battlefields in Bakhmut… in an effort to weaken Prigozhin and derail his ambitions for greater influence in the Kremlin.'

Prigozhin admitted that the situation was 'difficult, very difficult. The enemy is fighting for every metre… and the closer to the city centre, the fiercer the fighting'.

By 13 March the Ukrainians said pockets of Wagner troops had crossed the Bakhmutka River, but were then pinned down. Prigozhin then announced that Wagner mercenaries had taken control of the settlement of Zaliznyanskoye, nearly completing the encirclement of Bakhmut. Meanwhile, Ukraine's' supply lines were now under fire from the Wagners.

A week later, Ukrainian forces launched a counter-attack south-west of Bakhmut to push Russian troops away from the last remaining supply route to the besieged city. Geolocated footage shared on social media appeared to show Ukrainian troops in a position once occupied by Wagner mercenaries in the settlement of Ivanovske, almost four miles from the centre of the salt-mining town. The bodies of at least three Russian soldiers were shown on the heavily-mined battlefield, littered with anti-tank devices, and an abandoned Wagner foxhole.

Clearly, Prigozhin still refused to eat humble pie, however. Prigozhin had already written to defence minister, Sergei Shoigu, to warn that the Ukrainian army was planning an imminent offensive aimed at cutting off his forces from the main body of Russian troops in eastern Ukraine. The letter said the 'large-scale attack' was planned for late March or early April. Instead of apologising, Prigozhin intensified his personal attacks on Shoigu with the usual accusations, calling the minister's son-in-law, online fitness guru Alexei Stolaryov a 'scumbag blogger' and comparing him to armed robber Hayk Gasparyan, asking which one is better—Hayk, who committed a crime, joined Wagner and became a real hero, or the scumbag blogger who remained a vile creature. Stolaryov was the husband of Ksenia Shoigu, who was thought to be close with her father.

'How can Shoigu's son-in-law go to the United Arab Emirates and shake his bum around?' Prigozhin said. He also accused Shoigu's daughter of spending illicit funds on leading a life of luxury. Ksenia had recently posted photos of their holiday in Dubai, where they stayed at a luxury hotel.

To prove his usefulness to Putin, Prigozhin may have tried to develop new fronts for Wagner. Moldovan border police refused entry to an alleged member of the Wagner Group, fearing that Moscow was trying to destabilize Ukraine's neighbour after the country had gained EU candidate status. There were also reports of 2.5 tonnes of uranium going missing in Libya from a storage facility near where Wagner troops were stationed.

But his African operations also caused problems. As President of China Xi Jinping was heading to Moscow, 9 Chinese mine workers were killed in an attack in the Central African Republic that was blamed on the Wagner Group. Xi called on the authorities in the Central African Republic to 'severely punish' those responsible for the attack, which took place at a goldmine fifteen miles from the town of Bambari.

Wagner was certainly reorganising. Prigozhin admitted that his force in the Ukraine had 'reset and cut down its size' after the battle for Bakhmut. Yet he still thought he had a role in Ukraine. Recruitment notices were still posted inviting applicants to come forward for a six-month stint in Ukraine. But in addition, there was also the option to do nine to fourteen months rounds abroad in Wagner's African empire.

Prigozhin expressly denied he was preparing to withdraw Wagner from Ukraine. 'As long as our country needs us, we will remain fighting in Ukraine,' he said on Telegram. He must have received encouragement from some corners of Moscow that his services were essential in Ukraine. Short of men, a giant recruitment advert for the Wagner Group covering seventeen storeys went up on an office building next to a highway in north-east Moscow, showing the group's logo and slogans such as 'Join the winning team!' and 'Together we will win'.

Prigozhin used his public profile in unexpected ways to contradict official Kremlin policy indirectly. He stepped in when 53-year-old single father Alexei Moskalyov fled house arrest after his 13-year-old daughter Masha had drawn an anti-war picture at school. Her headmistress called the police after she drew a picture that showed Russian missiles falling onto a Ukrainian mother and child. It also featured the words 'glory to Ukraine' and 'no war'. Masha also refused to participate in 'patriotic' lessons that began in Russian schools after Putin ordered troops into Ukraine. Moskalyov was convicted over comments he had posted online and was convicted of discrediting the Russian army and sentenced to two years in a penal colony. Prigozhin issued a statement saying the decision was unjust and that it would be a 'great tragedy' if Masha was forced to grow up in a children's home.

An interview with Prigozhin aired by his own Federal News Agency (FNA) drew the attention of the analysts at the Institute for the Study of War who said it was 'noteworthy for its unique format'.

The ISW said: 'Prigozhin seemed to mimic the way that Vladimir Putin films his choreographed public meetings, either to mock Putin quietly or to suggest subtly that Prigozhin could become Russian president like Putin. The choreography and staging of Prigozhin's interview placed Prigozhin in the camera's frame at Prigozhin's desk across from his audience in the same way that Putin's filmed meetings and photo ops usually do. This film style is unusual for Prigozhin, as Prigozhin's public video statements typically do not employ such a sterile format.'

It was thought the Wagner Group boss might 'seek to parody Putin's cinematography style as part of a larger trolling campaign to attack the Kremlin or draw tacit parallels between Prigozhin and the office of the Russian presidency'.

'Prigozhin's recent behaviour—regardless of its intent—is advancing a narrative among Russian society that Prigozhin has larger political aspirations in Russia,' the analysis concluded.

Prigozhin certainly crowed about the impact on the Ukrainian army of having to fight Wagner in Bakhmut. 'The battle for Bakhmut today has already practically destroyed the Ukrainian army, and unfortunately, it has also badly damaged the Wagner Private Military Company,' Yevgeny Prigozhin said in an audio message.

He also claimed that if Wagner were able to achieve victory in Bakhmut it would be a 'major turning point in the war and in the entire modern history'. If Wagner were to 'perish in the meatgrinder of Bakhmut and take the Ukrainian army with it' it would give Russia space for a further offensive. He added. 'That means we played our historic mission.'

But daggers were drawn between those in Moscow who egged on Prigozhin and the Kremlin. On 2 April 2023, bank robber turned ultranationalist military blogger Vladlen Tatarsky (real name was Maxim Fomin) who had ties to Wagner was blown up and killed in the Street Bar café in St Petersburg that was reportedly owned by Prigozhin. Thirty others were wounded. The ISW assessed that the bombing may act as a warning to other Russian commentators to temper their criticism of the conduct of the war. Tatarsky had called for a tribunal for the Russian military leadership, describing Moscow's top officers as 'untrained idiots'.

Several hours before the explosion, Tatarsky praised advertising hoardings in Moscow seeking recruits for Wagner fighters.

'It's nice to see such outdoor advertising,' he said.

The bomb was in a small bust of Tatarsky given to him by twenty-six-year-old Darya Trepova in the café at a meeting of a weekend discussion club called Cyberfront Z—the Z clearly making an association with the Russian forces in the Ukraine. A native of Makiivka in the Donetsk region, Tatasky had fought for the separatists. His video of a ceremony at the Kremlin celebrating the annexation of Ukraine's occupied regions went viral. In it, Tatarsky was shown saying: 'We'll defeat everyone. We'll kill everyone. We'll rob everyone we need to. Everything will be as we like it.'

The day after the bombing Prigozhin claimed that Wagner had taken Bakhmut. Video footage showed Prigozhin raising the Russian flag on the ruins.

'Behind me is the building of city administration,' he said. 'This is the Russian flag. The message on the flag reads: "In kind memory of Vladlen Tatarsky".'

But the fighting was not over. It was reported that the Russians lost a thousand men—five hundred of them Wagner—that day. The Wagner cemetery at Bakinskaya was swelling. In a video showing Prigozhin visiting the vast field of graves are topped with a cross and wreath, he said: 'Those who fight sometimes die. That's how life works. They continue to bury Wagner fighters here, today there are no problems.'

Despite his boast of taking Bakhmut, two days later he admitted that Ukrainian forces were not abandoning the city. 'It must be said clearly that the enemy is not going anywhere,' he said on his Telegram channel.

Later Prigozhin took time out to attend Tatarsky's funeral. Hundreds turned out. His coffin was draped in a Russian flag with a sledgehammer alongside it. In his eulogy, Prigozhin said: 'Today I want to say thanks to Vladlen Tatarsky on behalf of myself and the fighters of the Wagner PMC. Vladlen Tatarsky did a lot so that we could go to victory and destroy the enemy. Thank you for this, we will always remember him. He is a soldier who stays with us, whose voice will live forever and speak only the truth.' But the message of the bombing—a signature FSB move—made clear, the infighting had moved beyond mere words.

16

UNDERMINING

Prigozhin's Moscow opponents were undermining him in sly ways. As Prigozhin was pausing Wagner operations in Bakhmut, a video appeared showing a Ukrainian prisoner of war having his head cut off with a knife. The video shows a Ukrainian soldier struggling on the floor, crying 'it hurts' and 'stop'. The attackers hold up the Ukrainian's tactical vest, displaying the patch worn by members of Kyiv's armed forces, to identify their victim to the camera.

'Get working, brothers,' a voice can be heard saying in Russian. 'Break his spine, f***, have you never cut off a head?'

There were cries of 'Do it, do it, do it' and 'Send it to Kyiv'.

At the end of the clip, there were cheers as the Ukrainian's decapitated head was held aloft towards the camera. The perpetrator and other men visible in the clip had white bands on their legs, which Russian soldiers wore as a means of identification. The footage was probably shot in summer 2022 given the amount of green foliage around the murder scene.

The Rusich Group, reacted to the footage with a smiley face emoji, adding: 'You will be surprised how many of these videos will gradually pop up.'

Another clip being circulated appeared to show the corpses of two Ukrainian soldiers lying on the ground next to a destroyed military vehicle.

'Got f**ked by a mine,' a Russian voice can be heard describing the incident. 'They killed them. Someone came up to them. They came up to them and cut their heads off.'

The dead soldiers also appeared to have had their hands cut off. Wagner defector Andrei Medvedev confirmed that the call signs, code words and cyphers heard in the video were distinctive of the group's mercenaries: 'It's a typical Wagner feature. A hundred per cent.'

Russian social media channels suggested the two videos were also shot close to Bakhmut.

'I am certain that this is not the last video of one of the [conflict] parties killing a prisoner of war,' said a post on the *Grey Zone* Telegram channel. 'In war, the enemies' heads, ears and other organs are cut off… This is bad, but this is the price of war.'

It was nothing that Prigozhin's trolls hadn't put out before intentionally to underline Wagner's approach to war. But Prigozhin was stopping the war machine and what was odd was that there were leaves on the trees and clearly the footage was old—from the summer of 2022. The video seemed to want to be aimed at Prigozhin rather than impress Ukrainian soldiers. Prigozhin himself, trying to clean up the image of Wagner PMC merely said: 'It is bad when people's heads are cut off, but I have not found anywhere that this is happening near Bakhmut or that fighters of PMC Wagner are participating in the execution.'

To underline his new tack, Prigozhin struck back. For Easter, Wagner announced it was releasing a hundred Ukrainian prisoners of war. 'Prepare all of them, feed and water them, check the wounded,' Prigozhin tells his men in a video posted on Telegram by his press service, ready for the handover 'before lunchtime' on Sunday. It showed his fighters wearing balaclavas as they watched the thin, dirty and unshaved Ukrainian soldiers walk down a muddy tree-lined road. They were still wearing the combat fatigues that they had been captured in. Many were wounded, one man was being carried on a stretcher and another was supported by two other soldiers as he hobbled along.

A group of Ukrainian prisoners was then shown being told that they would be passed back to Ukrainian forces to mark Orthodox Easter on 16 April.

'I hope you don't fall back into our hands,' an armed Wagner soldier was heard telling the men before they were ordered into a truck, some loading packs of water bottles.

More than a hundred men, some limping and some being carried on stretchers by their comrades were shown making their way in line along a muddy road as a man standing on a tank held a white flag. President Volodymyr Zelenskiy's chief of staff, Andriy Yermak, said 130 Ukrainian prisoners of war have been released and returned home in a 'great Easter exchange'. It was not clear how many Russians were sent back the other way.

Prigozhin was also shown greeting refugees in the city, including a boy named Vladimir, before they were evacuated. The people appeared to be sleeping in a cramped underground cellar of some kind. Prigozhin handed out chocolate bars to the children. In another video, Prigozhin was shown wearing a combat uniform and carrying a rifle as he lit a candle in what appears to be a dark and abandoned church to mark Orthodox Easter.

The battle of misinformation continued. On 13 April, Russia's defence ministry claimed that the last road in and out of Bakhmut had been cut off, 'blocking the transfer of the Ukrainian army reinforcements to the city and the possibility of retreat for enemy units'. The city was entirely encircled and Wagner troops were also advancing through the city.

But Prigozhin simply disagreed with Shoigu's officials and said: 'The harshest, bloody battles are still ongoing so it is too early to speak about a full encircling of Bakhmut.' He still claimed that only eighty per cent of the city—which now lay in ruins—was in Russian hands. Nevertheless, 'Wagner assault units were continuing high-intensity combat operations to oust the enemy from the central quarters' of Bakhmut.

Prigozhin said he had satellite surveillance that showed the Ukrainians had built up a reserve of 200,000 men. The US Institute of the Study of War said he was exaggerating, no doubt in the hope of securing more supplies and reinforcements to save his forces in Bakhmut.

He also resumed his attacks on Moscow and lashed out at the 'decadent and lazy' elite in Moscow, blaming them for undermining the war effort. Russia's 'Deep State' he said was 'mired in luxury and bureaucracy' and wanted to negotiate an end to the war.

'Their focus is not on a country or a people, their focus is on their own positions in society, their own comfort and their own capital,' he said.

'The ideal option is to announce the end of the special military operation, to inform everyone that Russia has achieved the results that it planned,' he said, 'and in a sense, we have actually achieved them... by destroying a large part of the active male population of Ukraine, and by intimidating another part of it, which fled to Europe.

'Russia cut off the Sea of Azov and a large piece of the Black Sea, seized a fat piece of Ukrainian territory and created a land corridor to the Crimea. Now there is only one thing left: to firmly gain a foothold, to claw in those territories that already exist.'

For years, Russia had considered that it had one of the best armies in the world, he theorised. This hubris had led to 'tragic events' in historic wars with Finland, in 1939-40 where a tiny Finnish army held off the gigantic Red Army, and Japan (1904-05 where the Russians effectively lost two fleets) as well as World War I which ended for Russia with the revolution in 1917.

'This can lead to global changes in Russian society,' Prigozhin said. 'The people are already looking for someone to blame for the fact that we are not the strongest army in the world, and in this situation they will look for 'the scapegoat'.' These were likely to be members of Russia's 'deep state'.

'At the same time, nothing threatens the supreme power of Russia, since it is a symbol of national unity and resistance to the West,' he said. 'I summarize—the Ukrainians are ready to attack. We are ready to repel the blow. The best scenario for healing Russia so that it rallies together and becomes the strongest state is the offensive of the armed forces of Ukraine, in which no negotiations will be possible. And either the armed forces of Ukraine will be defeated in a fair fight, or Russia will lick its wounds, build up muscles and tear its rivals again in a fair fight.'

Giving a hint that he was not a maverick acting off his own bat, Prigozhin announced that Nikolai Peskov, the thirty-three-year-old son of Putin spokesman Dmitry Peskov served as a gunner with Wagner Group. The Moscow-based newspaper *Komsomolskaya Pravda* published an interview with Nikolai where he said he had served as an artilleryman with the Kremlin's Wagner mercenary group for six months. Nikolai told the newspaper that he had served in Ukraine—a rare example of the son of a senior Russian official fighting in the war. To anyone in Russia, it would be clear that this story could only have appeared with Putin's agreement. Was Putin extending an olive branch?

'It was on my initiative,' Nikolai said in an interview. 'I considered it my duty.'

He added that he had served out his contract under an assumed name to hide his true identity and he received a medal for bravery, the newspaper said. Asked about his father's views of his service, Nikolai said: 'He's proud of me, I think. My father told me that I made the right decision.'

While the PR for Wagner was undeniable, there was scepticism about whether the patriotic story bore any relation to the truth. Nikolai had lived in Britain in the decade following the 1991 fall of the Soviet Union, according to *Kommersant*. In 2010, he was sentenced to fifteen months in a young offenders' institution for assaulting and robbing a teenager near a McDonald's restaurant in Milton Keynes. A few weeks earlier he had received a suspended sentence for stealing a mobile phone.

He then returned to Russia and reportedly served in the strategic rocket forces from 2010 to 2012, before spending a period as a correspondent with the Kremlin propaganda channel, Russia Today (RT). Instagram posts later showed him posing in front of expensive cars, playing polo and travelling either in first class or on private jets.

Then in 2022, an associate of the jailed opposition politician Alexei Navalny phoned Nikolai pretending to be a Russian recruitment officer and demanded he report for the draft. Nikolai told him that he was a 'Mr Peskov' so he would not be going anywhere and would 'resolve the situation at a different level', according to a recording of the call posted online.

In the newspaper interview, he claimed that he was researching how to sign up when he received the call. 'I was already getting ready to serve, for the trip,' he said. But there was a problem. 'I didn't know how to get there, because when it started there wasn't as much information as now. That's why, yes, I had to ask my father how to get in touch with a private military company. And he helped me with that.'

He said he considered it his duty to fight. 'I was just obliged to take part; I had to help all those who were there.' Adding: 'I couldn't sit to one side watching as friends and others went off there'.

His father told reporters: 'He took this decision. He's a grown man. Yes, he did indeed take part in the special military operation,' without giving further details.

Doubt was cast on this when an influential Russian military blogger with 500,000 followers published photos of a black electric Tesla in Moscow reportedly belonging to Nikolai Peskov.

'It was his favourite car, he always drove himself. From the beginning to the end of 2022, the car moved around Moscow. Data on fines was even kept,' said a post on a channel named after the Soviet Union's secret police. The recorded peregrinations of Nikolai's beloved car covered the period he said he was fighting with the Wagner Group in the Ukraine.

Prigozhin appeared somewhat mollified and went along with Nikolai's story. 'Of all my acquaintances, I will say this for the first time, one person, Dmitry Sergeyevich Peskov, who at one time had the reputation of being a complete liberal, sent his son. He came to me and said, 'Take him on as a simple artilleryman',' Prigozhin posted on Telegram. 'His son, who lived part of his life in America, if I'm not mistaken, or in England, came and asked to be taken on as a simple gunner. And he did absolutely fine as a simple gunner knee-deep in mud and shit in an Uragan [multiple rocket launcher]. Few people know about it.'

It was undeniable that Prigozhin was trying to mobilize public opinion, and Russian independent news site *Meduza* again reported Prigozhin was trying to gain control of the party A Just Russia, whose leader Sergei Mironov lauded Wagner as 'heroic'.

But Viktor Nikitin, a former Wagner employee who moved to southern Europe in the autumn of 2022, dismissed the notion out of hand that Prigozhin would seek to rule Russia. It was highly unlikely that Prigozhin suddenly thought of Russia as a democratic country where he could exert influence through a political party. He had failed to take Bakhmut and obviously harboured no expectation at all that he could take Moscow by force and control Russia.

'That will not happen,' he said. 'He is an outsider and the establishment will not accept him, the establishment will protect itself, he knows that. Would Prigozhin directly challenge Putin? That would be very foolish and dangerous.

Prigozhin is first and foremost a businessman and has no interest in political power. 'He has had a lot of money for a long time and now he has power at a time of war. But this type of power will not last in peacetime inside Russia. He can get political power abroad. He can try to run a small country in Africa through puppets for example. But I think he'll stay in Russia and try to re-establish good relations with the government. He'll need them to make his money in foreign countries.'

However, Prigozhin did start undermining Putin's justification for the war by publicly questioning whether there are actually any Nazis in Ukraine. In an audio message, he also announced: 'A decision has been taken to suspend artillery fire so that American journalists can safely film Bakhmut and go home.' But later added: 'Guys, this is military humour. Humour, and nothing more… it was a joke.'

He also appeared deadly serious when he threatened to withdraw from Bakhmut himself, saying his troops only had enough ammunition left for a few days. In a 90-minute video interview with Russian military blogger Semyon Pegov, Prigozhin said: 'If the shortage of ammunition is not replenished, then… most likely, we will be forced to withdraw part of the units.' He quoted from a letter he said he had sent to Russia's defence minister Sergei Shoigu, giving a 28-April deadline for the withdrawal.

In an incendiary comment he added, 'We need to stop deceiving the population and telling them that everything is fine,' he was quoted as saying in the interview. 'I must honestly say: Russia is on the brink of a disaster.'

Again he blamed the deaths of his men on the shortages. 'Nobody is giving them ammunition. Ammunition is stacked high in warehouses,' he fumed. 'Scumbags who made these decisions should be answerable to the mothers of those killed in action.'

He told Pegov: 'With regard to the need in general for shells at the front, what we want… Today we are coming to the point where Wagner is ending. Wagner, in a short period of time, will cease to exist. We will become history, nothing to worry about, things like this happen.'

He said that Wagner only had ten to fifteen per cent of the shells they needed, while predicting a Ukrainian counterattack in mid-May. 'This counteroffensive could become a tragedy for our country,' he said.

Still gloomy about the future of the Wagner Group, on 1 May 2023 (the founding day of Wagner PMC it would turn out), standing in front of a shattered building in Soledar, he said: 'If the company is fated to die one day, it won't be at the hands of the Ukrainian army or Nato, but our bastard bureaucrats at home.'

White House national security spokesperson John Kirby told reporters casualty figures, based on US intelligence estimates, included more than twenty-thousand Russian dead, half of them from the Wagner group. Around sixty to seventy per cent of Wagner's ground troops die in every assault, he said, when often the aim is just to dig a trench a bit closer to opposition lines. They were mainly convicts taken from the GULAG and in Russia few tears were shed.

News of infighting of Wagner with other troops intensified. Soldiers from Gazprom's private army, Potok, sent a video to Putin complaining that they had been transferred to a different private army—Redut which was formed by Russian Special Forces in 2003—and were then threatened by soldiers of the

Wagner group, who said they would shoot them if they retreated from their positions. Mobilized soldiers from the regular army in the Luhansk region disappeared after telling relatives that they had been sold to the Wagner Group by their commander.

A Kremlin insider since the beginning of Putin's rule, Prigozhin continued keeping up the pressure on Shoigu following the Kremlin's olive branch. Prigozhin renewed his appeal for ammunition. In a video posted on his Telegram channel, Prigozhin said he needs at least three hundred tonnes of artillery shells a day to withstand the assault.

'Three hundred tonnes a day is ten cargo containers—not a lot at all… But we are being given no more than a third of that,' Prigozhin said as he inspected boxes of rifles in a warehouse that he said was in the town of Soledar.

In another video a few days later, Prigozhin was blunter. Standing next to rows of bodies, he told the powers that be in Moscow: 'These are the Wagner lads who died today. The blood is still fresh. They came here as volunteers, they are dying so you can get fat in your offices.'

He maintained they had a 70 per cent shortage of ammunition.

Shouting, he continued: 'We have Shoigu, Gerasimov, where the f*** is ammunition…. These are Wagner lads who died today. The blood is still fresh…. Now, listen to me, you f***ing bastard. These are someone's f***ing fathers and someone's sons. And those bastards, who are not giving us any f***ing ammunition, will be in hell, munching on their f***ing insides.'

In his most aggressive video yet, he added: 'Look at them, bitches!… You scumbags are sitting in expensive clubs; your children are enjoying life and making YouTube videos. You think you are the masters of this life and that you have the right to control their lives. You think that if you have ammunition depots then you have the right to them. There are simple calculations: if you give the normal amount of ammunition then there will be five times fewer of them [dead]. They came here as volunteers and are dying so that you can fatten yourselves in your mahogany offices.'

'For the tens of thousands killed and wounded, they will bear responsibility in front of their mothers and children, I will achieve that,' he added threateningly.

17

RETREAT

Starved of ammunition, Prigozhin decided Wagner was pulling out. In a statement, he said: 'I declare on behalf of the Wagner fighters, on behalf of the Wagner command, that on 10 May 2023, we are obliged to transfer positions in the settlement of Bakhmut to units of the defence ministry and withdraw the remains of Wagner to logistics camps to lick our wounds. I'm pulling Wagner units out of Bakhmut because, in the absence of ammunition, they're doomed to perish senselessly.'

He explained: 'Wagner ran out of resources to advance in early April, but we're advancing despite the fact that the enemy's resources outnumber ours fivefold. Because of the lack of ammunition, our losses are growing exponentially every day.'

And he thought the Ukrainian spring offensive had started. 'I believe the advance of the Ukrainian army has already begun,' he said. 'We are seeing the greatest possible activity both on the perimeter and within the front lines.'

In full combat gear with an assault rifle hanging from his shoulder, he stood in front of dozens of his men and said: 'My lads will not suffer useless and unjustified losses in Bakhmut without ammunition. If, because of your petty jealousy, you do not want to give the Russian people the victory of taking Bakhmut, that's your problem.'

Perhaps in an effort to prevent Wagner's withdrawal, the Russian defence ministry assigned General Surovikin to work alongside Prigozhin. 'This is the only man with the star of an army general who knows how to fight,' Prigozhin said. He added that overnight he had been promised as much ammunition and weaponry as he needed to continue the assault on Bakhmut.

They quickly increased their shelling with the aim of taking the city by Victory Day—9 May. But then he said that there was no sign of the promised ammunition. 'The people who were supposed to fulfil the [shipment] orders have so far, over the past day, not fulfilled them,' Prigozhin said in a video post on Telegram. But he said he did not want to spoil the Victory Day parade.

As the celebration in Moscow was in full swing, however, it became clear that Prigozhin had been deceived with empty promises. Wagner was now receiving even fewer shells, only ten per cent of the ammunition they needed.

Worse, instead of defending or taking over Wagner's positions, the Russian army was retreating from Bakhmut. 'The 72nd Brigade pissed away three square kilometres this morning, where I had lost around five-hundred men,' Prigozhin complained bitterly. Some army troops exposed Wagner to Ukrainian attacks. 'Today one of the units of the defence ministry fled from one of our flanks… exposing the front,' he said in a video.

It was enough for Prigozhin to go back on his promise not to spoil the Victory Day parade and launched his own grenade at the Kremlin with 'grandfather'—aka Putin—'is a complete arsehole'.

In a matter of days, Prigozhin saw that his work was being undone and the mines would never be his. The advances 'are now being thrown away practically without a fight by those who should be holding our flanks', he complained.

Wagner trolls worked overtime. Documents were leaked showing that the convict *Wagnerovcis* were deliberately being starved of ammunition and were being replaced by regular conscripts. A video of a soldier named Ruslan signalling to a drone not to shoot and being led across no-man's land to the Ukrainian lines was shared worldwide.

As a former prison officer in one of Russia's brutal penal colonies, Ruslan said he was mobilized in September alongside 300,000 conscripts. In early May, his unit was told they were to travel to Bakhmut to replace Wagner Group mercenaries leaving their positions outside the town.

On 8 May, Ruslan arrived outside the town in a troop transport—where, to his surprise, he and three fellow soldiers were handed over to the charge of a Wagner fighter, who sent them over the top to secure a trench.

'If you fall behind, I will annihilate you. If you refuse to fight, I will annihilate you,' the man had said. '"If you are caught in fire on the way, no one will drag you out, we will just finish you off." That's how they escorted us to our positions.'

He and the two other newcomers spent hours in a trench lined with up to forty bodies of Ukrainian and Wagner troops. A mortar barrage wounded all three of them, but no one replied when they radioed for help. One of the men had both legs broken by a Ukrainian drone. He was thought to have shot himself soon afterwards.

Ruslan found a foxhole. The third man sprinted past him, along the trench searching for cover, pursued by the drone. 'There was an explosion, it caught him on his spine, he fell immediately, right in front of my eyes. He was alive but he couldn't move his legs,' Ruslan said. Moments later the man reached for his own grenade, whispered: 'Brother, I feel bad', and pulled the pin. 'At that point, I thought, I might as well give them a sign, the drone operator will by any case be a human,' Ruslan said.

Prigozhin was beside himself. 'This is not the problem of soldiers but of those who manage them and set their tasks,' he said. 'A fish rots from its head, and if decision-making is done through the a**e, soldiers leave because there is no point to die in vain.'

Prigozhin then struck back at the defence ministry's use of the media, saying their regular soldiers' flight was not a tactical retreat or regrouping but a rout.

'The taking of Bakhmut gives the Russian Federation nothing because the flanks are crumbling and the front is failing,' he said in a video. 'And the attempts of the defence ministry in the media space to somehow smooth over the situation are leading, and will lead, to a global tragedy for Russia!

'Therefore stop lying immediately. If you've run away, establish new lines of defence. But what you've trained for that defence—it's not capable of holding that defence. What has been happening recently, and what I have been warning about for a long time, is starting to come to pass. And it's leading to a great tragedy for our country.'

Ukrainian Armed Forces Storm Battalion Commander 'Rollo' countered, however, that even now Prigozhin was not telling the truth: 'Prigozhin is a liar, because the first to flee were Wagner. It was his units that fled, and our success is not due to the fact that they fled but the fact that we conducted a planned assault by circumventing and cutting them off. Actually, the unit he is bad-mouthing fought to the end, his Wagners were the first to flee.'

It was then reported that Prigozhin had offered to leak the locations of Russian soldiers to Kyiv if they withdrew their forces from Bakhmut. Kyiv rejected the offer.

An account on the messaging app Telegram called General SVR, which claimed to be run by a Kremlin insider, documented what it said was raging Putin's meltdown in the wake of his stalled offensive. He was reported to have told his generals: 'You f***ed it all up. Both Kherson and Artemovsk [Bakhmut] are p***ed away.'

Prigozhin also sent a message to Putin's defence minister Sergei Shoigu bluntly stating: 'Our positions in Bakhmut are successfully attacked from the flanks by the enemy. Given your super long experience, please can you come to Bakhmut.'

In another video message, he said the Ukrainians had seized high ground overlooking Bakhmut and opened the main highway leading into the city from the West.

'The loss of the Berkhivka reservoir—the loss of this territory they gave up—that's five square kilometres, just today,' Prigozhin said. 'The enemy has completely freed up the Chasiv Yar-Bakhmut road which we had blocked. The enemy is now able to use this road, and secondly they have taken tactical high ground under which Bakhmut is located.'

There were fears that the Wagners remaining in Bakhmut risked encirclement. But Prigozhin would have none of it. 'Stories of tactical withdrawals are nothing more than fleeing, skedaddling, total cowardice—something that will heap shame on the history of our country for many years,' he raged.

Even now, Prigozhin could not resist an opportunity for publicity. Footage on social media showed him inspecting a body and what he claimed were Pentagon identification cards showing that the man was a former US Army special forces soldier from Boise, Idaho.

'We'll put him in a coffin, cover him with the American flag with respect because he did not die in his bed as a grandpa but he died at war and most likely a worthy [death], right?' he said. According to CNN, Prigozhin said the deceased was 'shooting back' when he was killed.

A week after the Russian retreat had begun, Prigozhin uploaded a voice message to Shoigu and Gerasimov to Telegram, saying: 'Unfortunately, units of the Russian Defence Ministry have withdrawn up to 570 metres to the north of Bakhmut, exposing our flanks. I am appealing to the top leadership of the Ministry of Defence—publicly—because my letters are not being read. Please do not give up the flanks.'

Then, on 20 May, Prigozhin claimed to have taken the city. The working together of Wagner and regular troops seemed to have finally created a break-through. 'Today, at 12 noon, Bakhmut was completely taken,' Prigozhin said in a video in which he appeared in combat fatigues in front of a line of fighters holding Russian flags and Wagner banners. 'We completely took the whole city, from house to house.'

He said his own forces would pull out of Bakhmut in five days to rest, handing the ruins over to the regular military from 25 May to 1 June. The Ukrainians said that heavy fighting was still going on. But Putin went along with Prigozhin. A public statement from the Kremlin said: 'Vladimir Putin congrat-ulated the assault units of Wagner as well as all servicemen of units of the Russian armed forces who provided them with the necessary support and flank cover, on the completion of the operation to liberate Artemovsk. All those who distinguished themselves will be given state awards'.

However, Prigozhin still claimed full credit for the victory. 'During the taking of Arteomovsk [Bakhmut's Russian name], practically no one from the army helped us,' he said in a voice recording posted to his Telegram channel shortly after Putin's statement, insisting that his fighters had taken Bakhmut 'to the last centimetre'. The cost? 'I took 50,000 prisoners of which around 20 per cent were killed,' he said, adding that a similar percentage of those who had signed a contract with Wagner had also perished.

There was still confusion as the Ukrainians claimed they were now in a position to encircle them and the Wagner fighters were caught like rats in the trap. Denis Pushilin posted a video on Telegram. Dressed in military uniform he appeared to be planting the flag of the Donetsk People's Republic on a building. He said: 'Bakhmut had the misfortune to be Ukrainian. Now it's not Ukraine, it's Russia. And it's not Bakhmut—it's Artemovsk. The Russian flag over Artemovsk has already been hoisted earlier. Today I went to the liberated city to hang the flag of the Donetsk People's Republic and examine the settlement once again to work out the priority measures. Thanks to the Wagner fighters for completing the most difficult military task in the entrusted area! Now we will restore the Russian city Artemovsk again.'

Finally proclaiming victory in Bakhmut left Prigozhin again in a bullish mood. He again warned that the Kremlin's catastrophic war in Ukraine could trigger a violent revolution in Russia. Prigozhin said public anger over the 'fat, carefree' lives of the children of the Russian elite in wartime could lead to their villas being stormed by ordinary people armed with pitchforks.

'Everything might end as in 1917, with a revolution—when first the soldiers rise up, and then their loved ones,' Prigozhin told a pro-war blogger, referring to the uprising in World War I was swept Tsar Nicholas II from power.

'The guilty people will receive their punishment—as a minimum, they'll be hanged on the Red Square,' he warned, claiming Russian elites in Russia were living comfortably while troops were dying on the front lines.

'The children of the elite smear themselves with creams, and show off on the internet, while ordinary people's children come home in zinc [coffins], torn to pieces,' he said. 'I recommend that the elite of the Russian Federation gathers up […] its youth and send them to war.'

The reference to Putin as Tsar was unmistakable, even if most of the comments were aimed at the usual suspects in the Russian ministry of defence. He also took the Kremlin to task for not introducing martial law. 'We are in such a condition that we could f***ing lose Russia,' he said. Implicit was a rejection of the tactical nuclear option that Medvedev and Putin were increasingly touting internationally as the Ukraine invasion was stalling. The war was winnable with conventional warfare as long as the right resources were directed to the right place. Creating no-go radiation zones like Chernobyl through nuclear warfare was not the same as winning a war.

Again Prigozhin picked out Shoigu's son-in-law Alexei Stolyarov, who was on a holiday jaunt in Nepal at the time. He was among those who refused to commit. Ilya Medvedev, the twenty-eight-year-old son of Dmitry Medvedev, the former prime minister and president, said claimed had not received call-up papers. Zaur Tsalikov, the thirty-on-year-old son of a deputy defence minister, rejected the suggestion that he should fight in Ukraine. 'What do I have to do with the armed forces?' he said. 'There are military men.' Little, however, was known about Yevgeny Gerasimov, the grown-up son of General Vasily Gerasimov, Prigozhin's nemesis. He was believed to live in Moscow and to have taken holidays in Crimea.

Other members of the 'golden youth'—children of top officials—took luxury holidays in the West. Among them was Veronica Naryshkina, the thirty-five-year-old daughter of Sergey Naryshkin, the head of Russia's foreign intelligence service. Since the start of the war, she had visited Turkey, Italy and Greece, all Nato member states. Natalia Guseva, the daughter of Nikolai Gusev, head of Russia's Vympel missile factory, had lived and studied in Miami since 2020. America had become her second home. And, of course, there was Nikolai Peskov whose luxury car was racking up parking tickets in Moscow while he was supposedly in the trenches of eastern Ukraine.

Prigozhin's own son Pavel, in his twenties, had served in the army and then joined up to fight with the Wagner Group in Syria. 'Since then, he has constantly been in hotspots as part of Wagner,' Prigozhin said proudly.

By now Prigozhin's words were banned on Russian mass media. It made clear that he had no political ambitions. Even if his words weren't publicly reported (or maybe because of it) he continued to take down the policies of his former mentor, Vladimir Putin, even more directly than before. It was clear that the failures in Ukraine had unleashed a hidden war of recriminations in the Kremlin and that the faction that backed Prigozhin was flexing its muscle and using him as its mouthpiece to put pressure on Putin.

Prigozhin openly mocked the Kremlin's overall aim of 'demilitarizing' Ukraine in the most scathing way. 'If, at the beginning of the special operation, they had around five hundred tanks, now they have five thousand of them. If back then, twenty thousand [Ukrainian] soldiers fought skilfully, now there are 400,000. How did we demilitarize it?' he said. 'We have militarized it.'

The withdrawal of Wagner from Bakhmut was the opportunity for another critical video where Prigozhin said he would leave behind two visibly unfit fighters to rescue the army when they got into difficulty.

'We are withdrawing units from Bakhmut today. We are handing over positions to the military, ammunition and everything,' Prigozhin said in a video purportedly filmed in Bakhmut on the morning of 25 May. 'We pull back, we rest, we prepare and then we will get new tasks. Here are two guys we are leaving for the army. This is Biber and this is Dolik.' One was clearly very elderly, the other extremely young. 'As soon as the army finds things difficult, they'll stand in the way of the Ukrainian army. Be nice to the soldiers, lads,' he added.

'What is forbidden is always sweeter,' he said. 'Wagner is not a piece of slippery soap which the bureaucrats have got used to shoving all over the place; Wagner is an awl, a stiletto that you cannot hide… High-level bureaucrats, those very towers of the Kremlin, are trying to shut the mouths of everyone so that they don't speak about Wagner will only give another shove to the people.'

There was a more sinister turn, too. In an online video, three Wagner fighters threatened Viktor Sobolev, a high-ranking Russian MP who had warned Russian soldiers against joining the 'illegal' mercenary group. The masked Wagner mercenaries told Sobolev that if Russia lost the war they would 'come to Red Square and f*** you and people like you in the arse'.

Ilya Ponomarev, a former Russian opposition MP who took Ukrainian citizenship, thought that Prigozhin's support within the Kremlin no longer depended on Putin and that he wanted to force the Kremlin to remove Wagner from the battlefield so he could concentrate on lucrative interests in Africa. 'He wants to walk away with his head held high, like a winner who wasn't allowed to finish the job,' Ponomarev said.

When drones attacked Moscow, he immediately uploaded a diatribe on Telegram saying: 'You are the Ministry of Defence. You didn't do a damn thing to advance. Why the f*** did you let these drones get to Moscow? They're flying to Rublyovka [an upmarket suburb] to your houses—let your houses go up in flames! And what will ordinary people do when drones with explosives crash into their windows?

'So as a citizen, I am deeply outraged that these scum sit quietly with their arseholes smeared with expensive creams. And that's why I think the people have every right to ask them these questions, these bastards. But I have already warned about this many times, but no one wants to listen. Because I'm angry and I upset bureaucrats who have a great life.'

He told them to: 'Get your shit out of the offices you've been put in to defend this country!'

Prigozhin's message was received loud and clear. Igor 'Strelkov' Girkin concluded on 28 May that the Wagner group had graduated to taking on the Russian Federation.

'Prigozhin actually openly declared war against part of the military and state nomenclature. Naturally, he is not alone. He has a huge cover, including in the Ozero Co-operative,' Girkin said, referring to the senior elite who have country dachas near Putin. 'He is a member of the ruling mafia, one of its factions. We are witnessing how one of these factions is disrupting the *status quo*. A coup attempt has been announced. So far, it has been announced in the media. For now. What will happen next—I don't know.'

As if to underline what Girkin was saying, Prigozhin, rather than pull in his horns to recede in the background, only redoubled his efforts to irritate Moscow sufficiently to get removed from Ukraine.

He made public that he had asked prosecutors to investigate whether senior Russian defence officials had committed any crimes before or during the war in Ukraine.

'Today I have sent letters to the Investigative Committee and the Prosecutor's Office of the Russian Federation with a request to check on the fact of the commission of a crime during the preparation and during the conduct of the SMO [Special Military Operation] by a host of senior functionaries of the Defence Ministry,' he said.

It couldn't be clearer that Wagner PMC resented having to leave any of its troops under the orders of the ministry of defence. No doubt, Africa beckoned. Prigozhin's battle-hardened convicts would be able to far more effective in capturing economic targets from Africa's tin-pot armies than from Ukraine's unified and well-organised military resistance.

18

RUSSIAN CLOWNS

By 1 June, the Wagner Group had officially pulled out of the ruined city of Bakhmut, though, according to the Ukrainian military, some of its convict battalions were left behind under the direct command of the defence ministry in Moscow and renamed 'Storm Z'.

Assessing the Battle of Bakhmut and which side could claim victory, Ukrainian battalion commander Petro Horbatenko said: 'You win battles not by conquering and occupying land but by destroying your enemy and their equipment and their storage depots. We killed ten of them for everyone they killed of ours, and that is not counting artillery casualties. So we did kill off a lot of them, but they were mostly from the Wagner group. To them, they were just meat. So it is hard to say who won.'

Dmytro Kukharchuk, another battalion commander who had been in the fighting, said that Wagner lives were counted so cheaply by their own side that when they were in close-quarter fighting with Ukrainians, Russian guns would open fire on the frontline, killing both sides.

'We saw it with our own eyes, they used artillery to kill their own people,' he said.

Celebrating his 62nd birthday at a training camp, Prigozhin said that the remainder of his men would leave Bakhmut on 5 June. He also laid down his terms. The Wagner Group would continue fighting in the Ukraine if his men got a separate section of the front without having to depend on the 'clowns' who ran the Russian armed forces. 'If the whole chain [of command] is a hundred per cent failed and will only be led by clowns who turn people into meat, then we will not participate in it,' he said.

Prigozhin then turned his fire on rival PMCs whom he accused of attempting to steal his thunder—and, more importantly, his funding. He name-checked two of the five private armies run by Gazprom—*Potok* (torrent) and *Fakel* (torch)—claiming that such groups aimed 'to dilute Wagner'. He added an interesting comment and said that it was so that there would not be 'one big force that can play a role in domestic politics'.

The choice of the word 'domestic' sounded a dangerous alarm bell. But, if anyone was in doubt, he clarified what he meant. 'Everyone is saying that there will be a power struggle at some point, and everyone needs their own army', he said, as if that particular scenario was no longer one of his personal problems now that he had won and was withdrawing from Bakhmut and maybe even Ukraine altogether to focus once again on growing Wagner's economic colonies in Africa.

During his populist video rant—which only a small minority of Russians would ever see given his mass-media ban on Russian TV—Prigozhin drove past rows of destroyed homes near the frontline to trenches manned by these smaller battalions, including one he said was Gazprom's *Potok*. He described the men as being too poorly equipped to hold their ground and poured scorn on sponsors who were preoccupied with scoring political points rather than fighting Kyiv.

He suggested that another reason for Wagner's trouble in Bakhmut had been that Russia's immense war spending had attracted greedy rivals who wanted a cut and had been successful despite not having any combat experience directing mercenaries. 'People with money think creating a [battalion] is so hot right now. So they have begun to multiply… two of each kind,' Prigozhin said. 'They need to report to the Kremlin about how f***ing amazing they are for creating their own [units].'

Several of these smaller militias, such as *Potok*, fell under the auspices of a larger private military company called Redut, a competitor to Wagner that once provided a handful of staff to guard Russian interests in Syria. According to Ukrainian intelligence, Redut was believed to have roughly seven thousand troops in Ukraine who were involved in operations around Kyiv and Kharkiv.

As the *Wagnerovcis* were leaving Bakhmut, Prigozhin accused the official Russian military of laying mines that endangered the Wagner fighters who had captured the town and were now departing.

A video posted by his press office on social media on 4 June showed a man who identified himself as Lieutenant Colonel Roman Venevitin, commander of the 72nd Independent Motorized Rifle Brigade of the Russian armed forces, who confessed to leading the mining operation that endangered the Wagner fighters. He appeared to have a bruised face. Questioned by an interrogator he admitted opening fire on a Wagner vehicle while drunk. Asked why, he said 'personal animosity' towards the group, giving no further explanation, though he apologized to the mercenaries.

Alongside, Wagner published a written report filed by one of its commanders saying that their fighters had to stop around the village of Opytne on 17 May when they stumbled upon anti-personnel mines laid by Russian soldiers.

'The Wagner unit started the de-mining but had to halt the operation at around 3pm when they came under fire from the Defence Ministry soldiers,' the report said, adding that Wagner fighters 'had to deal with the aggression and detain them'. Prigozhin said the video of the Russian officer confessing to shooting at Wagner fighters, proved the veracity of their report.

Igor Girkin was quick to comment on his Telegram channel, 'Yevgeny Prigozhin, whose subordinates posted a video in which they mock a senior officer and an entire brigade commander… is allowed to do whatever he wants. He is considered as the highest caste!'

A representative of the Liberty of Russia Legion, a group of Russian men fighting alongside Ukrainian forces, suggested Prigozhin hand over the officer in exchange for the Russian troops and border guards they held captive in a cross-border raid. Prigozhin turned down their request, insisting that the officer was not a prisoner of war.

'He has been detained and handed over for an investigation,' he said. 'We definitely are not going to swap any Russians for other Russians.'

Prigozhin then claimed that the Russian regular forces who had taken over Wagner positions had already lost part of the village of Berkhivka to the north-west of Bakhmut, risking the encirclement of the city. 'The troops are quietly running away,' he warned. Describing the development as a 'disgrace', Prigozhin challenged Gerasimov and defence minister Sergei Shoigu directly in a social media post, saying: 'I urge you to come to the front, raise the army with pistols so that they advance.

'Come on, you can do it,' Prigozhin taunted. 'And if you can't, you'll die as heroes.'

'It would seem that there is not a single rule left in Russian politics that the Wagner boss has not violated. However, he gets away with everything,' Political analyst Abbas Gallyamov said.

There was a slight change in the atmosphere, though. Earlier, Prigozhin received rare public criticism from two close allies of his friend Ramzan Kadyrov, the leader of Chechnya. At the beginning of the war, Wagner mercenaries had joined gun battles with Chechen fighters and regular Russian troops in Kherson while it was still under Russian occupation. Kadyrov's allies now condemned Prigozhin as a 'hysterical blogger' who undermined Russia's war effort.

Again Prigozhin firmly denied rumours that he planned to challenge Putin at next year's presidential elections. Prigozhin's mind was focused on his mini empire in Africa. Close to Putin since the 1990s, he knew like no other that Russian elections were far from democratic and joked he would only form a Wagner political party if Russia was transformed into 'a desert and we drive across the sands in jeeps scalded on all sides, like in the movie *Mad Max*'. In other words, not a million years.

It seemed Prigozhin had had more than his share of politics for a lifetime. To vent his frustration, he continued sniping at the Russian army. An incursion into Russia's Belgorod Oblast had been thought to have been executed by a small band of pro-Ukrainian Russian nationals. But the Kremlin then released an official statement claiming its military had killed 'fifteen-hundred service-men' and destroyed 'a hundred armoured vehicles'.

Prigozhin was quick to dismiss the claim as a farce. 'To destroy one and a half thousand people, it must be such a massacre, within one day, over 150 kilo-metres, one hell of a massacre,' he jeered. 'Therefore, I think that these are just some wild fantasies.'

Flouting Russian federal law, Prigozhin then jokingly touted for Wagner business as a domestic PMC. He said he could defend the Russian border city Belgorod from Ukraine's partisan raids without permission of the Russian defence ministry. He would not wait for an invitation to take over border secu-rity if the army could not prevent further incursions, he said mockingly.

On 4 June, the Kremlin announced a second incursion, of what it called a 'large-scale offensive' by the Ukrainians in the Donetsk Oblast, and that it had been repulsed. More than three hundred troops had been killed and sixteen tanks destroyed, claimed the Russians. This time, a video was produced pur-porting to show vehicles in a field under heavy fire.

Russian defence minister Sergei Shoigu later updated enemy losses by a massive factor ten to '3,715 troops, fifty-two tanks, 207 armoured fighting vehi-cles, 134 motor vehicles, five aircraft, two helicopters, forty-eight pieces of field artillery and fifty-three unmanned aerial vehicles'. Kyiv dismissed the claims out of hand. They soon found a surprise ally in Prigozhin, who repeated that these claims of the ministry of defence were also 'wild and absurd fantasies, works of science fiction'. Prigozhin's video clip was published after Sergei Shoigu, the Russian defence minister, announced in another tall order that the Russian army had blown up eight Leopard battle tanks and more than 100 other Ukrainian armoured vehicles in the past few days.

Pro-war Russian bloggers soon noticed that the supposed tanks in Moscow's video bore a humiliating resemblance to farming equipment. The Rybar Telegram channel, which is in favour of Russia's invasion, identified the 'tank' as a John Deere 4830 tractor. Prigozhin promptly congratulated the Russian army on its wonderful work. The Wagner boss joked that Ukrainian forces had cunningly disguised German Leopard tanks as tractors and tank crews as farmers.

It was also noted that the crew of the Russian Ka-52 attack helicopter made no reference to Leopard tanks. The footage was more likely than not a Ka-52 helicopter destroying tractors during a training exercise recorded several months before Ukraine took delivery of the German battle tanks.

Prigozhin was not slow to drive home his full-scale offensive against the false claims of Shoigu's department. Dressed in a khaki sweatshirt and trousers, in the middle of a forest in a Wagner training camp, Prigozhin accused the

Russian army of lying about events in the Belgorod region—where anti-Putin partisans had been conducting cross-border raids from Ukraine since late May. He also repeated his warning of the risk of civil war. He called for Shoigu to be put on trial for facilitating 'the genocide of the Russian population' by being totally unprepared for the war in Ukraine, and more than once suggested that Shoigu and other senior military commanders should be shot.

Prigozhin also claimed that inhabitants of the Belgorod region had been writing to him, suggesting a Chile-type solution. 'Chile means Pinochet,' he explained. 'The Russian elite in a stadium surrounded by armed men with machine guns.'

He also berated Medvedev and Putin for mishandling the threat of using tactical nuclear bombs—which Medvedev had been ramping up—and their wisdom. 'The button should have been pressed earlier,' he said, 'even though it would have been the act of a fucked-up psychopath'.

He then poked fun at them for having conducted the one-and-a-half-year war in such a pusillanimous fashion that they had now created a situation where a dirty little bomb would have to be launched, not on Ukrainian, but on Russian soil itself. 'Could they [Russia] have the vile idea of dropping a tactical nuclear bomb on their own territory?' he asked. 'Is that why we are retreating in the Belgorod region, allowing them to advance, because it's frightening to throw [a bomb] at someone else's territory but we'll throw one on our own. We'll show them [how] cool [and] mentally ill we are. It's a big question if the [nuclear bomb] would work properly.'

It was all part of an hour-long interview followed by a tour of Russian cities where he spoke of the need to open a 'second front', on the web, to tell the population the truth about what was happening on the Ukrainian front lines. Rubbing salt into the wound, he recommended the raising of an army specifically to defend Russia.

That he could travel around Russia calling out the corrupt elites meant that he did not speak for himself alone but must have had protection at the highest level. Alexei Navalny and others had ended up in jail for much less.

The army tried to strike back in a video which featured the same Lieutenant Colonel Venevitin, now 'former commander' of Russia's 72nd Independent Motorized Rifle Brigade, who had appeared in a Wagner video. He accused Wagner of stoking 'anarchy' on Russia's frontlines, as well as kidnapping and torturing his soldiers during the battle for Bakhmut. He also accused the mercenaries of stealing arms, forcing mobilised soldiers to sign contracts with Wagner, and attempting to extort weapons from the Russian defence ministry in exchange for releasing kidnapped soldiers.

'The tension with the Wagners for me and my brigade began from the first days of our transfer to the [Bakhmut] direction,' said Venevitin in the new video, which was uploaded to the Internet and sent to journalists. 'This was due not only to provoking our fighters into conflicts with their audacious behaviour and constant threats to [kill] us but also by their concrete actions.'

Venevitin claimed that his soldiers had been systematically kidnapped, abused and sometimes subjected to sexual violence, using a slang word for 'prison rape'. He also claimed that Wagner had stolen two army T-80 tanks, and four machine guns, as well as a truck and an armoured fighting vehicle.

He accused Prigozhin personally of 'actively discrediting the armed forces of the Russian Federation, trying to present Wagner as the only effective force in this conflict'. Territorial gains claimed by Wagner, he said, would not have been possible without the army, reservists and other Russian units.

Venevitin said he had been detained by Wagner while on active duty for the Russian government, held in a basement, beaten, doused with petrol and subjected to three mock executions, before he was put on camera and forced to apologize. 'The video you published of my interrogation is the result of pressure, and that's all,' he said.

Commentators noted that Venevitin appeared to be reading prepared comments in the army video and that it was therefore not clear whether, as in the Wagner video, he was speaking under duress. In any case, Prigozhin rejected his accusations, calling them 'absolutely total nonsense'. Previously his mercenaries had detained Venevitin, interrogated him and then handed him over to authorities. Prigozhin had focused his ire on the 72nd Brigade since May when he first accused the army unit of abandoning its positions near Bakhmut and leaving Wagner open to counterattack by Ukrainian forces.

In response to Venevitin's accusation that Wagner stoked 'anarchism' on the frontlines, Prigozhin was careful still to pay loyal lip service to Putin; 'The anarchism that the Wagner is breeding at the front is the result of a game of political elites who, instead of strengthening our president, are trying to weaken him.'

Defence Minister Shoigu struck back and sought to bring the situation to heel by ordering all Wagner mercenaries to sign a contract with the defence ministry.

'Wagner will not sign any contracts with Shoigu,' Prigozhin counted, adding the insult that, 'Shoigu cannot properly manage military formations.'

He reckoned Shoigu would punish Wagner by depriving the PMC of its supplies. 'What could happen after this order is that they will not give us weapons and ammunition. We will figure it out, as they say,' Prigozhin said. 'But when the thunder breaks, they will come running and bring weapons and ammunition with a request to help', he bragged. Ukraine's armed forces had meanwhile retaken three frontline villages in western Donetsk, just a week after the launch of counteroffensive operations.

On television, President Putin backed Shoigu in a rare rebuke of Prigozhin, however, and confirmed the ministry would have 'volunteer' fighters in Ukraine sign contracts with the country's military command directly.

It made no difference to Prigozhin. The following day, he insisted: 'None of Wagner's fighters is ready to go down the path of shame again. That's why they will not sign the contracts.' He also said that he was unsure if his men would continue fighting anywhere in the Ukraine. 'When we started participating in this war, no one said we would be obliged to conclude agreements,' Prigozhin said.

It was getting difficult to keep up for outside observers with the infighting of Russia's forces in Ukraine and the reality on the battlefield. When the Ukrainians took the village of Blahodatne, they found a group of Russians who were holed up in the half-destroyed cultural centre. 'Those who resisted we killed, the others we took prisoner,' said a Ukraine machine-gunner.

All the prisoners turned out to be convicts fighting for the Wagner Group. One had shot himself to avoid capture. Another claimed he had never fired his weapon and, on inspection, the Ukrainians discovered he was telling the truth. 'These guys were prisoners before they came here. I guess they have nothing to lose,' their captor said.

19

REBELLION

When Defence Minister Shoigu issued his ultimatum to Wagner and other 'volunteer formations' to sign contracts by 1 July, Prigozhin responded by insolently drafting his own contract and sending it to the ministry of defence. Might his African Wagner also be forced to operate underneath Shoigu rather than alongside him? If that were the case, the Kremlin had shot to pieces the idea that Prigozhin could leave Ukraine with his head held up high to return to his African fiefdom unaffected.

Given the vast wealth Prigozhin had created abroad since 2014, this would be a blow for all Wagner stakeholders. From its mercenary origins as thugs without scruples, Wagner PMC was now an extremely profitable military empire that controlled diamond and gold mines as well as oil and gas concessions. Net income from mining was estimated to bring in $1 billion. Mafia-style, Wagner had used its military muscle to add regular commercial enterprises, raking in more money from the local population and the development aid that poured into the war-torn region. Dmitri Sytii had launched his own brand of beer, Africa Ti L'Or, in the Central African Republic as the brewery of French-owned rival Castel brand was firebombed by three white men wearing fatigues and carrying Kalashnikovs. A drone had also flown over the brewery that night, a Castel executive said. In Central African Republic, Prigozhin had also gone into the coffee business and Wagner PMC's brasserie in the capital Bangui was doing brisk business selling homemade beers and spirits to locals. A small distillery produced Wa Na Wa vodka with the logo of a rhino and the tagline: 'Made in the Central African Republic with Russian technology.'

Raising the stakes in its standoff with Moscow, the Wagner Group advertised for people aged twenty-one to thirty-five with a gaming background to join it as drone specialists as it seeks to expand its recruitment pool. The new Wagner recruitment campaign offered training with well-prepared instructors, health and life insurance (with Sogaz, the insurance company controlled by the Putin family), modern equipment and guarantees that all recruits would receive all promised payments. The recruitment billboard carried the slogan 'Join the winning team'. 'You do realize that this isn't a game? You'd be at war,' a recruiter reminded one caller inquiring about work.

Comments under the Wagner post ranged from enthusiastic to sceptical.

'I've got twenty years of experience on Call of Duty. Will you take me?' wrote one respondent. Another *VKontakte* user said that, while he had over seven thousand hours of experience in computer flight simulations, at forty-two he was considered too old to sign up as a combat drone operator. Wagner had replied that he could apply instead to fly a quadcopter as a member of a close-combat unit. Besides video game players, Wagner was also advertising for fluent French speakers to be interpreters in Africa, as well as welders, medics and drivers. Monthly salaries start at 240,000 rubles (£2,230), four times as high as the national average wage.

Gleefully Prigozhin continued to drive the point home that the Russian defence ministry was losing territory to Ukrainian troops. 'They are misleading the Russian people,' he said in an audio message released by his spokespeople. 'Huge chunks have been handed over to the enemy. All of this is being totally hidden from everyone.'

Prigozhin also alleged that Vladimir Putin was being told 'monstrous lies' by his military chiefs over Russia's 'colossal problems' in its resistance to Ukraine's counteroffensive. He accused the Russian defence ministry of covering up losses and said: 'Russia will wake up one day only to discover Crimea has already been handed over to Ukrainians.'

He also claimed that rocket attacks on his troops had left several dead. Russian infighting had reached such a level that the factions were killing one another rather than Ukrainian forces.

Furious, Prigozhin added: 'PMC Wagner Commanders Council made a decision, the evil brought by the military leadership of the country must be stopped. They neglect the lives of soldiers. They forgot the word "justice", and we will bring it back. Those, who destroyed today our guys, who destroyed tens, tens of thousands of lives of Russian soldiers will be punished.

'I'm asking: no one resist,' his rant continued. 'Everyone who will try to resist, we will consider them a danger and destroy them immediately, including any checkpoints on our way. And any aviation that we see above our heads. I'm asking everyone to remain calm, do not succumb to provocations, and remain in their houses.'

'Ideally, those along our way, do not go outside. After we finish what we started, we will return to the frontline to protect our Motherland. Presidential authority, Government, Ministry of Internal Affairs, the National Guard and other departments will continue operating as before.' Notably absent was the ministry of defence from his list.

But he also added less loyally of the Putin regime as a whole, 'We will deal with those who destroy Russian soldiers. And we will return to the frontline. Justice in the Army will be restored. After this, justice for the whole of Russia.'

No doubt careful attention was paid to what he said. It seemed that, finally, he had gone too far for those who had been protecting him from the usual consequences for those who dared to challenge the Kremlin.

Russian state media reported that the FSB had opened a criminal case against Prigozhin, accusing him of 'calling for an armed rebellion'. Not before time. For weeks US intelligence had been following the build-up of Wagner forces along the border with Russia. On 21 June, intelligence officials even briefed senior military and administration officials in the US that Prigozhin was preparing to take military action against senior Russian defence figures. They were also told that General Surovikin and others in the military and intelligence had advanced knowledge of the matter. The plan was to capture Shoigu and Gerasimov when they were in southern Russia in the area adjoining Ukraine. That done, Prigozhin thought that others would join the rebellion, US analysts thought.

Although the authorities knew something was afoot. The Kremlin thought of Prigozhin merely as an arch-opportunist who did not play by the rules and that the chances of his bloated words turning into an actual armed insurrection were nil. They thought he was bluffing in order to extract further concessions in Africa or Ukraine for Wagner PMC. Behind the scenes, feverish negotiations were continuing for the *Wagnerovcis* in Ukraine to stand down and lay down their weapons and submit to the army. It came to nought because, on 23 June, Prigozhin accused Shoigu of ordering yet another Russian military attack on a Wagner camp and published a video of what he said was his camp's remains. 'We were ready to make concessions to the defence ministry, surrender our weapons,' he said in an audio message released by his representatives. 'Today, seeing that we have not been broken, they conducted missile strikes at our rear camps.'

Shoigu's defence ministry issued a statement dismissing the claims that they were responsible for the attack. It read: 'All the messages and video footage distributed on social networks on behalf of Prigozhin about the alleged strike by the Russian Ministry of Defence on the rear camps of PMC Wagner do not correspond to reality and are an informational provocation.'

Prigozhin's response was to ramp up the rhetoric and call for action. He accused Russian generals of carrying out the air strike on his fighters in Ukraine and said a 'huge number' had been killed. Uncharacteristically, he provided no evidence. Prigozhin thought the time had come to strike first and show how useless Shoigu's army was at their job.

He made a direct call to arms. 'There are 25,000 of us and we are going to figure out what this chaos is happening in the country,' he said. 'Anyone who wants to join can. We need to end this mess.'

In an audio message late on Friday night, Prigozhin confirmed his troops were entering Rostov, a large city in the south of Russia that the Russian top military command in the Ukraine war was using as their high-command base.

'We crossed the state border in all places,' Prigozhin said. 'The border guards came out to meet and hugged our fighters. We are entering Rostov. Detachments of the ministry of defence, more accurately—conscripts, that jumped in to block our path, moved to one side. we don't fight children. It's Shoigu who kills children, throwing untrained soldiers, including conscripts, into war. He put eighteen-year-olds up against us, they're good to be our children and grandchildren. So these lads will live and go back to their mothers. We fight only against professionals.'

He now claimed to have taken control of Rostov, including all military establishments and he said sixty or seventy regular Russian soldiers had joined his cause. Prigozhin later claimed his troops had also shot down a Russian military helicopter after it started firing on Rostov's civilian population.

Inside Rostov-on-Don's southern military district headquarters, Prigozhin sent a dispatch to Yunus-bek Yevkurov, the deputy defence minister, with an ultimatum that Sergei Shoigu and Valery Gerasimov be handed over to Wagner or his fighters would march on Moscow.

'Until that [happens] we will be here, we will block the city of Rostov and we will head to Moscow,' he said, according to video footage that was posted to social media. He also said later that his troops had seized the city's airport. He insisted that Wagner's actions would not stop Russian troops from fighting in Ukraine.

'There were explosions overnight, the city is closed off, hell knows what is going on,' a local resident recalled. He confirmed that a helicopter had been shot down near his home on the outskirts of the city. 'Is this a civil war or what?'

Prigozhin vowed that he and his men would topple Russia's military leadership. 'All of us are ready to die. All 25,000, and then another 25,000,' he said in an audio message. 'We are dying for the Russian people.'

Showing how inept the military command was Prigozhin said, in audio recordings published by his press service, that his private army forces crossing from Ukraine into Rostov had faced no resistance. 'If anyone stands in our way we will destroy everything put in our path,' he threatened. 'We are holding out a hand to everyone, don't spit on that hand. We're going further; we're going to the end. Anyone who puts up resistance—we will consider this a threat and destroy immediately. Including any roadblocks on our way,' he added

Panic rapidly gripped the Kremlin. The FSB promptly declared Prigozhin 'a foreign agent'. Armed rebellion inside Russia,' the security service warned, 'is punishable with between twelve and twenty years in prison.' Its spooks also called on Wagner group members to ignore Prigozhin. They should 'not make irreparable mistakes, to stop any forceful actions against the Russian people, not to carry out the criminal and treacherous orders of Prigozhin, and to take measures to detain him'.

While Putin's motorcade sped from his home in the suburbs to the Kremlin, Russian state television interrupted normal programming to inform viewers that a video said to show the aftermath of a missile strike on a Wagner base was a fake. 'Security measures have been strengthened in Moscow; important sites have been taken under increased protection, as have the organs of state power and centres of transport infrastructure,' the Tass state news agency reported.

An emergency plan called '*krepost*', or fortress, was activated, deploying Russian soldiers around the capital and to strategic locations. According to several Telegram channels linked to the security services, emergency protocols were implemented in the city, involving the full mobilization of the local security services. Pictures published by local Moscow media showed armoured vehicles appearing on the streets of the city. *Baza*, a Telegram channel linked to the Russian security services, said that helicopters were seen flying over Rostov.

'All necessary measures are being taken,' said Dmityr Peskov as tanks were seen on the streets of Moscow and all mass outdoor events were suspended for at least one week.

As the city mustered what little protection it had and Prigozhin advanced with his troops, he doubled down and claimed that Russia's invasion was based on lies that Ukraine was a threat to Moscow and its citizens. Effectively, he took a sledgehammer to the case for the war that Putin and the Kremlin had built up since 2014.

In other words, Prigozhin still remained loyal to Putin whom he identified with the Russian people. 'The ministry of defence is trying to deceive the public and the president and spin the story that there were insane levels of aggression from the Ukrainian side and that they were going to attack us together with the whole NATO block,' Prigozhin said. Instead, he said the war was motivated by the personal ambitions of Shoigu and the avarice of Russian oligarchs, a special subject of which he, an oligarch himself, had much personal knowledge.

'What was the war for? The war needed for Shoigu to receive a hero star and become a marshal not in order to return Russian citizens to our bosoms and not in order to demilitarize and denazify Ukraine,' he said. 'The oligarchs needed the war. This is the clan that manages Russia today. And the second part of the operation was to install Medvedchuk as Ukraine's president.'

This was a reference to Viktor Medvedchuk, a pro-Russia Ukrainian oligarch living in exile in Russia who was also a close friend of Putin. He had been exchanged for the return of a hundred Ukrainian Azov fighters. Moscow could have struck a deal with Zelensky before the war, he said (quite accurately). Portraying the top brass as vodka-and-cognac-swilling fools who lunch on caviar, he said the Russian war effort continued to be hobbled by corruption.

'The Russian army is retreating in all directions and shedding a lot of blood… What they tell us is the deepest deception,' he said. 'We are bathing in our own blood. Time is running out fast.'

After securing all the military sites in Rostov-on-Don including the airfield, Wagner's column carrying around five thousand men headed up the M4 motorway which passed through Voronezh, three hundred miles south of Moscow.

'This is not a military coup, this is a march of justice. Our actions do not hinder the armed forces in any way,' the Wagner chief said, adding that the 'majority of soldiers' were on his side. He said that he wanted to avenge the ordinary Russian soldiers who have been killed by incompetent leadership since the start of the invasion of Ukraine last February. Russia has lost an estimated 220,000 men in the war.

The situation was becoming so critical that Putin had to appear on TV to show he was still in control of Russia. Standing in front of the Russian flag and his desk, Putin called Wagner's actions 'a stab in the back'. It was not clear where Putin was as he had installed copies of the same desk in all his residences. Rumour had it he had taken a plane and was no longer in Moscow. Without mentioning Prigozhin by name, he said: 'All those who deliberately embarked on the path of betrayal, who prepared an armed rebellion, embarked on the path of blackmail and terrorist methods, will suffer inevitable punishment. They will answer both before the law and before our people.'

Prigozhin responded in a video recorded at a military base in Rostov-on-Don. He denied Putin's authority and countered with an even more direct affront, 'The president is deeply mistaken about the betrayal of the motherland. We are patriots of our homeland, we fought and are fighting,' he said. 'No one is going to turn themselves in at the request of the president, the FSB or anyone else. We do not want the country to go on living in corruption, deceit and bureaucracy.'

General Surovikin, the deputy head of the armed forces in Ukraine and hitherto Prigozhin's ally, called on Prigozhin personally to 'stop the convoys and return them to their bases'. In a video posted on Telegram, Surovikin posed with his right hand on a rifle. 'I urge you to stop while it's not too late, you need to obey the will and order of the elected president of Russia,' he said. 'Stop the columns, return them to their permanent bases. We must resolve all problems peacefully.'

He continued his appeal to Prigozhin, with deeply personal references: 'Together we have been on a difficult path. We fought together, took risks, suffered losses and won together. We are the same blood. We are warriors. I urge you to stop. The enemy is just waiting for the internal political situation in our country to deteriorate. You can't play into the hands of the enemy in these difficult times for our country.'

The regime, however, was still teetering. Soldiers began to abandon their posts after threats from Wagner rebels advancing towards Moscow. Some offered them their support. In a video posted on social media, a masked paratrooper who was thought to be a part of the 217 regiment of the 98th airborne division, said that he and his unit backed the rebels.

'Wagner lads,' the paratrooper said, 'We are with and support you in your quest for justice against the greedy pederasts from the Ministry of Defence, who could not care less about the life of an ordinary soldier. We, like you, took part in difficult battles. We know the price of the life of a simple soldier. We know the price of our blood and we won't let them make cannon fodder out of us. So know this—we are with you and are ready to stand shoulder to shoulder with you in your just fight.'

A Russian security source revealed that Wagner fighters also controlled key military facilities in Voronezh. Some two hundred soldiers were reported to have surrendered to Wagner fighters in the Voronezh region, according to images on Telegram. There were reports of heavy fighting on the outskirts of the city. In a video posted to Telegram, the sounds of automatic gunfire and loud explosions could be heard and smoke could be seen billowing into the sky in a field.

This came after another group of Russian soldiers who said they were based in Ukraine pledged to support Prigozhin. 'We back you totally. If you need us, just whistle and we'll be there,' said one fighter, his face unmasked. Another soldier added that it was time to kick out the 'louses' in Moscow.

Many of the Moscow elite abandoned the city. Putin's private plane had taken off from Moscow's Vnukovo airport in the direction of St Petersburg with his deputy Medvedev. A spokesman for the Kremlin denied this while news outlet Visegrád 24 tweeted a picture of the flight tracker of a plane belonging to the Lukashenko family heading for Turkey.

Prigozhin's revolt was very well-prepared. Printed leaflets were distributed to Russian soldiers in the Ukraine. They urged the troops to ignore their orders and join the fight for justice. 'Shoigu and Gerasimov are traitors of the motherland,' the leaflet said. 'They have thrown you into the meat grinder to save their own skins. Their sons get fat, while you give your life for the motherland. Those creatures are hiding the truth. They have ruined the lives of hundreds of thousands of our lads. They even shoot their own soldiers! And make scapegoats out of you!'

'Instead of honour from the motherland, you pay with your lives for their brainlessness. We—the Wagner militia—are going on a march for justice to Moscow. Join us! It's not a coup. It's restoration of justice. Together we can stop this evil.'

Outside Voronezh, 500km from Moscow, the Wagner column came under air attack and at least one helicopter and an Il-22M airborne command-centre plane were shot down killing some 13 Russian military personnel. The rebels pushed on for Moscow.

20

PUTIN INC

As the Wagner column headed on northwards, a video showed it smashing its way through a roadblock of trucks blocking the highway. In the Lipetsk Oblast, 450km from Moscow, the highway was torn up by excavators. The bridges crossing the Oka river, 100km south of Moscow, were barricaded and defensive lines were set up.

Then it was all over. Just ten hours after leaving Rostov, the Wagner column did a U-turn halfway.

'We're turning around our convoys and going in the opposite direction,' Prigozhin said in an audio message. 'We left on 23 June for the march of justice. In a day we travelled, not reaching 200 km, to Moscow. During this time, we have not shed a single drop of the blood of our fighters.'

'Now the moment has come when blood could be shed, therefore, realizing all the responsibility for the fact that Russian blood will be shed on one of the sides, we turn our columns around and return in the opposite direction to the field camps, as planned.'

Prigozhin had achieved his goal and made his point that the Russian army was made of cardboard. Crowds gathered in Rostov-on-Don to say goodbye to Wagner troops as they left the city and headed back to their camps in Ukraine.

If attacking Moscow was risky, turning around was even riskier. Prigozhin continued to gamble that he remained untouchable from the Kremlin's repercussions, such as being arrested, or Wagner's encampment in Ukraine being annihilated by the Russian army. As he was on the way to Moscow, he had tried to speak to Putin himself, but Putin declined to take his call.

It turned out that, behind the scenes, negotiations were being conducted between Prigozhin, Putin's chief of staff Anton Vaino, and the secretary of Russia's Security Council and former head of the FSB Nikolai Patrushev, and the Russian ambassador to Belarus Boris Gryzlov. Also involved was President Lukashenko, whom Prigozhin had helped out with *Wagnerovci*s during the Belarus elections in 2020 when Lukashenk's position looked uncertain. Prigozhin, it was announced, would move to Belarus, and he and his men would be immune from prosecution in Russia. Those who wished to could accompany Prigozhin to Belarus. Others could still sign up with the Russian military. Their heavy equipment had already been taken, it was claimed. While it was clearly a face-saving exercise for the Kremlin, kicking a lot of decisions into the long grass, it did reveal the considerable power base Prigozhin represented.

More face-saving followed later. It was at last made public that the Wagner Group PMC really existed as an umbrella legal entity, despite the denials over the years. Released documents said the group was officially incorporated on 1 May 2014. At least, that was its incorporation date according to the group's purported founding charter. Apart from confirming that the Wagner companies formed in 2022 to recruit convicts and volunteers for the Ukraine invasion were Prigozhin satellites of the original Wagner Group PMC, it also confirmed indirectly something else: that Russia had been preparing militias to capture Ukrainian territory at least half a year before Ukraine's president Yanukovich ran into domestic trouble over the EU in November 2014. The Kremlin was going to strike Ukraine in 2014, no matter what.

The charter's publication papered over the yawning crack that had appeared in the Kremlin's authority by Prigozhin's unimpeded 24-hour march on Moscow. Creating space between the mercenary's incursion and Presidential authority, it sought to label what had happened not so much as a challenge of presidential power than as a minor departmental tiff that had regrettably spiralled. The document outlined Prigozhin's role as Wagner group director which included providing its weapons, funding and guarantees for those killed or injured in combat. But mainly, the main point the document emphasised was that Wagner Group PMC's charter was highly patriotic and not remotely anti-Putin (which of course was exactly what 23-24 June was) or the Russian Federation as such.

By appearances Putin was in complete charge again and he had pressed the 'destroy Wagner' button as expected. General Surovikin was taken for interrogation at an unknown location. Other Prigozhin sympathizers were purged. Prigozhin's opulent mansion was raided by the FSB and it found weapons, gold bars and a closet full of wigs. Photos were provided to the media. It was said his media outlets were closed down and propaganda assets taken over by the government and turned against him. Putin had taken control of Wagner's business interests in Russia and abroad it was said. State media also claimed Prigozhin had been working with Western intelligence and Andrey Gurulyov, a member of the Duma, called for him to be executed.

Some mud was slung at Prigozhin personally. In a lurid news report to outlets outside Russia, he was revealed to have a pleasure dome in St Petersburg. A Russian woman, 'Marsha', said she had sold her virginity to Prigozhin and claimed she was one of many. Her testimony was corroborated by a representative of a Russian sex worker's union.

Prigozhin, she claimed, believed virgins prolonged his youth. He kept a rotating harem of girls in rented rooms in the Solo Sokos Hotel in St. Petersburg. With them, 'he had sex without a condom' the sex workers' union representative said, because 'he believed that this is how he exchanges energy, fluids. It's as if he receives a charge of vitality from them.' She wasn't accusing him of being a paedophile, as she was careful to claim that all girls were 18 or older.

Prigozhin also had, she claimed, metallic spheres implanted in the foreskin of his 'very small' penis to enhance his sexual prowess and provide pleasure for his young partners. In fact, women found the balls to be painful during intercourse.

It happened in the Autumn of 2019 to Marsha. 'I met another girl, around my age, and she had been kicked out of her home and she really needed money. She asked me if I would like to sell my virginity for forty thousand roubles [$623 or £482]. She'd receive a commission. I was like, 'OK, let's,' although I didn't need the money that much myself.'

'She said I had to go to the clinic to have my virginity checked. I was sent to the Sogaz clinic, right there on the other side of Nevsky Prospekt', said Marsha. At the reception desk, you had to say a password—"women's sports".'

She was then sent to the Solo Sokos Hotel on Vasilyevsky Island on the western side of the city where there were rooms reserved for him. 'Everything was very fast,' she said. 'He just left the money in a pile on a chair.' He also told her to 'be nicer', complaining of the 'dour expression'.

Curiously, the detailed information on the 'pleasure dome' seemed to implicate Putin himself as much as Prigozhin. The Sogaz clinic and insurance company had deep family links to the Putins, including Putin's eldest endocrinologist daughter. It was also where the *Wagnerovcis* were treated for war wounds.

Nothing was heard from the usually voluble and outspoken Prigozhin. It was speculated that, soon, he would be found somewhere having committed suicide by falling out of a window like other executives who had caused far less commotion than he had. It was also speculated that the spoils of Wagner PMC business, mining and military were already in the process of being reorganised to be headed by someone else.

On 27 June, Putin himself revealed that the 'maintenance of the entire Wagner Group was fully provided for by the state'. It had paid Wagner 86.26 billion rubles ($1 billion) between May 2022 and May 2023. This admission tore the international veil the Kremlin had thrown over Prigozhin's mercenary empire around the world. Instead of a private enterprise, Wagner PMC had become by the Kremlin's admission a semi-governmental organisation in 2022. It would be hard for the Kremlin to deny involvement with, let alone the existence of, Wagner PMC's actions around the world going forward.

Suddenly, the image of Putin's restored omnipotence shattered once again when President Lukashenko announced—as if it was entirely to be expected—that Prigozhin had turned up in Belarus, but then returned to St Petersburg.

Heated negotiations were clearly still continuing. While Prigozhin had evidently agreed to complete radio silence and had to eat humble pie as the Kremlin steamrolled over him in the media, Putin however could still not rely on the complete obedience of the state apparatus he had enjoyed since 2000. He was unable to deal with Prigozhin himself, or other Wagner commanders who had taken part in the attack on Moscow.

Then, suddenly, Prigozhin himself was back in the Russian news. Kremlin spokesman Dmitry Peskov no less announced that a three-hour meeting took place on 29 June between President Putin and Yevgeny Prigozhin and his other Wagner commanders, presumably the members of the 'PMC Wagner Commanders Council'.

'The president gave an assessment of the company's actions on the front,' Peskov blandly told reporters. 'He also gave an assessment to the 24 June events.' Prigozhin and his commanders also had their say. It seemed that two Russias existed side by side—one without Prigozhin and one with the problem he presented.

'They presented their version of what happened and they emphasized that they are staunch supporter and soldiers of the head of state and the supreme commander. They also said that they were ready to continue to fight for the Motherland,' Peskov added. 'Putin listened to the commanders' explanations and suggested variants of their future employment and their future use in combat.'

According to Peskov, Prigozhin told Putin that Wagner unconditionally supported him. It was an extraordinary if not humiliating sign of Putin's diminished power as president that he had to admit to sitting in the same room as his subordinate Prigozhin without being able to arrest him there and then with all the other Wagner commanders.

Apparently, Prigozhin left the meeting unharmed. A few days later, he told Afrique Media television blandly 'I believe that the forum went well and we should see the results from it in the near future' according to a transcript posted on his Telegram channel that had resumed posting news. He also praised Putin and Wagner PMC's work in Africa.

Nonetheless, the sniping against Prigozhin continued in the Russian media and he continued to be portrayed as a parasite who enriched himself on the spoils of the Russian state.

As Putin opened the Russia-Africa Conference of 27-28 July in St Petersburg, Prigozhin's Telegram channel once again stole Putin's media thunder by releasing a photograph of him meeting the president of the Central

African Republic, the beating heart of Wagner PMC's mercenary empire.

In an audio recording of Wagner channel, he was also heard praising as 'a declaration of independence' the military coup in Niger, a country part of the second African cluster where Wagner PMC was fomenting civil war to build a satellite military-mining-commercial complex. 'It's getting rid of the colonizers', the Russian warlord commented on the ousting of Niger President Mohamed Bazoum.

On 21 August @Razgruzka Vagnera, one of the Wagner group's channels, released a recruitment video of Prigozhin in which he said, 'The temperature is 50 degrees—just the way we like it. Wagner is making Russia even greater on every continent—and Africa even more free.'

Prigozhin's rebellion lasted two months to the day. On its two-month anniversary, Russian state television released a video of a burning aeroplane. It was claimed that it was Prigozhin's private aeroplane and that its flight manifest from St Petersburg to Moscow confirmed that Prigozhin had been on board and that he was dead. Apart from the date, it was curious that it was a first in the aeroplane's model's long history that it had spontaneously developed a catastrophic fault. Then there was that Prigozhin had apparently thrown his standard (pre-coup) caution in the wind and filed his presence on the plane with Russia's central air traffic control. No doubles or aliases for him that day. Also dead was Utkin, the GRU colonel whose call sign Wagner had given the group its name. The last time sign of life of Utkin's was a flight to Rwanda in 2019 (his last visual sighting dated back to 2016). And yet here popped up suddenly, still dead.

There was no telling how or when Prigozhin had really died without independent verification, but it was abundantly clear that his story had come to a full stop.

Remarkably, Putin made a public address on the crash the next day and offered his 'sincerest condolences'. Defensively, he added that [Prigozhin] made a significant contribution to our common cause of fighting the neo-Nazi regime in Ukraine', that Prigozhin had vociferously punctured that balloon throughout May. He called Prigozhin a 'long-standing' friend and a 'talented person, a talented businessman', as well as 'a man with a complicated fate' who made 'serious mistake', suggesting it was just poor nature and nurture that drove Prigozhin. But, to remind everyone of his unquestioned control over the man, he added, 'he received the results… when I asked him, for the common cause, as in these last months'. Like a CEO after an oil spill, he also reminded everyone that the enormous risks associated with a flawed individual were reasonable because Prigozhin had built up their joint sprawling money-gushing empire: 'He worked not only in our country and worked with results but also abroad in Africa, in particular. He was involved in oil gas, precious metals and stones there.'

Although Prigozhin and 'Wagner' were dead, and presumably all the other members of the *Wagnerovcis'* commanders council, their deaths did solve the mystery of Wagner PMC's existence.

On the one hand, Wagner was a private military company set up in 2014 with an unambiguous commercial charter, on the other hand, it had the deepest support of the government of the Russian Federation. In Ukraine and Syria, its logistics were taken care of by the Russian army in a way that none of its competitors could ever dream of. Instead of being in the business of providing mercenaries, Wagner's main objective was entirely different. It was about capturing mineral and mining concessions outside of Russia. In this, the Kremlin, too, offered unparalleled support—even though the Russian Federation did not stand to benefit. In Africa, Prigozhin took meetings with African leaders alongside minister of defence Shoigu, even though he was just a private businessman and he could call on Shoigu for support of the Russian airforce (no doubt for a rental fee) to bomb Wagner targets. It gave Wagner the power to project the strength of a national army rather than merely that of a small band of soldiers. Even well-trained US mercenaries with the latest equipment would find it hard to compete, particularly as Wagner was both cheaper and unconcerned about the loss of its mercenaries' lives (as the 2018 Battle of Khasham in Syria had made clear). Efficiently deploying Wagner's unique clout, Prigozhin created his mining and mineral empire in Africa centred around Central African Republic's natural wealth. The only historical parallel for such a marriage of private enterprise and national support was the Belgian Congo, established as personal property by the Belgian King Leopold (1865-1909).

Prigozhin himself had certainly become a rich man. His fortune at his death was estimated to have grown to US$1 billion on the back of Wagner Group PMC: the former GULAG inmate had risen to join the ranks of Russia's oligarchs. But was he the equivalent of King Leopold and the owner of the territorial assets that Wagner Group PMC had put together, or did he have a far more powerful business partner who could make things happen?

Prigozhin had been able to build his mercenary empire despite a long-running feud with the third most powerful man in the Russian government, defence minister Sergey Shoigu. In every conflict, from the 2014 invasion of Ukraine to the occupation of Bakhmut, they had bitterly vied for the laurels. Yet, despite their professional hatred, the two continued to work together closely for a decade—even if the Russian military's support was less than enthusiastic, such as the late dispatch of fighter jets or poor coordination in Africa. It was only at Bakhmut, in the Spring of 2023, when Shoigu finally flexed the muscle of the ministry of defence and rationed Wagner troops of essential war supplies that Prigozhin's animosity boiled over publicly. From

February to June, his attacks on Shoigu became more and more personal, including attacks on Shoigu's children. In fact, not only Shoigu's children, but also the children of other powerful Russian figures, such as former President Dmitry Medvedev and the head of the SVR, Russia's equivalent of MI6 and the CIA—using words like 'scumbag', 'shake his bum around'.

It meant that the real ruler of the private Ukrainian, Syrian and African empire Prigozhin had cobbled together since 2014 was one person only—Vladimir Putin. He was the only man in Russia who could order Shoigu to continue to work together with Prigozhin. He was also the only man who could order the Russian military to focus on taking the salt mines in Bakhmut and Soledar for the financial gain of Wagner Group PMC, even though the town had no strategic importance whatsoever to the Russian Federation. If Wagner was Putin's Congo, no one in Russia dared take Prigozhin down without Putin's personal permission. This gave Prigozhin the extraordinary leeway from mere mortals in Russia. It also showed in the precision targets of Prigozhin's invective. The only child who was excluded from his abuse was the son of Putin's longstanding spokesperson Peskov. Instead of raking him over the coals for picking up parking tickets in Moscow, Prigozhin turned him into a *Wagnerovci* model for a promotional video claiming he had done a tour in Ukraine like Prigozhin's own son.

Putin finally began to move against *Wagnerovcis* in Ukraine when they failed to deliver the goods—despite Prigozhin's ceaseless bragging throughout the Autumn and Winter of 2022 that he could do a better job than the Russian military. In 2023, as Prigozhin failed to take Bakhmut, Putin gave Shoigu the freedom to support Wagner only to the extent the military wanted to for the first time since 2014. When Prigozhin didn't take the hint to submit to Shoigu, Putin next allowed the ministry of defence no longer to take Prigozhin's calls. Finally, Putin publicly intervened on 11 June on Russian TV and agreed expressly with Shoigu that Wagner mercenaries in Ukraine should henceforth sign up with the ministry of defence under Shoigu's direction. The message couldn't be clearer. The president who had encouraged for ten years the rivalry between the official Russian military and his own semi-private army of mercenaries had irrevocably cast his decisive vote that day against Prigozhin.

That is, it should have been decisive. But Prigozhin still didn't take Putin's no for an answer and stubbornly persistence his opposition against Shoigu and, in veiled comments, directly against Putin himself from 9 May, Victory Day, when he was promised but didn't receive ammunition and called Putin in veiled terms a 'complete a******e'.

There may have been several reasons. Having proven himself to be a successful commercial coloniser as well as an efficient organiser of turning GULAG convicts into a suicidal army, he had gained the respect of a dominant faction in the Kremlin, whereas the army and its planning had lost prestige for failing to grip the backwater that was Ukraine. As the Kremlin was reaching more and more vocally for the deployment of tactical nuclear weapons, this faction may have felt it was too little too late and more an act of desperation. Despite Putin washing his hands off of Wagner Group PMC in Ukraine and handing them over to Shoigu, they may have suggested to Prigozhin that Putin's *ukase* still left the escape route open for the regular Wagner cadre to withdraw from Ukraine and return to the Wagner colonies. After all, Wagnerovcis were on 6 months contracts anyway. Withdrawal would not endear him to the Kremlin, but as satrap of the loyal Wagner empire, his income streams were independent enough.

They may have seen Prigozhin as the perfect shot across the bow of the Kremlin since Prigozhin was vain, class-conscious and angry enough to turn on Putin—Prigozhin had certainly been dropping heavy-handed clues that his soldiers would revolt against the Kremlin. Unlike in Africa, Wagner troops were incurring colossal losses in Ukraine, yet in 2023 Prigozhin he had grown accustomed to as Putin turned off the charm. Any prior knowledge of Prigozhin's crazy plan to capture General Gerasimov, chief of the Russian military, and demand Shoigu's head was eminently deniable as Prigozhin would keep it a closely-guarded secret from anyone dutybound to report it to Putin. At the same time, an angry Prigozhin would prove how porous Moscow's military defences really were. If a tinpot soldier like Wagner could move up to the Kremlin in a day what would NATO be able to do if truly riled by a nuclear disaster? From 2014, the Kremlin's propaganda to the Russian population may have accused NATO of 'attacking' Russia through Zelensky's 'Nazi' regime, but that didn't mean anyone believed it even if they supported it. There was the awkward fact, for example, that NATO included Turkey to whom Russia regularly sold weapons.

With his obstreperous satrap out of the way, Putin was once again in control of the sprawling Wagner empire of home trolls and foreign troops. Wagner Group PMC continued to exploit death as a business and business was good. In a Stalinist retouching of history, everything stayed the same less Prigozhin. Putin remained president, Shoigu remained his trusted minister of defence, Gerasimov stayed on as the chief of the Russian military, and Prigozhin's reputation was redacted to what it had been until 2022. Ostensibly, the message was, the Kremlin will not yield to anyone's pressure.

Yet everyone in Russia knew that the Prigozhin business had exposed the Federation's Achilles heel. As Russia's president and ultimate ruler of the Wagner colonies, Putin had to decide whether he was still considered the only man to lead the state or whether he was in the 2020 position of his neighbour Lukashenko when he needed Wagner support as his praetorian guard. Were those around him reaching the decision that it was time for him to go in a paper revolution, the same way Stalin's successor Nikita Khrushchev was unseated by Leonid Brezhnev at the flick of a pen, or Mikhail Gorbachev suddenly found himself the powerless leader of a USSR shell? If the sentiment had changed, Putin would need to start purging the ranks before they purged him. He had nurtured Prigozhin as his most devoted acolyte—who would now go to hell and back for him, just for the money?

On 5 October, the Russian president addressed Prigozhin yet again. At the the Valdai Discussion Club—Russia's version of Davos—in the exclusive Blacksea town Sochi, where Russia's richest businessmen and *nomenklatura* meet, Putin explained that, 'Fragments of hand grenades were found in the bodies of those killed in the crash'. This seemed yet another twist to the story. He revealed that, surprisingly, the investigations team had discovered the fragments a month and a half later, but failed to do any toxicological analysis of the bodies on the plane despite the location of drugs in offices related to Wagner and Prigozhin. 'In my opinion, such an examination should have been carried out but it was not', Putin said. Presumably the bodies could no longer be tested. It was an unusual moment where the president felt he personally had to make public to his peers yet more disappointing work of Russian officials.